Language, Culture and Cognition

Multilingual Matters

Age in Second Language Acquisition
  BIRGIT HARLEY
Bicultural and Trilingual Education
  MICHAEL BYRAM and JOHAN LEMAN (eds)
Bilingual and Multicultural Education: Canadian Perspectives
  S. SHAPSON and V. D'OYLEY (eds)
Bilingualism and Special Education
  JIM CUMMINS
Cultural Studies and Language Learning
  M. BYRAM, V. ESARTE-SARRIES and S. TAYLOR
Cultural Studies in Foreign Language Education
  MICHAEL BYRAM
Current Trends in European Second Language Acquisition Research
  HANS W. DECHERT (ed.)
ESL: A Handbook for Teachers and Administrators in International Schools
  EDNA MURPHY (ed.)
Evaluating Bilingual Education
  MERRILL SWAIN and SHARON LAPKIN
Foreign/Second Language Pedagogy Research
  R. PHILLIPSON, E. KELLERMAN, L. SELINKER, M. SHARWOOD SMITH and
  M. SWAIN (eds)
Individualizing the Assessment of Language Abilities
  JOHN H. A. L. de JONG and D. G. STEVENSON (eds)
Investigating Cultural Studies in Foreign Language Teaching
  M. BYRAM and V. ESARTE-SARRIES
Key Issues in Bilingualism and Bilingual Education
  COLIN BAKER
Language Acquisition: The Age Factor
  D. M. SINGLETON
Language Acquisition of a Bilingual Child
  ALVINO FANTINI
Language Distribution Issues in Bilingual Schooling
  R. JACOBSON and C. FALTIS (eds)
Mediating Languages and Cultures
  D. BUTTJES and M. BYRAM (eds)
The Role of the First Language in Second Language Learning
  HÅKAN RINGBOM
Schooling in a Plural Canada
  JOHN MALLEA
Second Language Acquisition — Foreign Language Learning
  B. VanPATTEN and J. F. LEE (eds)
Teaching and Learning English Worldwide
  J. BRITTON, R. E. SHAFER and K. WATSON (eds)
Variation in Second Language Acquisition: Vol. I and II
  S. GASS, C. MADDEN, D. PRESTON and L. SELINKER (eds)

Please contact us for the latest book information:
Multilingual Matters,
Bank House, 8a Hill Road,
Clevedon, Avon BS21 7HH.
England

MULTILINGUAL MATTERS 69
Series Editor: Derrick Sharp

Language, Culture and Cognition

A Collection of Studies in First and Second Language Acquisition

Edited by
Lilliam Malavé and
Georges Duquette

MULTILINGUAL MATTERS LTD
Clevedon · Philadelphia · Adelaide

Library of Congress Cataloging-in-Publication Data

Language, Culture and Cognition: A Collection of Studies in First and Second Language Acquisition/Edited by Lilliam Malavé and Georges Duquette.
p. cm. (Multilingual Matters: 69).
Includes bibliographical references and indexes.
1. Language acquisition. 2. Bilingualism. 3. Language and Culture. 4. Cognition in children. 5. Language and languages—Study and teaching.
I. Malavé, Lilliam M. II. Duquette, Georges. III. Series: Multilingual Matters (Series): 69.
P118.L258   1991
401'93   dc20

British Library Cataloguing in Publication Data

Language, Culture and Cognition: A Collection of Studies in First and Second Language Acquisition (Multilingual Matters: 69).
1. Development. Psycholinguistic aspects.
I. Malavé, Lilliam. II. Duquette, Georges
401.93

ISBN 1–85359–103–3
ISSN 1–85359–102–5 (Pbk)

Multilingual Matters Ltd

UK: Bank House, 8a Hill Road, Clevedon, Avon BS21 7HH, England.
USA: 1900 Frost Road, Suite 101, Bristol, PA 19007, USA.
Australia: P.O. Box 6025, 83 Gilles Street, Adelaide, SA 5000, Australia.

Typeset by Photo·graphics, Honiton, Devon.
Printed and bound in Great Britain by Billing and Sons Ltd.

Contents

Acknowledgements

While the responsibility for the contents of this publication remains with the editors and authors, the editors would like to acknowledge the contribution of colleagues and friends who facilitated the development of this book. We would like to thank the University at Buffalo, Saint Mary's University, and Laurentian University for providing the support system necessary to complete a project of this magnitude. Acknowledgement is also made to Mrs Carolyn P. Singletary, Mr Esteban Lopez, and Ms Ann Rodrique for their support and invaluable assistance with manifold publication procedures. Special recognition is extended to Professor Bernie Davis for his recommendations on research methodology and procedures. Finally, the generous co-operation of the contributing authors is recognised.

Lilliam M. Malavé
Georges Duquette

Preface

This collection of essays, studies and research is unique. 'Unique', for it brings together a number of authors of national and international reputation who, together, deal with themes of great interest. Professors Malavé and Duquette are to be congratulated not only for their excellent initiative of extending an invitation to these colleagues who have distinguished themselves in their field, but also for collecting, in a single volume, a series of essays and studies which focus on topics of current interest.

A quick glance at the Table of Contents will show that, while the emphasis is on research, topics range from theoretical to practical, and such topics attract the attention not only of researchers but also of practitioners. It is encouraging to see such a variety of themes, of studies focusing on both first and second language development, and of discussions that deal not only with the 'good language learner' but also with the less able student. Papers dealing with the latter are generally rare and, therefore, welcomed indeed.

It is generally impossible to treat so many topics in a single volume, topics whose aim is to interest a multiplicity of readers. Professors Malavé and Duquette have succeeded where many other editors have failed; they have provided us with an anthology of previously unpublished readings of interest to researchers, the 'seasoned' practising teacher and the teacher who is about to enter the profession.

There is very little doubt in my mind that *Language, Culture and Cognition* will be a success. It provides a superb overview of research and studies currently under way in North America, and shares with other colleagues findings which will be read with great interest not only by North Americans but also by readers on the other side of the Atlantic.

It only remains for me to wish every success to this publication. *Language, Culture and Cognition* will surely make a significant contribution and will leave an indelible mark in the field of first and second language research.

Anthony S. Mollica, Editor
The Canadian Modern Language Review/
La Revue canadienne des langues vivantes

Introduction

LILLIAM M. MALAVÉ and GEORGES DUQUETTE

The relationship between the linguistic and cultural characteristics of bilinguals and their cognitive abilities has attracted the scholarly attention of many social scientists. The literature on bilingualism and multiculturalism is heavily influenced by pedagogical assumptions that explore the performance of bilinguals. The academic success or failure of bilinguals has been explained in terms of educational notions that range from cultural and linguistic deprivation theories to premises that support the differential and superior performance of bilinguals' cognitive and academic ability. In contrast to the majority of the literature that uses pedagogical constructs to explain the behaviour of bilinguals, this publication provides current research findings to critically analyse and interpret the academic and cognitive performance of bilinguals.

This book aims to provide up-to-date research findings and conceptualisations in order to explore the relationship between native culture, first and second language acquisition, and cognitive development. It is divided into three parts: Part I, consisting of five chapters, focuses on the cognitive processing of language systems; Part II, consisting of four chapters, discusses the nature, role and effects of culture in language acquisition; Part III, consisting of eight chapters, centres on aspects and considerations of the teaching/learning process.

Part I, on the cognitive processing of language systems, begins with a look at cognition and language processing inside the learner. John Oller, Jr explores the relationship between language, kinesics and sensory systems, and offers comments concerning the development of interlanguage systems. This topic is continued by Larry Selinker's overview of some concepts comprising the development of interlanguage systems in academic discourse domains. The chapter by Herbert Seliger discusses long-term incremental changes in the composition of an interlanguage grammar and other processes to achieve short-range goals that may lead to language-like behaviour rather than acquisition. The last two chapters of this part

1

focus on the processing of specific languages: Spanish and Pilipino. Joan E. Friedenberg investigates the roles that native language, age, and learning situation play on error and implied learning strategies used to acquire Spanish. Erlinda Reyes and William Fagan analyse the profiles of Filipino low-achieving readers processing two languages, Pilipino and English.

Part II, on language and culture, explores the nature, role and effects of culture in language acquisition. Sandra Weber and Claudette Tardif discuss the primacy of culture as a major determinant of meaning in the French immersion classroom and how it structures the child's learning experiences. Alvino E. Fantini presents a framework to explain a significant link between language and culture: language as a paradigm of a view of the world, continually reflecting and affecting the speaker's perception of reality. The relationship between language and culture is further explored within the framework of minority language students with special needs in the next two chapters. Georges Duquette examines the relationship between the home culture and the acquisition of languages, and identifies culture-relevant and special needs of language minority children. Henry Trueba's ethnographic study provides statistical information, raises the question of attended or neglected minority needs, presents a series of case studies, and discusses child-centred pedagogical approaches that consider the background culture and first language of minority children.

Part III, on language learning and instruction, presents a comprehensive discussion of teaching approaches, and instructional issues and frameworks. Jim Cummins establishes what school administrators and policy makers need to know about language development and bilingualism in order to institute educational programmes that promote high levels of English language skills and academic achievement of students from language minority backgrounds. Lilliam M. Malavé presents a conceptual framework that focuses on the acquisition of content and procedural knowledge by handicapped students who are culturally and linguistically different. Janice Chavez, David Lopez and Louise Burton examine the nature and level of communication between Hispanic parents of learning handicapped children and their special education teachers. Five additional chapters discuss schooling and language minority students: Rodriguez Landry and Réal Allard introduce a model of the sociological and psychological determinants of additive and subtractive bilingualism; Birgit Harley examines students' use of verbs in an oral interview setting; Doug Hart, Sharon Lapkin and Merrill Swain explain the results of two evaluations of secondary level immersion programmes conducted in

Ontario; Margaret S. S. Yau explores the interplay of linguistic and cognitive ability on ESL students' writing performance; and Joan Netten reappraises teaching practices in selected classrooms with respect to aids to comprehension, the use of affect in motivating and responding to pupils, and the amount of and techniques used for correcting the oral production of pupils.

Some may take issue with this book on the grounds that it provides a very broad spectrum of topics and limits the opportunity for extensive discussion of any particular one. In a sense, this is a valid criticism since there is a great need to further the exploration of the concepts examined in this publication. At the same time, it should be noted that the purpose of this book is to present recent research findings in the field of bilingualism and multiculturalism. However, many of the research topics included in the book have not generated the same level of scholastic enthusiasm. Therefore, to delay the publication of these studies in order to gather more information about the topics would have created a conflict with our aim to provide readers with up-to-date conceptualisations, instructional approaches and research findings in bilingual and second language education. It is hoped that this book will stimulate the generation of ideas for new research studies and encourage the publication of more research-related books in the areas of bilingualism and multiculturalism.

Part I:

Cognitive Processing of Language Systems

1 A Theory of Intelligence as Semiosis: With a Couple of Comments on Interlanguage Development

JOHN W. OLLER, JR

> . . . symbolization is a necessary condition of all inquiry and of all knowledge, instead of being a linguistic expression of something already known which needs symbols only for the purposes of convenient recall and communication. (John Dewey, 1938: 263)

The Pentateuch says that the universe came into being in response to the utterance of God: this teaching is encapsulated in the Greek account by the proposition that 'in the beginning was the word'. The Russian genius, Vygotsky (1934), adjusted this proposition by quoting Faust, who said that 'in the beginning was the deed'. Vygotsky elaborated by saying that 'the word is the end of development, crowning the deed'. A few months later he died, never dreaming that his remarks would be tested in scarcely three decades by one of the most remarkable advances in the history of science — the discovery of the genetic code.

From a scientific point of view, perhaps it would be better to say that the word is both the beginning, middle, and end of development. While it may be true that mature expression of human capacity for language may indeed be the crowning evidence of intelligent action, deeds without plans can hardly be termed intelligent at all. If there were no semiotic system in which to formulate a plan, there could be no intelligent action at all. Therefore, if 'language' is taken in the broadest possible sense as 'semiosis', or the representation of meaning, intelligence is a problem of symbolisation from start to finish.

Interestingly, John Dewey also understood 'language' in the sense in which it is used in the present discussion. He saw it as properly applied to all modes of conventional semiotic representation. He wrote:

> Language in its widest sense — that is, including all means of communication such as, for example, monuments, rituals, and formalized arts — is the medium in which culture exists and through which it is transmitted. Phenomena that are not recorded cannot be even discussed. Language is the record that perpetuates occurrences and renders them amenable to public consideration. On the other hand, ideas or meanings that exist *only* [his emphasis] in symbols that are not communicable are fantastic beyond imagination. (1938: 20)

Moreover, Dewey contended, and correctly I believe, that actions themselves are governed by a kind of grammatical system — a fact generally unappreciated by classical logicians, not to mention modern-day psychologists, linguists, and language teachers:

> The authors of the classic logic did not recognize that tools constitute a kind of language which is in more compelling connection with things of nature than are words, nor that the syntax of operations [actions; or Vygotsky's 'deeds'] provides a model for the scheme of ordered knowledge more exacting than that of spoken and written language. (p. 94)

In other words, actions are governed by a kind of grammar that is more rigorous and unyielding than the grammars of natural language systems such as English or Navaho.

For example, to test Dewey's claim, consider the order of events necessary to start your car: it is necessary first to have the keys before you get in the car (or else go back to get them); to insert the right key in the ignition; and so on. Or take any physical routine whatever and think it through in terms of the sequence of specific acts required to perform it.

In the present discussion, life's own language is considered — the biological code, which is, it would seem, as close as science has yet approached to the basis of all living things — and it is construed as a microcosm of intelligence itself. In developing the argument, findings are drawn primarily from biology and the neurosciences. Linguistics, especially Chomskyan generative theory, is only alluded to in reference to the nature of grammatical systems, as is the measurement of intelligence. Interlanguage systems are taken to be approximative attempts to produce and/or comprehend one or more varieties of some targeted language norm. The principal thesis to be developed, somewhat less tentatively than before (Oller, 1981), is that intelligence has a propositional and grammatical character — that it is ultimately based on abstract, non-physical, word-like concepts or categories — and to explore gingerly the implications of this thesis. Or, putting the thesis in a slightly different form, it is that intelligence is essentially semiosis — the capacity to represent systematicity or meaning.

The primary evidence to be appealed to comes from the character of the genetic code, the biological basis for the organisation of living things. In a classic textbook on the subject, Carl Woese (1967) writes about the 'vocabulary' which the cell uses 'to construct messages in nucleic acid language', messages which are then 'translated into amino acid language by means of a dictionary or codebook' (p. 4). He says that every living cell uses 'a tape-reading process in the synthesis of protein' (p. 4). He even goes so far as to suggest that 'the cell can be considered as consisting of a collection of genetic tapes' — that the cell itself *is* a collection of tapes realised as certain complex linear molecules. Indeed, he says that the DNA molecule itself is not merely a long string of tapes, but a whole 'library' of them. Carl Sagan (1978) estimates that a single human DNA molecule consists of roughly 500 million words of text; each DNA text a unique library, that is quite perfectly replicated and deposited in every single cell of each unique organism.

Another biologist, Brian Clark (1977), says that the discovery and partial deciphering of the genetic code is one of the most significant scientific advances in the twentieth century. It is owing to the genetic library of life-discourses, according to Clark and other biologists, that species have hereditary continuity. In fact, this library of texts, biological words strung together in meaningful ways, ultimately directs all of the processes required for sustaining life and provides the foundation for all intelligent biological action. Therefore, contrary to Vygotsky's claim, the meaningful arrangement of biological words into genetic texts must, it would seem, predate the existence of living organisms in order to make possible that existence and thus the various activities of life. Deeds, in this sense, cannot predate words, at least not in the sense of semiosis as defined in the present discussion.

It was realised with the discovery of DNA in the early 1950s that proteins were genetic products rather than genetic materials in the raw. With the discovery of DNA, an almost unbelievably complex polymer, began the search for its relationship to the proteins. The key to the pragmatic linkage between the two was the genetic code. Interestingly, this code, once it was deciphered in part, proved to be the basis of all living things; it turned out to be, apparently, a universal system governing all biological organisms. The code is as rigidly followed in the construction of an amoeba as in the making of a human being. Even viruses, which are possibly derivative corruptions, it seems, fall almost entirely within the scope of the same biological system. In fact, careful research has demonstrated that even minute changes in the system as a whole would be lethal not just to some, but apparently to all living species (Hinegardner & Engelberg, 1963, 1964). The genetic code appears to be an exceedingly articulate system in an improbable and delicate ecological balance (cf. Hoyle, 1983).

However, the approach of this discussion is not merely to look into the cell for clues concerning the character of intelligence. It is to examine the analogical linkage of the genetic texts contained within living cells to the very character of those cells themselves, as well as the differentiation and integration of those cells into a complex organism, their development into various organs, and, ultimately, their organisation in the human brain. In other words, the argument for the proposition that intelligence is based on words appeals to the remarkable hierarchy of languages beginning with the genetic code *per se* and extending through various intermediate levels of organisation to the point where human intelligence becomes able to relate purely abstract linguistic structures to experience of the physical world in such a way as to make sense of both the structures themselves and of experience.

At every discernible point along the way, at every link in the hierarchy, we see analogies of the pragmatic mapping process whereby it is possible for any normal human being to create utterances which are somehow appropriate to the facts of not only that person's experience, but to some extent, those of the common experience of all human beings. The process of pragmatic mapping, viewed at the level of normal human discourse, is an active, intelligent, articulate linking of signs (meaningful semiotic elements — words, phrases, clauses, etc.) with facts of experience. This linking, in all cases it would seem, depends on certain types of grammatical relations; for instance, such a linking depends on an infinitely rich set of subject–predicate relations (both dependent and independent, subordinate and superordinate), as well as negations of such relations, conjunctions of them, and other complications of all of the foregoing.

If these grammatical relations did not exist prior to any given event in experience, it would be impossible (apparently) to conceptualise or represent the experience of any event as humans in fact are able to do. As the philosopher Kant (1724–1804) and other rationalists before and since have argued, if it were not possible to represent events, it would be impossible to experience them at all (Kant, 1783). Or as John Dewey put it in 1938, that which cannot be represented in communicable symbols is 'fantastic beyond imagination'. That is to say, experience itself, or any kind of knowing whatsoever, depends on representation. Consciousness presupposes a rich ability to utilise conceptual relations between abstract categories. Or, putting the matter in different words, intelligence presupposes semiotic capacity — the ability to represent meanings. All of which implies grammatical complexity from the outset.

In fact, the genetic code itself appears to be a kind of grammar which governs the construction of certain kinds of texts. Apparently, the code sets limits to the kinds of strings of biological words that will turn out to be well-formed texts — ones that define viable organisms. For any given species, for instance, the shape, size, functions, and metabolic processes are pre-determined by the arrangement of genetic-words in the biological text that specifies the character of the type of organism in question.

The biological material is passed from parent to offspring in reproduction and thus ensures the continuity of the species. Within any given text, or library of texts specifying the character of a given organism, there are marks of punctuation indicating how given segments of the string are to be read. From DNA molecules, interpretations are generated (transfer RNA molecules) together with instructions (ribosomal RNA) about how to manufacture proteins, and even instructions (messenger RNA) about how to interpret the instructions (e.g. how to set up the protein manufacturing plant, the ribosome, at the outset). Even now, as work in genetics progresses apace, the detailed character of this grammatical structuring is just beginning to be understood (cf. Denton, 1986).

Not only is the structure of biological organisms programmed into the code, but in a dimly understood manner, the genetic library of texts that determines any given species also provides for certain regulatory processes (e.g. metabolism) and sets limits to what a given organism can be. The structure of any given cell is determined more or less directly by a particular arrangement of proteins which are built from amino acids according to detailed instructions coming from the DNA. The proteins themselves, then, perform a regulatory function in their own right as governors of metabolic processes of various sorts (cf. Clark, 1977; and Woese, 1967); for example, insulin as an enabler for glucose to be converted to energy in muscle cells.

Since DNA is more or less linear text (though with some overlapping portions as in a dialogue, as we will see below) which specifies the character of an organism, the linguistic analogy probably fits better than any other that might be imagined. Even proteins are more or less linear in surface structure, though, again, like the elements of a text, their parts (which consist of other proteins) often lead lives of their own (have independent functions), all of which again suggests the aptness of the textual analogy. However, the biological argument for intelligence as having a propositional, textual, grammatical character does not end with the systematic translation of DNA language into protein language. On the contrary, the mystery only begins to unravel there.

When we progress from the structure within a given cell, the substructure of the single cell, to interactions between cells, we find additional evidence for the semiotic (word-like or language-like, textual) basis of intelligence. For example, consider the behaviour of a single-celled organism such as an amoeba. Take, for instance, the amoeba's response to light or heat. When exposed to light above a certain threshold, the amoeba will flee into its medium until its comfort level is restored. How is this possible? In some way, the amoeba must represent (or take notice of) the fact that brightness (or heat) is making it uncomfortable. Then, in some manner, it must internally issue an order to its protoplasm to move until it is out of the light (or heat). This order then is executed until some previously defined equilibrium is restored. All of this activity requires taking account of states of affairs external to the amoeba itself, triggering operations which will tend to bring about some different state of affairs. Is this sort of activity intelligent? Perhaps so, perhaps not. Everything depends on our definition of intelligence.

It is certain, however, that the amoeba's behaviour does involve a kind of complexity which can be accounted for only by appealing to the sorts of propositional relations previously mentioned — subject–predicate relations, together with such constructive operations as superordination, subordination, negation, and conjunction. The whole process, implicit in the amoeba's tropic behaviour, is even discourse-like: 'It's getting uncomfortable here. I'd better move. Okay, I'm moving. Ah! That's better. I'll quit moving now.' To the extent that such propositional complexities (regardless of what molecular or other form they may take) are involved in the amoeba's behaviour, then, it might be said that the behaviour in question is intelligent. Moreover, and more to the point of this discussion, this elaboration of the amoeba's behaviour may help, I think, to illustrate the sort of thing that intelligence is.

While pondering these ideas some years ago, I was mildly surprised to learn that the famed author of the precursor of our modern intelligence tests, the biologist-turned-psychologist, Alfred Binet, had discussed much the same constellation of problems before the turn of the century, and had come to somewhat the same conclusion about the behaviour of single-celled organisms as I am suggesting for consideration here — that they demonstrate a surprising degree of propositionally complex intelligence. As far back as 1888 Binet had written a charming treatise whose English translation was entitled *The Psychic Life of Micro-Organisms*. Actually the book was originally published in French, and the title, *La Vie Psychique . . .*, would no doubt have been better translated as *The Mental Life. . .*, or perhaps even, *The Cognitive Experience of Micro-Organisms*.

Binet contended that all ciliated infusoria (single-celled protozoans with oar-like appendages, such as *Paramecium Aurelius*) could be frightened by placing a drop of acetic acid in the organism's medium. If this were done under a microscope, the organisms, Binet wrote, would be seen to flee in all directions 'like a flock of frightened sheep' (1888: vi). He claimed, therefore, that such organisms could be said to demonstrate the seemingly advanced state of mind called 'fear', along with other psychological traits. In addition, Binet argued that such organisms could be shown to demonstrate intelligent behaviours such as hunting for a particular type of prey, memory of the way out of a certain type of enclosure, planning for the future as demonstrated by preparing a perfectly suited housing for an offspring, courtship behaviour including the game of hard-to-get, and other mental behaviours commonly believed to occur only in higher species.

Of course, the point here is not merely to praise the mental skills of an amoeba, but to argue quite simply that considerable propositional complexities are involved in any activities of the sort demonstrated by Binet. He himself observed that somehow the behaviour of a single-celled organism was controlled by the powers contained within its nucleus, which he described as 'an essential factor in the cell's vitality' (1888: 100). Beyond this, he wondered by what mechanism certain internal states of the organism were set in correspondence with states external to the organism. In his view, 'what would be necessary to explain, is how and in consequence of what mechanism of structure, one form of molecular movement, corresponding to a given excitation, is followed by a certain other form of molecular movement corresponding to an act likewise determined' (p. 65).

A similar problem arises in any attempt to explain the manner in which cells in a more complex multicellular organism are able to know their respective functions, or how they are able to communicate with each other. In fact, an analogue of this problem arises in the world of single cells that have special, short-lived, functions. For example, consider a male sperm cell. How does it know its objective of uniting with a female egg cell, and how does it know when to stop looking and start uniting? Regarding this feat, Binet quoted contemporary biologist, Balbiani, who said: 'I believe that the spermatozoids do not move about blindly, but . . . act in obedience to a kind of inner impulsion, to a sort of volition which directs them to a definite object' (1888: 78). Or, how does a cell of a developing embryo know whether it is to be part of a hand, or eye, or ear, or whatever? Or, how do cells know their proper functions when in fact so many functions are metabolically and otherwise differentiated?

In a popular article, Lewis Wolpert some years ago noted that there had already been widespread speculation among microbiologists and embryologists about whether 'cells have complex conversations with each other during development' (1978: 157). Regardless of the answer to that question, he concluded that 'a large number of experiments indicate that most patterns arise as the result of cell-to-cell interaction' (p. 164). The mystery is, what kinds of physico-chemical mechanisms are employed in this process? For the most part, biologists (not to mention the rest of us) remain somewhat in the dark (again, cf. Denton, 1986).

Still, there is evidence that communication both within and between the cells of complex organisms is extensive. Further, it is clear that the genetic basis of life and its relationship to the basic protein building blocks is essentially one of design and governance. Apparently the system is anything but haphazard and chaotic. To illustrate this point consider the following remarks from microbiologist Michael Denton in 1986:

> Viewed down a light microscope at a magnification of some several hundred times, such as would have been possible in Darwin's time [and Binet's too], a living cell is a relatively disappointing spectacle appearing only as an ever-changing and apparently disordered pattern of blobs and particles which, under the influence of unseen turbulent forces, are continually tossed haphazardly in all directions. To grasp the reality of life as it has been revealed by molecular biology, we must magnify a cell a thousand million times until it is twenty kilometers in diameter and resembles a giant airship large enough to cover a great city like London or New York. What we would then see would be an object of unparalleled complexity and adaptive design. On the surface of the cell we would see millions

of openings, like the port holes of a vast space ship, opening and closing to allow a continual stream of materials to flow in and out. If we were to enter one of these openings we would find ourselves in a world of supreme technology and bewildering complexity. We would see endless highly organized corridors and conduits branching in every direction away from the perimeter of the cell, some leading to the central memory bank in the nucleus and others to assembly plants and processing units. The nucleus itself would be a vast spherical chamber more than a kilometer in diameter, resembling a geodesic dome inside of which we would see, all neatly stacked together in ordered arrays, the miles of coiled chains of the DNA molecules. A huge range of products and raw materials would shuttle along all the manifold conduits in a highly ordered fashion to and from all the various assembly plants in the outer regions of the cell. (p. 328)

Leaping over the middle ground between the micro-cosmic world of DNA and the organic complexities of a human being, we discover that the most complex organ known to science, a human brain, may also best be described in linguistic terms. We have already seen that the grammatical complexity of a cell is substantial, but by comparison with a single living cell, the complexity of the human brain is awe-inspiring. Michael Denton (1986: 330) writes:

An individual cell is nothing when compared with a system like the mammalian brain. The human brain consists of about ten thousand million nerve cells. Each nerve cell puts out somewhere in the region of between ten thousand and one hundred thousand connecting fibers by which it makes contact with other nerve cells in the brain. Altogether the total number of connections in the human brain approaches 10^{15} or a thousand million million. . . . Imagine an area about half the size of the USA (one million square miles) covered in a forest of trees containing ten thousand trees per square mile. If each tree contained one hundred thousand leaves the total number of leaves in the forest would be . . . equivalent to the number of connections in the human brain!

The semiotic metaphor with reference to brain studies was canonised in the book *Languages of the Brain*, by Karl Pribram in 1971 — a person referred to a few years later in *Psychology Today* as 'the Magellan of brain science'. Another brain scientist, distinguished Oxford professor J.Z. Young, extended the language metaphor still further:

To understand the language of the brain it is necessary to know how the nerve cells combine, like letters or the phones of speech, to produce units that have meaning, like words. . . . If grammar is the system that regulates the . . . use of language, we migh⁺ say that the brain operates a sort of metalanguage with a metagrammar, which regulates the . . . conduct of life, including speech. (1978: 46)

Furthermore, the brain does not merely function in the control of mental behaviours, though we non-specialists often tend to see it as if it were limited to that role. In much the way that DNA controls organismic development at the micro-level, the brain (indeed the whole central nervous system) seems to play a crucial role in the global architecture and construction of the entire body at the macro-level. Lenneberg (1967) cited the research of Critchley (1955) showing that damage to either of the parietal lobes in infancy results in stunting of the corresponding body parts on the opposite side. Moreover, Lenneberg argued that mere 'disuse' is an insufficient explanation of this stunting since it is apparent in pre-natal stages. Thus, muscular and skeletal development seem to be under the control of the developing central nervous system in much the way that cell architecture and metabolism fall under the control of DNA.

Summing up and extending the whole thesis of this discussion, it might be argued that the genetic code sets limits and also specifies the underlying possibilities for living organisms. Particular expressions (interpretations) of that grammatical control mechanism or governance system are realised in the DNA molecules that specify particular living organisms. However, the DNA molecules themselves, in like manner, constitute a kind of grammar governing the development of proteins. The latter, in their turn, and again in a similar fashion, seem to constitute grammatical systems in their own right, and in like manner, also control a whole constellation of factors (cf. Woese, 1967; and Clark, 1977) including cell architecture, metabolism, defence, etc. Skipping the intermediate ground of embryology and the differentiation of distinct organs in complex life-forms, we come to the advanced complexity of mammalian nervous systems including the brains of human beings. Here, again, we see a sort of grammatical governance relationship, to both physical development and mental behaviour.

Thus, from the DNA upward, biological development is somewhat like the cascading network of relationships of subordination and superordination, of implication, presupposition, and association. However, when we examine more closely the increasingly complex developments of the upward cascade in the case of biology, each step seems quite miraculous in its own right. Also, from the lowest level upward, what charms the linguist in us (if there is one), is that there is a surprising text-like quality from start to finish. Michael Denton comments on the densely packed information system which is apparently unpacked in a cascading series during biological maturation. For instance, concerning proteins, Denton comments that

> the breakdown products of proteins [are used] to perform all sorts of functions often quite unrelated to the function of the 'mother' protein. Thus, many protein functions are compacted into an original molecule. The process begins by the synthesis of the original protein which, after performing its function, is broken down into still smaller proteins capable of yet further functions. The device is somewhat analogous to having a whole tool kit compacted within the first tool we require to initiate a particular operation; and when the initial operation is complete, the tools required for the next operation, and so on until the operation is complete. (1986: 337)

The whole process appears to depend on the sort of multi-layered hierarchical structuring that is characteristic of natural language systems, and of texts expressed in natural languages, except for the fact that the wisdom of the biological solution with respect to functions served by particular proteins cannot be fully appreciated until the anticipatory character of each component step in the process is understood.

Another sort of textual compacting is observed in interpretations of DNA so as to produce more proteins than are theoretically possible to derive from a single linear sequence. This is accomplished, in Denton's own words, 'by a mechanism of wonderful ingenuity' (p. 336), by simply parsing the same structure in a variety of ways so as to produce a considerable variety of interpretations (proteins, in this case). Just as the sequence of letters 'n-o-w-h-e-r-e' may be read as 'now here' or 'no where' the same sequence of DNA words may provide for the synthesis of different proteins on different readings.

However, in order for the process to work as efficiently as it does, there must be internal marks of punctuation, or instructions about how distinct parsings are to be achieved. Denton writes:

> Overlapping genes are not the only recently discovered ingenious device for compacting information with great economy into DNA sequences. DNA does not consist entirely of genes containing encoded messages for the specification of proteins; a considerable proportion is involved in control purposes, switching off and on

different genes at different times and in different cells. This was considered, again by analogy with human information retrieval systems such as might be used in a library or filing system or computer, to be positioned adjacent to, but separate from, the genes under its control. There was some empirical support for this very logical view, but once more, as in the case of overlapping genes, biological design turned out to be far more clever than was suspected, for it has now been found that many sequences of DNA which perform the crucial control functions related to information retrieval are situated not adjacent to the genes which they control but actually embedded within the genes themselves. (1986: 337)

While Denton sees 'no strict analogy in our own technology' for such 'compacting devices', it might be argued that the processes he describes are not unlike the embedding of structure within structure within structure, and so forth, which is so characteristic of the grammar of natural language systems.

Is it possible that the cascading network observed in forward gear with reference to the physical growth and development of biological organisms (moving apparently uphill through increasing levels of complexity) is merely observed in reverse motion with reference to psychological development and language acquisition (moving apparently downhill by fixing and fleshing out innate categories with reference to particular experiences)? This is a possibility to which we return shortly. Let it be noted here only that the direction of movement may be somewhat incidental: the innateness or pre-programmed aspect of both processes may be their more important quality (just as Chomsky, Fodor, and others have been arguing; cf. Piatelli-Palmarini, 1980, and the contributions by both Chomsky and Fodor included there).

With that in mind, the shared mystery of both embryological development (including perhaps the problem of speciation and phyla) and psychological maturation may be, as Denton's arguments together with those of Chomsky, Fodor, and others (cf. Piatelli-Palmarini, 1980) seem to imply, a single problem of design. As intractable a problem as it may seem, the principal issue would be to find a way to characterise the text-like interrelatedness, the connectedness, of the entire continuum of development ranging from inert matter through the full spectrum of biological order. We need, not merely 'a theory of learning', but a better articulated 'theory of evolution' in the broadest possible sense of the latter term.

In fact, part of the embryological aspect of the problem, as Denton points out, can be construed as suggested by Von Neumann (1966) as a question about automata: namely, how to design one capable of self-replication. Von Neumann, according to Denton, saw the problem as consisting of three parts: (1) information storage; (2) duplication of the stored information; and (3) self-replication — that is, setting up the information in such a form that it will fully specify the means for its own duplication. These are scarcely trivial engineering problems, and yet all of them are solved in the design of living organisms. Denton comments:

> So efficient is the mechanism of information storage and so elegant the mechanism of duplication of this remarkable molecule that it is hard to escape the feeling that the DNA molecule may be the one and only perfect solution to the twin problems of information storage and duplication for self-replicating automata.
>
> The solution to the problem of the automatic factory is the ribosome. Basically, the ribosome is a collection of some fifty or so large molecules, mainly proteins, which fit tightly together. Altogether the ribosome consists of a highly organized structure of more than one million atoms which can synthesize any protein that it is instructed to make by the DNA, including the particular proteins which compromise [sic; apparently 'comprise' is intended] its own structure — so the ribosome can construct itself. (pp. 337–8)

The sheer difficulty of the engineering problems that are perfectly solved in the ribosome defies the imagination. Denton writes:

> It is astonishing to think that this remarkable piece of machinery, which possesses the ultimate capacity to construct every living thing that ever existed on Earth, from a giant redwood to the human brain, can construct all its own components in a matter of minutes and weigh less than 10^{16} grams. It is of the order of several thousand million million times smaller than the smallest piece of functional machinery ever constructed by man. (p. 338)

But is the mechanistic analogy appropriate? Denton replies:

> In every direction the biochemist gazes as he journeys through this weird molecular labyrinth, he sees devices and appliances reminiscent of our own twentieth-century world of advanced technology. In the atomic fabric of life we have found a reflection of our own technology. We have seen a world as artificial as our own and as familiar as if we had held up a mirror to our own machines. (p. 340)

Inevitably, therefore, as astronomer Johannes Kepler (1571–1630) (who correctly predicted the elliptical orbit of the planets) and others have often observed, design implies a designer. The story is told that Kepler had built a model of the solar system which elicited an exchange with an atheistic acquaintance. Upon seeing Kepler's model, the man said, 'It's beautiful, who built it?' 'No one,' Kepler said with a twinkle, 'It just happened' (Naismith, 1962: 7).

While few moderns may be willing to embrace the full force of its teleological implications, the existence of design is a fundamental fact of science. It can no longer be construed, at least not in the eighth decade of the twentieth century (if ever it could have been), as an argument based on some dope-smoking ritual of some long outmoded superstition — the opiate of the poor, ignorant, oppressed masses. As Denton says, far from being an a priori argument as often argued in modern intellectual circles, 'the inference to design is purely a posteriori induction based on a ruthlessly consistent application of the logic of analogy. The conclusion may have religious implications, but it does not depend on religious presuppositions' (p. 341).

With all of the foregoing in mind, we may now conclude with the promised comments on the matter of language acquisition and more particularly the theory of interlanguages as some sort of approximation to a target norm, short of the norm and perhaps influenced by the grammatical character of some other better known system.

First, it may be suggested that advances in microbiology lend credence to the innateness hypothesis as put forward by Chomsky, and as championed more recently by Fodor, and others. If the syntax/semantics of all possible natural languages and even some sort of skeletonised variant of all possible lexicons should turn out to be essentially in place at birth and just waiting to blossom in the course of development at the gentle prodding of few and meagre experiences, interlanguages (as approximative systems) may be as much products of default settings in some universal grammar as they are of an interactive meshing of the native language system(s) and one or more target languages.

If correct, this hypothesis would suggest a sort of contrastive analysis not merely between native and target languages, but between both of them and hypothesised elements presumably of universal grammar. Perhaps interlanguages of a wide-ranging sort will tend to show some of the tendencies predicted by Bickerton (1981), for instance, in the rapid creolisation of multiple variants of some pidgin language in a single generation.

More specifically, for example, we might expect for pragmatic reasons that SVO order, for instance, will tend to be the universal grammar default setting whenever the learner/acquirer is not coerced into some other order by the native or target grammar. SVO is pragmatically more natural because of the fact that an agent must ordinarily conceive a plan prior to carrying it out by acting so as subsequently to influence a patient or object.

Second, if experience is to have a role, I still suppose that it will be along the lines laid down in Vigil & Oller (1976) — that unexpected negative feedback on the cognitive dimension will prove to be the primary cause of destabilising a developing grammatical system and thus pushing the learner/acquirer to a higher level of proficiency in a given target language. Otherwise, to the extent that the learner/acquirer finds his or her communicative requirements fully met by any particular variant of a grammar, that variant (interlanguage), I suppose, will tend to stabilise and will therefore become a plateau (or 'fossilised' system) beyond which there will be no impetus to proceed. Of course, as noted in the original paper with Vigil (though seemingly misunderstood and therefore disputed by Selinker & Lamendella, 1979, 1980), the learner/acquirer may be his or her own best source of destabilising feedback through the sort of self-monitoring that asks, 'Is that what I meant to say?' That is to say, there is no need to suppose that feedback must be 'extrinsic' (as Selinker & Lamendella, 1979, argued) in order for it to function as such. If the learner/acquirer sets a high enough standard of performance, there seems to be no necessary intrinsic limit to the approximation to nativeness eventually to be achieved — unless, of course, the 'critical age' hypothesis were correct.

At this point, I remain sceptical about the latter hypothesis, and continue to believe that nativeness can be achieved long past puberty. Perhaps the changes taking place at or about puberty may be used to define a 'sensitive period' beyond which it becomes more difficult to acquire native proficiency in a non-primary language system, but the claim that it becomes impossible is, I believe, refuted by appropriate case histories.

References

BICKERTON, DEREK. 1981, *Roots of Language*. Ann Arbor, MI: Karoma.
BINET, A. 1888, *The Psychic Life of Micro-Organisms*. Chicago: Open Court.
CLARK, B. 1977, *The Genetic Code*. London: E. Arnold.
CRITCHLEY, M. 1955, *The Parietal Lobes*. London: E. Arnold.
DENTON, M. 1986, *Evolution: A Theory in Crisis*. Bethesda, MD: Adler and Adler.

DEWEY, J. 1938, *Logic: The Theory of Inquiry.* New York: Holt.

HINEGARDNER, R.T. and ENGELBERG, J. 1963, Rationale for a universal genetic code. *Science* 142, 1083–5.

— 1964, Comment on a criticism by Woese. *Science* 144, 1031.

HOYLE, F. 1983, *The Intelligent Universe.* London: Michael Joseph.

KANT, I. 1783, *Prolegomena to Any Future Metaphysics.* New York: Liberal Arts (1950).

LENNEBERG, E. 1967, *Biological Foundations of Language.* New York: Wiley.

NAISMITH, A. 1962, *1200 Notes Quotes and Anecdotes.* Chicago: Moody.

OLLER, J.W., JR 1981, Language as intelligence? *Language Learning* 31, 465–92.

PIATELLI-PALMARINI, M. (ed.) 1980, *Language and Learning: The Debate between Jean Piaget and Noam Chomsky.* Cambridge, MA: Harvard University Press.

PRIBRAM, K. 1971, *Languages of the Brain.* Englewood Cliffs, NJ: Prentice-Hall.

SAGAN, C. 1978, *The Dragons of Eden: Speculations on the Evolution of Human Intelligence.* New York: Ballantine.

SELINKER, L. and LAMENDELLA, J.T. 1979, The role of extrinsic feedback in interlanguage fossilization. *Language Learning* 29, 363–75.

— 1980, Fossilization in interlanguage learning. In K. CROFT (ed.) *Reading in English as a Second Language: For Teacher and Teacher Trainees.* Cambridge, MA: Winthrop, 2nd edn, pp. 132–43.

VIGIL, N.A. and OLLER, J.W. JR 1976, Rule fossilization: A tentative model. *Language Learning* 26, 281–95.

VON NEUMANN, JOHN 1966, *Theory of Self-Reproducing Automata.* Urbana, Ill.: University of Illinois.

VYGOTSKY, L. 1934, *Thought and Language,* tr. E. Hanfmann and G. Vakar (1962). Cambridge, MA: Massachusetts Institute of Technology.

WOESE, C. 1967, *The Genetic Code.* New York: Harper and Row.

WOLPERT, GORDON 1978, Pattern formation in biological development. *Scientific American* 239, 154–64.

YOUNG, J.Z. 1978, *Programs of the Brain.* Oxford, England: Oxford University Press.

2 Along the Way: Interlanguage Systems in Second Language Acquisition

LARRY SELINKER

Introduction

This essay will provide an overview of some of the concepts comprising the interlanguage (IL) hypothesis.[1] The word 'hypothesis' should be stressed here since much of what follows, it must be emphasised, is still in the realm of hypothesis and not of certainty. This is because, quite honestly, we haven't been around that long. The field of second language acquisition (SLA), of which IL is a part, is a relatively new field.

Most scholars agree that the field of SLA began in 1967 with a classic paper by Pit Corder (Corder, 1967). That is, searching the literature for several centuries back, there exists no previous systematic field of study of learner languages, under any name. This is striking, since there are 'sibling fields', such as the study of grammar and the thinking and talking about language pedagogy which are at least 2,500 years old. It is not surprising that in SLA we are still in the stage of struggling for a way to do things with a relatively new subject matter.

The concepts comprising the IL hypothesis to be discussed below relate to bilingual and multicultural education in the following way: it is the main thesis of a strong view of the IL hypothesis that, from a productive point of view, non-native (NN) speaking students do not learn to produce second languages; what they do in fact is to create and develop ILs in particular contexts, specifically for our purposes here, that IL in academic discourse domains is real. From a comprehension point of view, however, things may be quite different since NN students do seem to learn to understand second languages as well as native speakers (NSs) do. That is, to my knowledge the existence of a 'perceptual IL' has not been seriously suggested in the literature. The forces leading to NN ILs are many, but prime among them is language transfer, or the influence on the developing IL of the native language (NL). One of the key practical aspects of such IL learning is what has been termed 'fossilization', or the permanent cessation of IL learning often far from target language (TL) norms. The issue of the permanency of fossilization, that is, what will not go away no matter how much correction is given, is highly contentious, but it appears to be accepted that fossilization is real; that is to say, from a practical point of view, non-learning in IL is a serious problem. One of the premises that I will argue for, however, is that given the reality of contextually based ILs, it is none the less possible to 'teach round' fossilization.

One of the important research points I will return to is that it is not known which sorts of IL are associated with academic success. It is my hypothesis that such knowledge is essential from a practical point of view since the use of such forms may actually help promote subject matter or content learning. Davies (1984) argues that the recognition and rewarding of certain types of IL may actually promote SLA. Namely, we would like to know which IL forms are associated with content success whether the IL behaviour is classified as 'errors' or not. A corollary issue of great importance would be: which sorts of IL (whether TL-like 'non-errors' or not) are associated with unsuccessful academic achievement? In general, note that we would like to know how context-bound IL behaviour is.

A key question which underlies this work then is 'along the way to where?' With fossilization an apparent reality, the answer cannot be along the way to NS competence, i.e. the full range of contexts in which NSs control a language. But in the setting of bilingual and multicultural education, such complete NS mastery, even if it were possible, would not be enough; content learning to a certain level of success is, of course, also required and IL here is clearly involved, but to an unknown degree. A true IL perspective does not take TL NS norms as the only legitimate goal. It depends. In fact, the IL hypothesis has always been friendly to local varieties of English, whether in Singapore or Seattle, Nepal or New York.

Another introductory point of importance is that the terms 'interlanguage', 'transitional competence' (Corder, 1971, 1981) and 'approximative systems' (Nemser, 1971) are not synonymous and should not be treated as such. In my view, they reflect different theoretical positions that have practical ramifications. The transitional competence hypothesis emphasises the in-flux phenomenon of only certain ILs. This hypothesis does not pretend to account for those ILs which are permanently fossilized, or even for the real possibility of those parts of developing ILs which may be fossilized relative to particular contexts. The approximative systems hypothesis is different from the other two in its emphasis on directionality towards the TL. This latter hypothesis is, I believe, fundamentally false in its view that SLA evolves in stages which gradually more closely approximate the TL. It is in fact a denial of the strong possibility of the reality of permanent fossilization. To hold this hypothesis, one would have to conceive of SLA as a type of acquisition where non-learning is not a serious problem. We know that that position would not reflect reality. The problem with rejecting this hypothesis is that the classical assumption seems to have a strong grain of truth to it: at some level of consciousness, learners on some occasions do in fact try to approximate some sort of 'target'. The difficulty is that the resultant IL productive systems do not march inexorably towards that target.

These then are some of the themes to be discussed in this essay.

Some Concepts Related to IL

Relevant data

It was rashly claimed in Selinker (1972) that the only data which are relevant to a theory of SLA should be gathered in 'meaningful performance situations'. This was surely too strong, for it denies legitimacy to studies which gather data from SLA experiments or from the intuitions of IL speakers. This extreme claim had put me in the unfortunate position of denying the validity of some of my own experimental work (e.g. Selinker, 1969), but, none the less, there is a grain of truth in it. I still feel that if we are interested in a teaching/learning approach and not just a learning approach independent of content learning in educational settings, then we must admit that experimental results are hard to extrapolate from. In the last few years, I have taken the working position that my own studies (e.g. Douglas & Selinker, 1985, 1987; and Selinker & Douglas, 1985) should remain close to the actual teaching situation concerned, involving the micro-analysis of IL data in such situations.

As regards the use of IL intuitional data, I also argued against this in Selinker (1972), but clearly once again the case was overstated. Over the years interesting results have come out of studies which use elicitation procedures. However, a caution by Labov (1966) is still worth considering in bilingual and multicultural settings: when two forms of a language are in a subordinate and superordinate relationship, the intuitions one gets from speakers in the subordinate situation may reflect the superordinate system. This may very well happen in a school setting where standard English is the superordinate dialect and an English IL is perceived as the subordinate dialect.

One of the strongest reasons in IL studies to investigate this issue of relevant data is that we must be sure of the status of the following claim of the IL hypothesis: that learners create second language systems that have forms (and possibly meanings) which appear neither in the NL nor in the TL, as well as TL-like forms which may not have TL meaning, but an IL-particular semantics. We need to know exactly what these form/meaning correlations are. This is a methodological problem which has not been addressed very well in SLA because, essentially, it is a problem of comparing non-equals. This is the situation which holds especially if one takes an 'error analysis' (EA) point of view, whether in an empirical sense or in teacher statements to students about the errors they make. It turns out that in EA, the epistemological problem is that one is comparing what students actually say, i.e. actual data, with what the researcher (or teacher) infers would have been said by a NS if — and this is important — the NS had been trying to express the same meaning that the learner appears to have intended. So, in an EA perspective, one is comparing actual data with inferred data, two unequal types of data. (Kellerman, 1987, presents more discussion on problems inherent in an EA perspective.)

Now there is a type of intuitive data we recommend using in SLA and that is 'secondary data', the primary data usually being the N/NN or NN/NN IL talk that one is interested in analysing. There are two types of secondary data: 'retrospective' and 'expert' data. In the methodology we recommend (cf. Douglas & Selinker, 1985, 1987; Selinker & Douglas, 1985), videotape technology is employed to record a communicative event, such as a conversation about the subject matter being studied. The resulting videotape (the primary data) is then reviewed by the co-participants as a retrospective event and, depending on the purpose of the study, by various sorts of relevant expert reviewers (e.g. an expert in the content or subject matter being discussed in the primary data) to comment on the technical correctness, appropriateness and precision of the language being used. The secondary data is audio-recorded and co-ordinated with the primary data. One type of instruction recommended by Frankel & Beckman (1982) is to ask reviewers of the primary data to stop the tape 'where you see anything surprising, unusual or interesting'. They report a high correlation of places on the primary tape where various types of reviewers stop the tape. Of course, there are often differences as to what is commented on. Each type of data contributes to our understanding of the original communicative event, with the secondary data helping to guide the analysis. (See the references cited above for technical details.)

Age

In the original IL paper (Selinker, 1972) it was hypothesised that puberty was a cut-off point for the formation of ILs; that before puberty, learners in some mysterious way became NSs of the TL. One thing we feel sure about is that this notion is false. That IL can be found in young school learners under certain sociolinguistic conditions has been known for quite some time (cf. Selinker, Swain & Dumas, 1975; Tarone, Frauenfelder & Selinker, 1976; and for an update: Harley & Swain, 1984). As alluded to in the introduction to this chapter there are important perceptual/production differences in the IL situation that may strongly differ from the NL situation. There is evidence in French immersion settings that this is indeed the case. For example, Harley & Swain (1984: 291) cite previous research which shows that from a comprehension point of view, 'immersion students develop a remarkable ability to comprehend oral and written discourse in the second language'. In spite of this, they conclude that 'there is evidence to show that after six to seven years of an immersion program, productive use of the second language still differs considerably in grammatical and lexical ways from that of native speakers'. They document in considerable detail an area that is central to the learning of second languages, the verb system. Describing this work would take us too far afield; suffice it to say here that they integrate into their discussion 'target-like performance', the 'continuing role of the mother tongue in immersion interlanguage', and 'the extent to which fossilization occurs'.

Does all this mean, then, there is an earlier cut-off point, say five years old, under which ILs cannot be formed? I know of no empirical evidence concerning this question. However, on a trip to India in 1983, several colleagues (Prahlad and Tirumalesh, personal communication) argued that in the multilingual settings that one finds in central institutes in India where the father's language is, say, Tamil, the mother's is Hindi, the maid's may be one of any local number and the language, including language of play, of the community is English, then one sees ILs in children as young as three. But here one runs into the question of 'target' in IL setting versus non-native variety setting, that has recently been much discussed (cf. Zuengler, 1989, for a survey of results and issues). Eisenstein (1986) discusses this question of 'target' regarding SLA in New York City.

The conclusion must be that IL learning should be of concern to those working with even young school-age children.

Language transfer

This topic concerns the role and influence of one language upon the formation of another, usually — but not always — the role of the NL in forming IL. This topic is often subsumed under a slightly broader topic called 'cross-linguistic influence' (CLI). The most extensive recent work on this subject is that of Kellerman (1987), who concludes:

> There is crosslinguistic influence and it exists in many forms . . . the phenomenon is so pervasive that it cannot be considered peripheral to the study of [SLA] . . . There is now evidence to suggest that CLI not only acts as a source of surface forms in the learner's IL at levels beyond and within the sentence. Furthermore, where the adult L1 pattern is also consonant with a putatively universal developmental stage in L2 learning, the learner may proceed to that stage faster than those learners who do not pattern may lead to delay in the acquisition of the L2 target or even fossilization. (Kellerman, 1987: 49) (L1 = NL, and L2 = the second language)

Finally, he concludes that 'It is misleading to say that CLI does not afflict the more advanced learner to a greater extent than the less advanced'. One painful lesson that we have learned over the years is that a learner does not transfer an entire NL subsystem to the IL, but 'selectively' transfers bits and pieces (cf. Gass & Selinker, 1983, *passim*): that is, the influence of NL is variable. As Kellerman puts it: 'learners do not bring fully determined L1s to the acquisition of L2s' (Kellerman, 1987: 69). Much empirical work has gone into trying to figure out exactly what gets transferred and why and, in my opinion, given the range of IL situations actual and potential in the world, the present period of research will eventually be looked on as just scratching the surface. The two references cited in this paragraph and the references cited in these sources should provide the interested reader with more detail than perhaps he/she would like to know. A type of language transfer, 'internal-IL transfer' will be discussed below in the section on discourse domains.

One of the key problems in language transfer research is methodological. It is not always clear how an analyst can identify that a transfer has occurred in an unambiguous sense. Several things are clear from the research literature: structural congruence between the two systems is not enough and error counts and simple percentages can be misleading. It is now recognised that there must be a comparison of behaviours in a common L2 with different L1s. Also, although an extreme view of contrastive analysis is misleading, it remains a good place to start in searching for hypotheses to be tested. Finally, it is clear that language transfer interacts with other processes and constraints throughout the IL experience. As Kellerman (1987) points out, one important constraint is fossilisation.

Fossilization

This is the term used to cover the complex phenomenon of the cessation of IL learning often far from TL norms. It is what appears to make second language different from first. Like the other concepts discussed here, its application is individualistic and variable. Fossilization may be empirically described by looking at forms in IL speech and writing that remain over time, despite all attempts to eradicate them.

It turns out that fossilization has been more assumed than studied. A main reason, once again, is methodological. Short-term studies by definition are irrelevant for we are talking about the 'permanent' cessation of IL learning or forms that remain in learner speech for a very long time. How long? It looks as if researchers have agreed (Gass, personal communication) that if an IL form remains in learner speech for five years, we will call it 'fossilized'. Even so, such longitudinal studies seem to be beyond research agendas as they are currently arranged. And what about learner writing? It is not inconceivable that TL-like competence, when it occurs in IL talk, might not extend to IL writing. This has been speculated about with regard to Native American children (Charley Basham for Alaska settings and Sue Foster for Arizona settings; personal communications).

We need to build a large body of empirical as well as experiential data here, and this is where teachers in bilingual and multicultural settings can help. We need to find out about the following sorts of things:

— The nature of fossilization. We think that fossilization is peculiar to IL learning: might it be a part of other types of learning as well?
— The source of fossilization. Many variables have been suggested as

sources: are the sources more related to restricted L2 input or to motivational factors, as well?

— The objects of fossilization. It looks as if any part of IL can fossilize from phonology through syntax through rhetoric through conversational and communication strategies. Is this indeed true for 'all' items of IL or is there variation here, as well?

— The manner of fossilization. We have no idea about sequences of fossilisable items. Is fossilization an abrupt event or a gradual process occurring over years?

— Point at which fossilization begins. We have some idea that it can set in quite early in certain situations (cf. Perdue, 1984, concerning 'guest worker' immigrants in Northern Europe). In general, is there a lower bound when fossilization could possibly occur?

— Persistence of fossilization. Though I know of no research literature on this, it seems clear, anecdotally, that some things that were thought to be fossilized have only been temporarily 'stabilised' and have later developed. How do we find out about this?

— Candidates for fossilization. Anecdotally again, it seems that some individuals are more prone to fossilization than others. This seems especially true regarding child SLA. We need to find out about the relative contributions here of variables such as age, sex, motivation, intelligence, language aptitude, opportunity to learn, opportunity to practise, etc.

The practising teacher will see by perusing this list that, regarding fossilization, we are still at the primitive stage of formulating adequate questions. I believe that teacher wisdom can help here to set the agenda for those perspectives on this problem which would be most productive and for which purposes. (Cf. Selinker & Lamendella, 1978, for technical detail.)

But it is most important for teachers to realise that, regarding fossilization, nowhere is it claimed that learners cannot be taught to communicate in a second language. If, as suggested above, IL learning and use is bounded by context, we must explore the strategy of 'teaching round' fossilization and for that we need the concept of 'discourse domains'.

Discourse domains

It is clear that IL varies by context. Tarone (1983) has shown that IL varies by task, that one will get more or less 'vernacular' IL form depending on the task used in the particular study. In a series of studies (e.g. Douglas & Selinker, 1985, 1987; Selinker & Douglas, 1985) we have empirically extended this notion to say that IL varies by discourse domain, by which we mean the cognitive experiential[2] way an individual 'slices up' the content domains of language use that he/she must talk or write about. Prototypical domains are such things as 'talk about work' and 'talk about life story'. We have spent several years in trying to come up with a composite methodology to study contextually based IL learning, use and fossilization; details are given in the references cited above.

Our intention is to take a true IL perspective in studying IL forms and attendant rhetoric, semantics, programmatics and discourse, not focusing on 'error', but linking variation in IL form to learner-constructed domains of content and subject matter use. Our claim is that learners construct ILs within discourse domains, so that they possess a number of different domains with a somewhat different IL associated with each. The connection with language transfer and fossilization — as well as communication and learning strategies — is that these SLA strategies and processes do not occur globally across ILs, but rather differentially within discourse domains. That is, not only is there IL variation by domain, but fossilization, language transfer, communication and learning strategy variation, as well. In the papers cited, and in several others, we have presented evidence that we think is congruent with these hypotheses.

In language use situations, we hypothesise that learners cognitively engage a discourse domain and the IL associated with it. We have found, for example, that in the work talk domain, one subject used the modal words 'can' and 'could' pretty much in a TL-like fashion to indicate factual or hypothetical possibility. However, in the life story domain, he distinguished concrete, specific topics from abstract, general ones by switching between 'could' and 'can' in his discourse in what seemed to us to be an IL-particular use. In other words, he was using modals, and other features, differentially in the two domains. Though it is more complicated than that, we concluded that ILs can change longitudinally within domains, but that such changes may not carry across domains. Note that we could have made an error in judgement had we concentrated on testing IL modal knowledge and use in only one of the domains.

This is an important point. It relates to the concept mentioned above of 'internal-IL transfer' and is very much a teacher topic. We know that when a form enters the IL, it does not enter the entire IL, that the learner cannot use that form precisely and correctly in all contexts. So, if it enters one context, what is its 'life history'? Does it remain in that one context forever or does it transfer internally in the IL to other contexts? Schumann and colleagues (e.g. Master, Schumann & Sokolik, 1987) have followed the introduction of IL forms in 'pidginized ILs' and have followed the life history of such forms context by context. The work is promising, but it is too early to come up with general conclusions. This is another area where teacher-directed practical research could prove of great value.

The idea of 'teaching round' fossilization is relevant here. Teachers should become aware of those domains in which particular learners may wish to or need to communicate. Teachers might wish to adjust teaching to such contexts, since it appears that system-wide IL changes are more difficult to induce than domain-specific IL change. The important practical conclusion here is that it may be the case that the onset of fossilization will be slowed in domains that are new to learners if domain knowledge is induced slowly while productive IL is restrained. But these ideas remain to be tested.

Conclusions

We will conclude by discussing fossilization a bit more and then consider where we might wish to put our research emphasis in the next few years.

It is most important for teachers to try to come to grips with a deep understanding of why fossilization exists, persists and is so pervasive. What ecological functions could such a strategy have for learners? In a paper written in 1984, Klein suggests that there are advantages for fossilized learners' ILs, if the freezing takes place 'at not too elementary a level'. Klein (1984) claims that such ILs are stable, first of all, and, second, that they are 'easy to master'. Third, it has been empirically shown over and over that learners can perform many linguistic and pragmatic functions with very limited and non-TL-like linguistic means.[3] These insights could prove especially important to teaching colleagues who, by their own admission, worry about this phenomenon. We might wish to devote some research effort to investigating the positive aspects of fossilization (to the learner!), as well as its negative aspects, especially within relevant and important discourse domains.

One of the background ideas underlying some recent work in IL is that cognitive information, where communicative intent is elicited, is important to understanding the IL forms that learners produce in school settings. This is where discourse domains in different activity types comes in. We thus need to be interested in the linguistic content of academic achievement in an IL. Our perspective implied that students need to become more precise in the IL they are producing relative to particular contexts. The students becoming a 'knower' or an 'expert' in certain areas and the IL associated with that have to be looked at, and Zuengler (1987) is beginning to do that.

In taking an IL perspective within bilingual and multicultural settings then we need to discover several sorts of things: (a) we need to discover which IL forms are associated with successful completion of specific learning tasks. We also need to have (b) some understanding of how factors such as age, language transfer, fossilization and backsliding affect the IL that learners create relative to particular sorts of learning tasks in school. We also need to have some understanding of (c) the current IL base of learners related to specific learning tasks in specific domains, for this will be the base upon which learners need to grow in terms of becoming more precise relative to the linguistic content of academic achievement in the TL. Also, it would be helpful to really find out (d) how true it is that learners, in creating second language systems, do in fact create forms which appear neither in the NL nor in the TL. Then we must find out (e) about the semantics/pragmatics of these IL-particular forms relative to important contexts. Also, we cannot assume that TL-like forms produced by IL users have actual TL-particular semantics/pragmatics; we need to find out (f) which TL-like forms are congruent with TL semantics/pragmatics and which have IL-particular pragmatics/semantics. We need to discover (g) what are the sorts of IL which successful users of the TL (here most particularly content teachers) can 'tolerate' in particular discourse domains as successful completions of particular learning tasks in terms of relevant IL form. We should try to become aware of (h) what 'targets' learners are trying to 'approximate', if indeed they are doing such a thing. Does a more conscious attempt at approximation make a difference and under what conditions? And, finally, for the various bilingual and multicultural contexts that exist, we must become empirically more certain about (i) the age factor and IL development, use and fossilization.

It is clear to me that this sort of knowledge can help teachers prepare relevant materials and lessons. But, in the final analysis, one of the practical benefits to be derived from studying IL in bilingual and multicultural settings is a humane one: that this sort of information should help teachers help their students understand their own learning along the way to more successful school achievement.

Notes

1. Some of the ideas presented in this chapter are developed in a more technical way in Selinker (1984, 1991), Douglas & Selinker (1985, 1987), Selinker & Douglas (1985), Selinker & Lamendella (1978) and in the introduction to Gass & Selinker (1983). Additionally, the studies presented in the latter on language transfer provide useful empirical detail. Where I have offered overall interpretations for what these studies might mean, the usual claims of responsibility apply.
2. This was shown quite convincingly with Alberto (Schumann, 1978) and with the many studies of guest-worker learners in Northern Europe (Perdue, 1984, and the special issue (*passim*) of *Studies in Second Language Acquisition* (8, 4, 1986) which reports on ten years of SLA work in France).
3. Domains of experience as cognitive models are discussed in a most useful way in Lakoff, 1987.

References

CORDER, S.P. 1967, The significance of learners' errors. *IRAL* 5, 161–70.
— 1971, Idiosyncratic dialects and error analysis. *IRAL* 9, 147–60.
— 1981, *Error Analysis and Interlanguage*. Oxford: Oxford University Press.
DAVIES, A. 1984, Introduction. In A. DAVIES, C. CRIPER and A.P.R. HOWATT (eds) *Interlanguage*. Edinburgh: Edinburgh University Press.
DOUGLAS, D. and SELINKER, L. 1985, Principles for language tests within the 'discourse domains' theory of interlanguage: Research, test construction and interpretation. *Language Testing* 2, 205–26.
— 1987, U.S. TAs vs. FTAs: Comparative Features of Discourse Domains. Paper presented at TESOL 1987, Miami.
EISENSTEIN, M.R. 1986, Target language variation and second-language acquisition: Learning English in New York City. *World Englishes* 5, 31–46.
FRANKEL, R. and BECKMAN, H. 1982, *IMPACT: An Interaction-Based Method for Preserving and Analyzing Clinical Transactions. Explorations in Provider and Patient Transactions*, ed. L. Pettigrew. Memphis: Humana.
GASS, S. and SELINKER, L. (eds) 1983, *Language Transfer in Language Learning*. Rowley, MA: Newbury House.
HARLEY, B. and SWAIN, M. 1984, The interlanguage of immersion students and its implications for second language teaching. In A. DAVIES, C. CRIPER and A.P.R. HOWATT (eds) *Interlanguage*. Edinburgh: Edinburgh University Press.
KLEIN, W. 1984, *Some Remarks on the Syntax of Learner Varieties*. Unpublished ms., Nijmegen.
LABOV, W. 1966, *The Social Stratification of English in New York City*. Washington: Center for Applied Linguistics.
LAKOFF, G. 1987, *Women, Fire, and Dangerous Things: What Categories Reveal About the Mind*. Chicago: University of Chicago Press.
MASTER, P., SCHUMANN, J. and SOKOLIK, M. 1987, The experimental creation of a pidgin language. Paper presented at Second Language Research Forum, Los Angeles.

NEMSER, W. 1971, Approximative systems of foreign language learners. *IRAL* 9, 115–24.

PARRISH, B., TARONE, E. and TAGHOVI, E. 1986, Article usage in interlanguage: a study in task-related variability. Paper presented at TESOL 1986, Anaheim.

PERDUE, C. (ed.) 1984, *Second Language Acquisition by Adult Immigrants: A Field Manual*. Rowley, MA: Newbury House.

SCHUMANN, J. 1978, *The Pidginization Process: A Model for Second Language Acquisition*. Rowley, MA: Newbury House.

SELINKER, L. 1969, Language transfer. *General Linguistics* 9, 67–92.

— 1972, Interlanguage. *IRAL* 10, 209–31.

— 1984, The current state of interlanguage studies: An attempted critical summary. In A. DAVIES, C. CRIPER and A.P.R. HOWATT (eds) *Interlanguage*. Edinburgh: Edinburgh University Press.

— 1985–86, Attempting comprehensive and comparative empirical research in second language acquisition. Review article of Perdue (1984). *Language Learning* 35, 567–84 and 36, 83–100.

— 1986, LSP and interlanguage. Interlanguage and LSP. *ESPMENA Bulletin* 22, 1–13.

— 1991, *Rediscovering Interlanguage*. London: Longman.

SELINKER, L. 1985, Wrestling with 'context' in interlanguage theory. *Applied Linguistics* 6, 190–204.

SELINKER, L. and LAMENDELLA, J. 1978, Two perspectives on fossilization in interlanguage learning. *Interlanguage Studies Bulletin* 3, 143–91.

SELINKER, L., SWAIN, M. and DUMAS, G. 1975, The interlanguage hypothesis extended to children. *Language Learning* 25, 139–52.

TARONE, E. 1983, On the variability of interlanguage systems. *Applied Linguistics* 4, 142–63.

TARONE, E., FRAUENFELDER, U. and SELINKER, L. 1976, Systematicity/variability and stability/instability in interlanguage systems: More data from Toronto French immersion. *Language Learning* Special Issue No. 4, 93–134.

TICKOO, M.K. 1986, *Language Across the Curriculum: Proceedings of the Annual RELC Seminar, 1985*. Singapore: Regional Language Center Press.

ZUENGLER, J. 1989, Identity and IL development and use. *Applied Linguistics* 10, 80–96.

3 Strategy and Tactics in Second Language Acquisition

HERBERT SELIGER

Literature describing the processes (as opposed to the product or output) of second language acquisition has used the term 'strategy' somewhat indiscriminately. Elaine Tarone's 1979 paper addressed this problem with regard to the notion 'communication strategy'. It is often not clear whether, in studies discussing acquisition strategies, the term refers really to acquisition, production, discourse, communication or something else.[1]

In short, we have reached a point of semantic satiation with regard to the term 'strategy' and in many ways the term itself has become empty of any distinctive content. To call everything we observe in second language (L2) acquisition a strategy, divests the term of meaning. Everything to which the term is attached appears to have the same importance or psychological status in the hierarchy of events that lead to L2 acquisition. For example, in a study by Cohen & Aphek (1979), activities carried out by learners in order to retain new vocabulary, such as associating the new word with an L1 or L2 equivalent or conjuring up a mental picture of the word, are referred to as strategies. Assuming without hesitation that finding out more about how learners in classrooms learn and retain new vocabulary is important to language teaching, can we describe these procedures (which are often idiosyncratic) on the same level as other processes which have been called strategies, such as hypothesis testing, simplification or overgeneralisation?

This chapter will be concerned with distinguishing between processes which bring about long-term competence in the second language and other processes which do not. It will be claimed that there are activities carried out by the learner that bring about long-term incremental changes in the composition of an interlanguage grammar while other processes are used to achieve short-range goals and may in fact lead to language-like behaviour rather than acquisition.

36

It is proposed that long-term acquisitional processes should be defined for all learners in the same way because (1) they are human, and (2) they are acquiring a human language and all that that entails from linguistic to communicative competence. That is, the nature of the learner and the nature of the object of acquisition define the processes. While these basic processes, which shall be referred to here as acquisition strategies, are the same for all learners, learners develop individual mechanisms which affect the use of these unconscious strategies. This mechanism is a filter which is the result of various developmental and experiential factors in the learner's background. The filter predisposes the learner to apply the basic acquisition strategies in idiosyncratic ways.

Strategies may be described as superordinate, abstract, constant and long-term processes. What learners do to meet the immediate demands of a particular learning task or situation may be called *tactics*; these are short-term processes used by learners to overcome temporary and immediate obstacles to the achievement of the long-range goal of language acquisition. The function of tactics is to provide language material upon which the emerging grammar may be built. Strategies are applied to this basic material provided by tactics, and extract from these 'protocols' the underlying grammatical principles that will become the interlanguage grammar. Tactics are defined or delineated by the interaction of the local conditions of language learning (an external factor) and the individual's filter for language acquisition (an internal factor). The tactics resulting from this interaction may be referred to as the acquisition style of the learner.

Strategies may be viewed as having a distilling function in the sense that they distil rules or principles from data. Since strategies are abstract programmes, they need input of some kind in order to be stimulated into operation. This input is supplied by tactics which selectively provide language data from the language to which the learner is exposed. With regard to adult–child differences in language acquisition, since the strategies are the same, research could focus on differences in the source language material from which adults and children develop grammar, in terms of (1) parameters such as complexity of input material, quantity and contexts and opportunities for use; (2) since there must be a fit between strategies and tactics which derive from them or feed input into them, in which learning environments can strategies be most efficiently utilised?

Where tactics are an outgrowth of underlying basic strategies, it is predicted that they will lead to successful long-term acquisition. Where

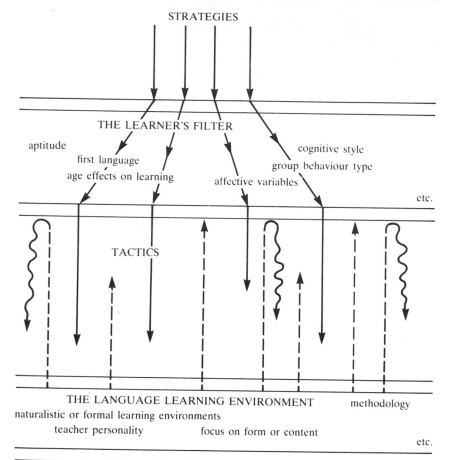

STRATEGIES

THE LEARNER'S FILTER

aptitude

first language

age effects on learning

affective variables

cognitive style

group behaviour type

etc.

TACTICS

THE LANGUAGE LEARNING ENVIRONMENT   methodology

naturalistic or formal learning environments

teacher personality   focus on form or content

etc.

Key

Tactics which are refracted versions of underlying strategies.
Composition of individual filter changes or refracts strategies.

Tactics which are generated by the interaction of the learner's filter and the learning environment. These tactics reflect the conditions of learning context, e.g. rule memorisation, early imitative drill before interim grammar is ready, etc.

Input characteristics of Learning Environment as perceived by the learner.

FIGURE 3.1 *Biologically determined human learning*

the individual's filter or conditions in the language learning environment preclude the use of tactics which emerge from underlying strategies, language-like behaviour or short-term acquisition is most likely to result rather than long-term increments in the interlanguage grammar. That is, since the individual learner's selection of tactics is idiosyncratic, some acquisition styles will lead to successful learning while others will lead to reduced or slower rates of acquisition.

Figure 3.1 indicates that some activities (tactics) carried out by learners are not refractions of underlying strategies passing through the learner's filter but reflections of characteristics of the learning environment. That is, learners do things in a classroom because they are expected to: the expectation is stimulated externally. In the case of learner tactics that are caused by what learners expect from the language classroom, such activity emanates from within the learner's filter as a result of previous experience with language learning. It is part of the classroom 'culture' that the learner plays the game by the rules established by the teacher. Learners may do many things that they feel intuitively do not lead to real learning, but because they are basically conformist will do them. On the other hand, because the learner has been conditioned through classroom experience to expect certain kinds of activities, they may demand them. That is, learners may develop cultural expectations of the language classroom. A common example is the foreign student who demands more grammar rules or who voluntarily sits for hours in a language laboratory because of an expectation that technology will provide a magic solution to whatever problem he may have.

If we examine the literature on strategies, we will discover that the processes or activities which are described as second language acquisition strategies may be divided into the two general categories described above as strategy and tactic.

1. There are those activities carried out by language learners which are intrinsic to the learning or acquisition process itself, are unconscious and which are found among all language learners regardless of language background, age, attitude, or language acquisition context. Examples of such activities or processes would be hypothesis testing, simplification and overgeneralisation, although it is not clear that these would exist at the same hierarchical level. (See Macnamara, 1975; Selinker, Swain & Dumas, 1975; Richards, 1971; Adjemian, 1976 for just a few examples.) This first type of activity has been described above as an acquisition *strategy*.

2. Strategies, however, are general, abstract operations by which

the human mind acquires and organises new knowledge. Such abstract operations must be translated in accordance with the built-in predispositions of the learner in response to the particular learning task. That is, while all language learners have the same built-in programme for reasons described above, the process of maturation, language development and interacting with the environment lead to a differentiation in the preferred ways to realise these abstract learning principles in concrete situations. The translation of *strategies* into concrete behaviours called *tactics* is affected by what the learner brings with him or her in terms of built-in predispositions, attitudes and so on. The tactics carried out by language learners are often, but not exclusively, conscious and stimulated or initiated by the specific conditions of the immediate learning context.[2]

Tactics may be traced to a number of various sources. For example, different tactics will be generated by language learning taking place in a classroom or in a naturalistic environment or by the particular method used by a teacher. Adults are able to use a rule-oriented approach to initiate acquisition while children seem to prefer an inductive approach. The communicative demands placed on the learner will generate different tactics. A reading knowledge of the language is a limited goal requiring a different level of competence and a different focus on the language material than the need to know how to communicate in the language. Even a teacher's instruction may initiate different tactics on the part of different learners in the same class. For example, the instruction 'Learn these words for tomorrow' may cause some learners to memorise the words as a list of L1 and L2 equivalents while others may learn them by creating meaningful sentences or exotic images to represent the new vocabulary. (See Blum & Levenston, 1978; Cohen & Aphek, 1979; Bialystok & Froelich, 1977; and Bialystok, 1979, for examples of what are referred to here as tactics rather than strategies.)

Of these two basic types of learner activity, strategies and tactics, it appears that the latter is amenable to some degree of outside intervention and manipulation while the former is both inaccessible and unamenable to change. As will be discussed below, only some forms of tactics are malleable while others may be so much a part of the learner's make-up that they are probably impervious to outside intervention.

The Biological and Cognitive Foundations for Strategies and Tactics

Basically what is being suggested is that we return to more universal, biologically founded criteria for what is called a strategy. This is not an original position, obviously, and has been implied in Slobin's work (1978) and explicitly stated by Lenneberg (1967). Both Slobin and Lenneberg refer exclusively to the acquisition of a primary language. The learner in such cases is a child and the environment for acquisition is more narrowly defined. However, since the cognitive mechanisms used for such acquisition are not thought to be substantively different but rather elaborated through the process of maturation, there is no reason to believe that the same mechanisms are not used for the acquisition of a second language whether by adult or child. In fact, it is the position of this chapter that no other mechanisms are available for true acquisition but that set of human language acquisition strategies.

Lenneberg (1967) has formulated what he terms general premises for a biological theory of language. Firstly, cognitive function is species-specific. That is, there are specifically human and non-human ways of behaving, of acquiring knowledge about our environment and of surviving in our environment. Lenneberg goes on to describe what he calls the neurophysiological correlates of cognitive functioning or propensities. He describes these as a set of capacities, such as the capacity for categorising information in different ways, the capacity for problem solving, the formation of learning sets, and the tendency to generalise in certain directions (p. 372). Without arguing the details of these capacities, it is important to keep in mind at this point that we are concerned with functions that are general or universal to the species and which are capacities; that is, we have the potential for these functions. Lenneberg also states, under his second premise, that such properties are replicated in all members of the species but that not every member is able to realise the full potential for these capacities. This last point may explain some of the variance we find with so-called language aptitude and at least some of the variance found between children and adults.

Another premise proposed by Lenneberg is that cognitive processes and capacities are differentiated spontaneously with maturation. What this essentially means is that the plan is present from birth but its realisation changes with the maturation of the organism.[3] In order for these cognitive functions to emerge properly, however, there is a need for a conducive social environment. In Lenneberg's scheme the environment acts as a trigger to set off the maturationally appropriate responses in the organism. Lenneberg refers to this process as the actualisation of latent structure and by way of metaphor states that the organism may be said to 'resonate' to environmental stimulation.

When applied to interpreting second language acquisition, Lenneberg's views may be construed to mean that while strategies are constant across learners, they are potentials, and the characteristics of the learning situation (the Learning Environment in Figure 3.1) may or may not cause such potentials to be activated or, in Lenneberg's sense, to be actualised. This also means that while this activity is common to all second language learning contexts, there will still be individual variation in the outcomes of the application of these strategies.

A distinction must be made between what a learner is capable of doing and what he actually does, and between universal second language acquisition strategies and the outcomes of these strategies which may be affected by factors outside of biologically given operations possible to the learner. In other words, a distinction must be made between the potentially available set of strategies and the actual implementation of these capacities in real language learning contexts. Some learners will successfully translate these abstract capacities into real acquisition, between strategies as the universal abstract set of capacities and their relative realisation as tactics, which should be the focus of second language acquisition research.

The Filter

While it is reasonable to claim that long-term incremental changes can take place in the learner's grammar only through the utilisation of the basic set of abstract learning operations (strategies), it is not reasonable to expect that learners translate these basic strategies into tactics in the same manner in actual learning contexts. There will be widespread variation in the way in which individuals acquire a language in actual learning environments, though they must still utilise some local realisation (tactic) of these general underlying operations in order to effect long-term acquisition.

This variability or individual pathway to second language acquisition is defined by the Learner's Filter (see Figure 3.1). The composition of the filter will be determined by another set of factors which, while not biological in nature, still dictate the way in which the individual will approach the second language. In other words, in the realisation process of translating basic strategies to the specific task of learning a second language, the learner will be predisposed to approach the learning task in a particular way. These individual approaches are unconscious and determined by the learner's previous experience, causing him to adopt individualised responses to the local conditions of language learning.

There are, of course, precedents for claiming that there can be both universal strategies and at the same time individual or idiosyncratic ways of applying these strategies. In an article devoted to the topic of linguistic universals, McCawley (1979) dissociates himself 'from the assumption that people who talk the same have the same linguistic competence'. Rather, he advocates a conception of language acquisition 'in which many details of acquisition are random or influenced by ephemeral details of one's linguistic experience'. As an example, McCawley brings two alternative linguistic analyses to explain plural formation, concluding that some people may have learned plurals one way and others according to the second analysis. He states that 'the assumption that all normal adult members of a linguistic community have the same internalized analysis is . . . gratuitous'.

There is also a large body of literature in first language acquisition which describes variability in individual styles of acquisition. Bloom, Lightbown & Hood (1978) found children who were imitators and those who were not. Peters (1977) describes analytic and *gestalt* learners; the *gestalt* learner relies more on imitation of phrases or routines, fewer nouns and lots of pronouns and even uses what Peters refers to as place holders such as 'uh-uh' to stand for the words that he doesn't know rather than resort to some form of circumlocution. The analytic learner is the standard L1 acquirer who follows the route familiar to us of one-, two- or three-word sentences and increments in the MLU. Catherine Nelson (1979) claimed that the type of acquirer seemed to correspond to such factors as the birth order of the child and the level of education and income level of the home. Rosenblum & Dorman (1978) also found variation in first language development to be traceable to birth order; good imitators in their study were almost aiways first-born or only-born.

Among adult second language learners different styles of social interaction have been found to affect the rate of progress of the learner because of the kind of hypothesis testing being carried out by the learner. In that research (Seliger, 1977), it was found that High Input Generators (HIGs) were better at using data-getting tactics; that is, they were better at getting language data directed at them and, because it was individually focused, converting those data into intake for the purposes of developing and testing hypotheses about L2. The other type of learner described in this research was the learner who interacted at a low level and was referred to as the Low Input Generator (LIG). This second type adopted tactics of linguistic and social avoidance which removed him from much contact with the language. In a subsequent study of HIGs and LIGs (Seliger, 1978), it was found that in an error analysis of the output of both types, HIGs showed a much higher percentage of L2 overgeneralisation errors than L1 interference errors, while LIGs showed the opposite relationship for error type when the learners were matched for level of proficiency and language background. This finding would seem to indicate that one style of learner may be characterised as relying on L1 as a source of hypotheses about L2, while a second type evolves or 'matures' out of this stage to one in which the source of hypotheses becomes L2. The difference in orientation towards L1 or L2 as a source of hypotheses with which to build the grammar seems to be a function of interactor type.

In a paper on communication strategies, Tarone (1979) proposed that High Input Generators may be using different kinds of communication activities to gain input. That is, the tactics used in communication activities by this type of learner may be data- or input-getting tactics in addition to communicative tactics. As noted above, whether communication tactics can simultaneously serve an acquisition function, or whether the learner changes focus from communication to attention to form or meaning through the use of some kind of switching mechanism, is a question that must be investigated.

There are, of course, other factors in the filter which predispose the L2 learner to an individual pathway or set towards L2. One obvious factor would be the language background of the learner. What is being suggested here is a modified version of Whorf's relativity hypothesis; that is, the first language of the learner will cause him to focus on L2 input in a particular way and cause him to employ basic strategies differently than someone from a different L1. That is, the first language affects cognitive function and not just the output of that function.

Early studies support the view that language does have an effect on cognitive function. A study reported by Carroll (1964) showed that Navaho-speaking children performed a sorting task differently from English-speaking Navaho children. Children from English-speaking Navaho families sorted objects according to colour while children from Navaho-speaking families demonstrated a tendency to sort according to shape. It was explained that the difference in sorting behaviour stemmed from the fact that the Navaho language requires a different form for a verb of handling depending on the shape of the object being handled. Thus Navaho-speaking children develop a sensitivity for conceptualising shape and focusing on it earlier than English-speaking children from the same background. The same study found a similar effect for socio-economic background. Middle-class children performed the task in the same way that Navaho-speaking children did when compared with children from low socio-economic background. These results might be interpreted to mean that either language or social environment will have an effect on cognitive development and function. Such findings should also not be interpreted to mean that the first language causes a permanent set for cognitive development and function, since the findings were only with regard to time of onset of such functions.

Recent work by Schachter & Rutherford (1979) shows that not only the structure of the language but also the typology of the language will affect the output of the learner. It is reasonable to assume that the speaker of a topic-prominent language will apply hypothesis testing procedures differently to second language data than a speaker of a subject-prominent language. Topic-prominent language speakers pay more attention to discourse features beyond the sentence, while subject-prominent language speakers pay more attention to grammatical relationships within the sentence. Again what is suggested by this is that the set of the learner will be affected by language typology which, in turn, will determine where he will apply the strategies he has at his disposal; that is, how speakers of different types of languages will convert the same basic strategies into tactics. In short, speakers of different languages, while using the same basic strategies will apply them differently to the language data because of a pre-determined focus.[4]

Another factor which will decide how basic strategies are refracted through the filter will be the social environment in which language acquisition, first or second, takes place. A study by Geffner & Hochberg (1971) indicates that children of low socio-economic class develop different neurological specialisation functions which in turn would determine what in the environment they pay more attention to. This study showed that these children demonstrated different laterality patterns (indicating different processing) from upper-class children.[5] In this case, what is again suggested is that early experience by a human being may predispose him to approach future learning tasks with a particular set or focus.

Cognitive style is still another factor built into the learner's filter. A large body of research conducted by Herman Witkin and his associates using the field-independent/field-dependent construct suggests that (1) such predispositions are found early in life, and (2) cognitive style causes the learner to approach the learning task according to cognitive style variants. It must be assumed that, since the claim is that field sensitivity is a universal cognitive trait, learners of L2 bring this predisposition with them to the second language acquisition task. Again such a predisposition will determine what in the language data is focused on by the learner and will determine how and where he will translate basic strategies into tactics. Seliger (1977) found that High Input Generators learning English as a second language tended toward field independence while Low Input Generators tended towards field dependence. Genesee & Hamayan (1980) found this tendency for successful child learners of French as a second language.

An additional factor which must be considered to have an effect on the way in which a learner will apply strategies is the age of the learner or his level of cognitive development. The critical period concept would imply that in spite of using the same basic underlying strategies, certain acquisitions would be beyond the capabilities of the learner. This, of course, does not mean that acquisition is prevented, but rather that the results of learning will be different for learners of different ages (see Seliger, 1978, 1980 for a discussion of the interface between cognitive and biological potentials).

There are of course many additional factors which would be part of the make-up of the learner's filter. All of those factors normally described in the literature on L2 acquisition as 'learner variables' may be considered part of the filter. The mention of age as a factor in the composition of the filter of course raises the additional question of the relative stability or constancy of the factors which make up the learner's filter. As basic strategies are pre-determined and intrinsic to the biological nature of the human learner (for example, it would be illogical to claim that some humans learn according to a behaviourist habit paradigm while others follow a cognitive operations pathway), it must be assumed that some factors which comprise the filter and which affect the conversion of strategies into tactics are immutable and stable while others may be temporary.

It is unlikely that external intervention can change a true LIG into a HIG. That is, the constellation of characteristics which make up the Low Input Generator are probably the result of long-term personality development and unlikely to change because of the superficial manipulation of certain conditions within the language learning environment. At this point we would have to distinguish between real changes in learning behaviour brought about by methodology and learner behaviour which is reflective of the demands of the learning environment (see below). Given an emphasis on communicative activity in a language lesson, even a LIG will respond with communicative-type responses. However, such behaviour is not the result of tactics emerging through the filter from underlying strategies but a reflection of external conditions. In a situation such as this we would get 'communicative-like' behaviour since the basic make-up of the learner would prevent true uninhibited communicative behaviour.

An assumption implied in the literature on the good language learner (Naiman *et al.*, 1975; Rubin, 1975) is that if we can identify the strategies used by the good language learner, we can somehow apply this knowledge towards helping the learner who is not successful. This is probably a false assumption. It may not be possible to do very much for some learners, even under optimal conditions. This would be true if, at the level of translating strategies into tactics, the make-up of the individual learner's filter hinders or prevents a high level of acquisition. The qualities of the good language learner which make up his filter, such as cognitive style and personality, may be determined so early that it is highly unlikely that such qualities may be taught in the normal sense. Conversely, the learner who does not possess these qualities at the time of instruction will be unlikely to acquire them within the limited conditions of formal instruction. This means, as stated above, that a LIG or any of the other unsuccessful learner types identified in the literature will be unlikely to adopt tactics which allow him to gain access to language material in the same way that HIGs do. If anything, learners such as LIGs adopt tactics which keep them distant from the language.

The point is, that while we can assume that learner types such as High Input and Low Input Generators must use the same language acquisition strategies, it is the translation of these strategies into tactics as characterised by the learner's filter which will determine the success of either type. What is needed therefore is a hierarchical categorisation of learner activities showing the relationship between strategies and tactics. Understanding the mismatch or agreement between individual constraints on the local translation of strategies may aid us in prescribing individual pathways for second language acquisition in formal environments and in having realistic expectations about the outcomes of language instruction.

The Language Learning Environment

As indicated throughout this chapter, the Language Learning Environment (see Figure 3.1) consists of the external features of the setting in which tactics are employed. These local conditions may be conducive to the use of strategy-derived tactics or may simply encourage the development and use of tactics which lead to successful functioning within the particular context, but not necessarily to true acquisition as measured by incremental changes in the interlanguage grammar.

One obvious feature of formal language learning environments is that of the teacher, whose function is not merely to serve as a surrogate interlocutor. Much current research is concerned with detailed descriptions of teacher behaviour (Bowers, 1980). If such research has a major weakness, it must be that it ignores the fact that the same teacher behaviour elicits different responses in the form of tactics from different learners. Teacher behaviour is not in itself a predictor of learner behaviour and must be viewed as one dependent variable in the total relationship between learner tactics and the learner's filter.

In addition to reflecting teacher behaviour, tactics will reflect the features of the particular methodology being used. Learners have adopted tactics of mimicry and memorisation because they have been led to believe that such behaviour will lead to language proficiency. Another reflective tactic has been to practise mechanical substitution or transformation with semantically discrete patterns in the belief that the facile manipulation of such patterns will at least give the impression of speaking the language fluently and somehow result in an equivalent facility to communicate in naturalistic language environments.

The fact that learners of a particular age, cultural or educational background seek second language acquisition through the classroom rather than in naturalistic environments should lead us to question the source for this predisposition (see for example, Krashen & Seliger, 1975). Classroom-based language acquisition calls for the use of certain kinds of tactics which may not be appropriate for some learners. Classroom language data are presented to the learner differently than they would be presented to him in a naturalistic environment; the classroom predisposes the learner to focus on formal aspects of language while naturalistic environments, because they are totally communicative, require a focus on content. In fact, classroom language learning may be encouraging the use of tactics which, while leading to formal analysis of linguistic form, interfere with the use of tactics which are based on language acquisition strategies.

If it is assumed that both successful and unsuccessful learners must employ the same underlying set of universal acquisition strategies in order to accomplish second language acquisition, it must be the tactics that each employs in formal and naturalistic learning environments that should be the focus of research. To what degree are tactics related to underlying strategies? Where there is such a relationship, it is expected that tactics will lead to increments in acquisition. Some tactics simply lead to language-like behaviour such as the memorisation of word lists, dialogues, or grammar rules. The behaviour resulting from the employment of reflective tactics will be performance without affecting the underlying competence of the learner. HIGs, while responding to regular classroom demands for such performance (because it is part of the language learning game), also develop a set of compensatory tactics such as increased interaction with peers and native speakers which provide data for the use of underlying acquisition strategies (Seliger, 1977). LIGs, while responding with reflective tactics of performance, also develop what might be characterised as an avoidance tactic which emanates from the composition of the learner's filter: that is, they avoid situations which are related to real language use and interaction. What remains to be researched is why the pseudo-learning brought about by the use of reflective tactics appeals to and satisfies some learners while others develop compensatory tactics which, because they allow for the use of strategy-derived tactics, lead to real acquisition.

There are L2 learners who exhibit characteristic LIG behaviour and yet seem to acquire the second language. LIG behaviour for a few such learners may be a local response to the classroom environment itself; that is, LIG behaviour in a few cases may be a temporary locally stimulated reflective tactic rather than an individual pathway or style determined by the acquisition filter. For example, if one compares the behaviour expected of a student in a class in Taiwan with that expected in an American language class, it is readily seen how classroom behaviour may not be a reflection of the student's true group behaviour but rather what he/she has been taught to expect as appropriate group behaviour in the classroom. A survey of Taiwanese students in the Queen College English Language Institute has shown that in a Chinese classroom, the students never ask the teacher a question because of fear that the teacher may not know the answer and thus lose face. Students never speak to each other in class and responses consist primarily of recitation. This description is probably not too different for many other countries. When students coming from this background enter a second language classroom with its emphasis on student participation and interaction and in some cases where the teacher plays the role of counsellor or is silent, one can readily imagine the confusion.

In such cases, research should examine which local conditions cause LIG-like behaviour and which conditions stimulate more language interaction. In the case of tactics which result from contrasts in classroom culture, an awareness of these contrasts coupled with classroom activities which allow for gradual adjustment may remove some of the cultural barrier.

It is often stated that learners acquire a second language in spite of the methods used to teach them. What this means essentially is that learners adopt what may be called 'subversive tactics': that is, they employ tactics that either supplement or avoid the outcomes which are defined by the teacher or the method. Many learners still succeed in acquiring language under conditions that research would indicate to be unproductive, such as grammar translation method or audio-lingual habit method. These learners probably succeed because they are able to develop tactics to overcome obstacles raised by the classroom method. Some seek out native speakers, others talk to themselves, to peers or to a tape recorder. With methods which tend to be more naturalistic, learners surreptitiously compile their own verb charts or acquire grammar books which deal with the more paradigmatic aspects of language.

Summary

This chapter has proposed that learners' acquisitional behaviour exists at two levels:

(1) The level of strategy, consisting of a set of abstract universal cognitive functions which are used to acquire knowledge. These functions are biologically determined, age-independent and constant. Acquisition cannot take place without employing these strategies. They represent a set of capacities or potentials which may or may not be realised by the individual learner. Strategies distil general principles from the data supplied by tactics and assimilate them into the underlying competence grammar.
(2) The second level of acquisition behaviour consists of activities carried out by the learner in response to the local conditions of language acquisition (the Language Learning Environment). These local, immediate and temporary responses are referred to as tactics. Ideally, tactics are locally translated realisations of strategies, but not necessarily. Tactics are determined by the interaction of learner variables (the Filter) and the contextual features of the Language Learning Environment. Tactics are data-collecting processes and act as mechanisms which provide input upon which strategies operate.

The relationship between strategies and tactics is decided by the individual learner's filter, consisting of factors which contribute to making up the learner's idiosyncratic style of learning or acquisition, that is, the way he translates strategies into tactics.

It is proposed that L2 research should be concerned with delineating the hierarchical relationship between strategies and tactics and learner filters to find which combinations lead to successful L2 acquisition, which do not, which may be affected by instruction and which are unteachable. The facilitative role of instruction will be strengthened by understanding what tactics are appropriate for what learner styles and how tactics are related to underlying strategies.

Notes

1. This is a problem intrinsic to many of the models proposed to explain second language acquisition. These models confuse variables affecting communication and performance in the second language with variables affecting acquisition. While it is quite likely that in a particular discourse sequence, both acquisition and communication can take place, it is improbable that these processes take place simultaneously. Rather, cognitive focus or set switches from communication to acquisition function. It is therefore not unlikely to find hypothesis testing as both a language acquisition strategy and a clarification-communication strategy in the same sequence, but not with the same item (Seliger, 1980). (See also Bever, 1970 for the same notion applied to linguistic processing.)
2. The strategy–tactic dichotomy obviously raises questions about other dichotomies proposed to explain second language acquisition, such as the learning–acquisition dichotomy and the extension of this idea into the monitor model proposed by Krashen (1978). I have discussed elsewhere (Seliger, 1979) why formally taught rules cannot become part of the acquired grammar.

   According to the strategy–tactic dichotomy, if one wishes to distinguish learning from acquisition in a technical sense, learning may be said to be the externalisation and concretisation of abstract unconscious principles for the acquisition of knowledge. Learning takes place in actual situations; learning activities are related to specific tasks and may be changed or adapted in accordance with varying conditions. In light of this, monitoring, because it is related to very specific conditions such as time, focus, even learner type (under-, over- and optimal users) and only to output and not input, is a tactic in the sense used here and, most importantly, a production or editing tactic rather than a grammar-building tactic. It is unlikely that such monitoring is related to incremental changes in the abstract grammar of the learner. As demonstrated in Seliger (1979), verbalising a rule or consciously using a rule may or may not demonstrate actual competence. Monitoring therefore is more likely to be a *reflective* production tactic.
3. Felix (1980) has recently proposed that cognitive development must be considered independent of linguistic development. In other words, he believes that the best explanation for language acquisition, first or second, is an independent set of linguistic abilities not related to general cognitive abilities. This position is part of the general Piaget–Chomsky debate regarding the

source of linguistic abilities. Felix's argument is that if cognition were the major determining factor, 'L1 and L2 acquisition should be totally dissimilar as a result of learner's different cognitive status'. This argument, of course, ignores the role of major factors such as the environment and the biological effects of age in the development of language. This position also assumes that the picture presented by the Piagetians is the only possible framework within which to claim that language abilities are subsumed under general cognitive abilities. Bruner (1979) has proposed an intermediate position which combines the concept of abilities specific to language but as part of general intellectual and social development: 'His [the child's] hypotheses are based in part upon his knowledge of the requirements of action and of interacting with another' (p. 283). See Seliger (1977) for a similar view of second language acquisition.

In fact, it may be claimed that the formal operations stage described by Piaget may play a negative role in L2 acquisition in the classroom. That is, formal educational settings impose a structuring based on arbitrary systems (e.g. a particular linguistic theory) and a focus on formal operations to the point of verbalisation and reliance on formal, introspective kinds of learning (tactics). LIGs and monitor over-users may be learners who have converted formal operations into a preferred tactic for dealing with any learning taking place in a classroom, including language. It is conscious focus on formal operations to the exclusion of natural unconscious learning, which is a characteristic of all formal educational settings, that may hinder the acquisition of a language in the classroom.

4. The cognitive set caused by language typology could be viewed as a temporary factor in language acquisition and may be characteristic of early stages of L2 learning. One might theorise that figuring out the distinctive typological features of topic-prominent versus subject-prominent languages is part of the general matching and contrasting that takes place in hypothesis testing.

5. Kinsbourne & Hiscock (1977) have suggested that such differences in laterality effects as found for children of different socio-economic backgrounds would not indicate different neurological organisation so much as the predisposition for non-verbal versus verbal processing strategies. Such a view would leave intact the claim of this chapter that the basic set of language acquisition strategies is universal and constant but that such strategies may be refracted by experience and environment: that is, nurture affecting nature.

References

ADJEMIAN, CHRISTIAN 1976, On the nature of interlanguage systems. *Language Learning* 26(2), 297–320.

BEVER, THOMAS 1970, Perceptual strategies and the competence–performance issue. In G.B.F. D'ARCAIS and W.J.M. LEVELT (eds) *Advances in Psycholinguistics* (pp. 4–30). New York: American Elsevier Publishing Co.

BIALYSTOK, ELLEN 1979, The role of conscious strategies in second language proficiency. *Canadian Modern Language Review*.

BIALYSTOK, ELLEN and FROELICH, MARIA 1977, Aspects of second language learning in classroom settings. *Working Papers on Bilingualism* 13, 1–26.

BLOOM, LOIS, LIGHTBOWN, PATSY and HOOD, LOIS 1978, Pronominal–nominal variation in child language. In LOIS BLOOM (ed.) *Readings in Language Development*. New York: Wiley.

BLUM, SHOSHANA and LEVENSTON, E.A. 1978, Universals of lexical simplification. *Language Learning* 28(2), 399–416.

BOWERS, ROGER 1980, Verbal behavior in the language teaching classroom. Paper presented at the 3rd Annual Colloquium on Classroom Centered Research, 14th International TESOL Convention. San Francisco, 4–9 March 1980.

BRUNER, JEROME 1979, Learning how to do things with words. In DORIS AARONSON and ROBERT W. RIEBER (eds) *Psycholinguistic Research: Implications and Applications* (pp. 265–84). Hillsdale, NJ: Erlbaum.

CARROLL, JOHN B. 1964, *Language and Thought*. Englewood Cliffs, NJ: Prentice-Hall.

COHEN, ANDREW D. and APHEK, EDNA 1979, Retention of second language vocabulary over time. Paper presented at the 13th International TESOL Convention, Boston.

FELIX, SASHA W. 1980, On the (in)applicability of Piagetian thought to language learning. Paper presented at the 14th International TESOL Convention, San Francisco.

GEFFNER, D.S. and HOCHBERG, I. 1971, Ear laterality preference of children from low and middle socioeconomic levels on a verbal dichotic listening task. *Cortex* 7, 193–203.

GENESEE, FRED and HAMAYAN, ELSE 1980, Individual differences in second language. *Applied Psycholinguistics* 1(1), 95–110.

KINSBOURNE, MARCEL and HISCOCK, MERRILL 1977, Does cerebral dominance develop? In S.J. SEGALOWITZ and F.A. GREUBER (eds) *Language Development and Neurological Theory*. New York: Academic Press.

KRASHEN, STEPHEN D. 1978, Second language acquisition. In WILLIAM ORR DINGWALL (ed.) *Survey of Linguistic Science*. Stamford, CT: Greylock Publishers.

KRASHEN, STEPHEN D. and SELIGER, HERBERT W. 1975, The essential contributions of formal instruction in adult second language learning. *TESOL Quarterly* 9(2), 173–83.

LENNEBERG, ERIC H. 1967, *Biological Foundations of Language*. New York: Wiley.

MACNAMARA, JOHN 1975, Comparison between first and second language learning. *Working Papers on Bilingualism* 7, 71–95.

McCAWLEY, JAMES 1979, Language universals in linguistic argumentation. In B.B. KACHRU (ed.) *Linguistics in the Seventies: Directions and Prospects* (pp. 205–20). Urbana, IL: Department of Linguistics, University of Illinois.

NAIMAN, N., FROEHLICH, M. and STERN, H.H. 1975, *The Good Language Learner*. Toronto: Ontario Institute for Studies in Education.

NELSON, CATHERINE 1979, Lecture on first language acquisition presented at Queens College, C.U.N.Y., March, 1979.

PETERS, ANN M. 1977, Language learning strategies. *Language* 53(3), 560–73.

RICHARDS, JACK C. 1971, Error analysis and second language strategies. *Language Sciences* (October 1971), 12–22.

ROSENBLUM, D. and DORMAN, M. 1978, Hemispheric specialization for speech perception in language deficient kindergarten children. *Brain and Language* 6, 378–89.

RUBIN, JOAN 1975, What the good language learner can teach us. *TESOL Quarterly* 9, 41–52.

SCHACHTER, JACQUELINE and RUTHERFORD, WILLIAM 1979, Discourse function and language transfer. *Working Papers on Bilingualism* 19, 1–12.

SELIGER, HERBERT W. 1977, Does practice make perfect? A study of interaction patterns and L2 competence. *Language Learning* 27(2).
— 1978, The evolution of error type in high and low interactors. *Indian Journal of Applied Linguistics* 4(1), 22–30.
— 1979, On the nature and function of language rules in language teaching. *TESOL Quarterly* 13(3), 359–69.
— 1980, Data sources and L2 speech performance. *Interlanguage Studies Bulletin*.
— 1984, Exceptions to the critical period hypothesis. In ROGER ANDERSEN (ed.) *New Dimensions in Research on the Acquisition and Use of Second Language*. Rowley, MA: Newbury House.
SELINKER, LARRY, SWAIN, MERRILL and DUMAS, GUY 1975, The interlanguage hypothesis extended to children. *Language Learning* 25, 139–52.
SLOBIN, DAN I. 1978, Developmental psycholinguistics. In WILLIAM ORR DINGWALL (ed.) *Survey of Linguistic Science* (pp. 267–316). Stanford, Conn.: Greylock Publishers.
TARONE, ELAINE 1979, Some thoughts on the notion of 'communication strategy'. Paper delivered at the TESOL Summer Institute, University of California at Los Angeles, July 1979.
WITKIN, HERMAN A., OLTMAN, PHILIP K., RASKIN, EVELYN and KARP, STEPHEN, 1971, *Embedded Figures Test*. Palo Alto, CA: Consulting Psychologists Press.

4 The Acquisition of Spanish as First and Second Language: Learner Errors and Strategies

JOAN E. FRIEDENBERG

Everyone makes errors when learning a language. Errors are deviations in pronunciation, structure, or vocabulary from what is considered to be normal by adult native speakers. Small children make errors when they are first learning to speak their native language. Foreign language learners make errors in their classrooms, and second language learners make errors while getting to know their new neighbours, much to their own dismay. While small children's baby-talk has always been considered to be cute, foreign and second language errors have caused embarrassment, inhibition, and lower test scores for these learners.

At one time, errors were considered to be an indication of what a learner did not know, but since the early 1970s researchers have looked at them as indicators of what learners *do* know and how they approach the task of learning a language. For example, although an error such as *Yesterday we goed fishing* indicates that the speaker does not know that *went* is the past form of *go*, it also indicates that she/he has acquired a regular structure, namely the *-ed* morpheme for past tense, which can be interpreted as a sign of accomplishment. By analysing the errors language learners make, we can have a good idea of the learning and communication strategies they employ. But this information alone cannot help language learners and teachers find the ideal conditions for language learning. There are many variables which can influence language learning. Yorio (1976), for example, identifies the following six: (1) native language, (2) age, (3) learning situation, (4) motivation, (5) intelligence and aptitude, and (6) educational background.

The purpose of the research described in this chapter was to investigate the roles that native language, age, and learning situation play

55

in the errors and strategies used to learn Spanish. To investigate the role of native language, the errors of first and second language learners of Spanish were compared. To determine the role of age, the errors of child and adult second language learners were compared. To consider learning situation, a comparison was made of the errors of persons learning Spanish in a formal classroom setting with those of persons learning Spanish in a natural environment.

Related Literature

Until the 1970s, the most significant research addressing the question of the influence of the native language on second language learning was that proposed by the Contrastive Analysis Hypothesis. During the 1940s and 1950s, with the help of behavioural psychology and structural linguistics, the Contrastive Analysis Hypothesis was developed as an attempt to predict and prevent the errors occurring in one language because of interference from another.

While Contrastive Analysis seemed to be theoretically sound, its validity could never be established by language teachers or researchers. As a result, Error Analysis was adopted in the 1970s. Unlike Contrastive Analysis, which was designed specifically to catch the errors which the analysis predicted and no others, error analysis looks at all errors and seeks to find a cause for them. Many studies then emerged which usually categorised errors as being either the result of interference, or developmental cognitive strategies that oversimplify the target language (Dulay & Burt, 1974a,b; Taylor, 1974; Jain, 1974; Duskova, 1969; and Richards, 1974a,b). Although these studies strongly suggest that errors are due to more than native language interference, many have been plagued with such methodological difficulties as not establishing clear criteria for interference or oversimplification, inability to categorise sizeable portions of data, inability to compare results reliably with first language studies, and inappropriately basing conclusions about second language learning in general on the results of carefully controlled written data or on unstructured natural data where avoidance can mask errors.

More recently, researchers have further developed and refined error analysis. Ahukanna, Lund & Gentile (1981), for example, examined 40 Igboo (Nigerian) learners of French and found that a learner's susceptibility to interference was influenced by the amount of experience in the native language and knowledge of a third language. Le Compagnon (1984) suggests from her study that native language interference can actually influence how overgeneralisation will occur. Gass (1984) indicates that the best way to test for interference is to make a carefully controlled comparison of the second language errors of speakers of a first language that has a transferable pattern with those of speakers of another first language without the transferable pattern. Besides native language, the variable of age has also been investigated. Many researchers in disciplines ranging from Education to Linguistics to Neurophysiology support the assumptions that there is a lateralisation of the brain that occurs at around puberty which causes the atrophy of the so-called Language Acquisition Device (LAD). In other words, they claim that pre-adolescent children are specially equipped to learn language and that this capacity becomes unavailable after puberty, forcing post-adolescents to use other strategies to acquire language. One such pioneer in the idea of a 'critical period' for language learning is Lenneberg (1967) who states: 'there is evidence that the primary acquisition of language is predicated upon a certain developmental stage which is quickly outgrown at the age of puberty.' He uses as evidence to support this statement biological research in areas such as aphasia, lateralisation, cerebral dominance, and hemispherectomies, and the structural, physiological changes in the brain which occur prior to puberty.

Behavioural evidence also supports the notion of a critical period. For example, most foreign language learners never really gain more than a minimal reading knowledge of the new language; many adult immigrants fail to learn the new language even after 20 years while their children learn it in a matter of months; and most adults are unsuccessful at ridding themselves of foreign accents.

However, Hill (1970) suggests that the apparent inability of adults to acquire a second language successfully is more culturally influenced than biological. Hill studied a group of 10,000 South American Indians who between them speak 24 languages. Tribal rules dictate that Indians marry individuals who do not speak the same language and each ends up speaking at least two tribal languages (with native-like proficiency), Tukano (a lingua franca) and usually Spanish or Portuguese. Like Hill, other researchers point out that many adults *do* successfully learn a second language, and that failure can best be attributed to such variables as preoccupations with work and other problems, lack of motivation, and the artificial environment of language classes (Krashen, 1982; Macnamara, 1973; Richards, 1976; and Wolfe, 1967). Much of the evidence favouring a critical period for language learning then could be the result of the differences between the learning situations of the child and the adult: that is, adults often learn in the limited and artificial environment of a language class while children usually learn in the natural environment of playground and school. Macnamara (1973) points out that even children perform poorly in a classroom language learning situation. In fact, Schumann (1976a) notes that morpheme acquisition is actually quite similar for children and adults when both are instructed learners.

The most frequently cited research concerning formal versus informal language learning is that by Krashen (1976) who found that formal second language classroom instruction was ineffective if the learning is in the second language environment, and that living in the second language environment contributes more to second language proficiency than does formal language instruction providing that exposure to the second language was consistent and meaningful.

Fathman & Precup (1983) examined the second language learning strategies of children and adults in formal and informal settings and found that informal learners used a greater variety of communication strategies and rarely relied on native language transfer, while instructed learners were more concerned with form and engaged in more monitoring (i.e. self-correction) than the other learners. Adults and children differed in that adults were more hesitant, repeated words more frequently, and apologised for their errors more often. This difference in behaviour suggests that affective factors have an influence on second language learning strategies.

Research Design

The research reported here investigated the roles that native language, age, and learning situation play in the errors and implied learning strategies made by learners of Spanish. Unlike most previous studies, this research compared the errors of second language learners with the errors made by child first language learners who have no other language from which any transfer can take place. One hundred and ten learners of Spanish were given a structured oral interview in Spanish. Learners included 20–25 persons from each of the following groups:

(1) Middle-class English-speaking children learning Spanish in a classroom in an English-speaking environment in a New York suburb. Average age is 11 (range is 10–12) and average contact with Spanish is three years.

(2) Middle-class English-speaking older (post-pubescent) students learning Spanish in a classroom in an English-speaking environment in a

suburb of New York City. Average age is 17 (range is 15–18) and average contact with Spanish is three years.

(3) Middle-class Spanish-speaking children learning Spanish in their native monolingual environment in Puerto Rico. Average age is 5.5 (range is 5–6).

(4) Middle-class English-speaking children learning Spanish in the natural second language environment in Puerto Rico. Average age is 7.5 (range is 3–11) and average contact with Spanish is 3.5 years.

(5) Middle-class English-speaking adults learning Spanish in the natural second language environment in Puerto Rico. Age is 30+ and average contact with Spanish is five years.

Testing materials and procedure

The test for this study, which was designed to investigate the transfer and simplification errors in Spanish determiners, verb inflections, adjective and noun gender, and in copula (i.e. *ser/estar*) use, consisted of 45 items and their corresponding pictures. The testing method consisted of asking the subjects questions about the pictures in order to elicit the grammatical structures desired.

Research Questions

This research was specifically designed to address the following questions:

(1) What role will *native language* play in the errors and implied learning strategies of L2 learners?

(2) What role will *age* play in the errors and implied learning strategies of L2 learners?

(3) What role will *environment* play in the errors and implied learning strategies of L2 learners?

Results

Results for each of the four aspects of Spanish grammar investigated appear below.

Determiners

Both English and Spanish have two sets of determiners: *definites* and *indefinites*. In some cases, the use of determiners in both languages is comparable, in other cases it is not. For example, neither Spanish nor English uses a determiner with the use of nouns in general terms when the noun represents *part* of a substance or class.

Example: Manzanas crecen en Chile.
Apples grow in Chile. (But apples also grow elsewhere.)

On the other hand, a determiner is used in Spanish and not in English when a noun represents *all* of a substance or class, with the use of most person titles, with certain prepositional phrases denoting location, and with the names of the days of the week.

Example: *El* dinero es malo.
Money is evil.

La doctora Gomez esta aqui.
Doctor Gomez is here.

Vamos a *la* escuela.
Let's go to school.

Patino *los* sabados.
I skate on Saturdays.

Table 4.1 illustrates that *all* learners made more errors in situations where English and Spanish are incongruent than vice versa. In addition, instructed second language learners made a relatively high proportion of errors where the two languages are congruent, compared with non-instructed second language learners and primary language learners.

Verb inflections

Spanish verbs exhibit inflectional morphemes isolating the following grammatical categories: verb class, mood, tense, person, and number. The present study will mainly be concerned with verb class, person, and number. In addition, it will examine the verb root in irregular verbs.

All Spanish verbs fall into one of three verb classes. These classes are identified by the thematic vowel *a*, *e*, or *i*: Class I infinitives end in -*ar*, Class II in -*er*, and Class III in -*ir*.

TABLE 4.1 Determiner errors and their proportional frequencies for all five groups of subjects

	Instructed American children (/)	(%)	Non-instructed American children (/)	(%)	*Instructed American adults (/)	(%)	Non-instructed American adults (/)	(%)	Monolingual children (/)	(%)
#Type 1 errors #Type 1 answered	23/73	32	4/90	4	50/164	30	10/103	10	2/95	2
#Type 2 errors #Type 2 answered	48/67	72	41/59	69	43/93	46	36/60	60	30/63	48

*High denominators are due to higher number of subjects in this group.
Type 1 situation — English = Spanish   Type 2 situation — English ≠ Spanish

Class I	Class II	Class III
hablar	comer	dormir
cantar	beber	sentir
bailar	comprender	partir

The following are the regular (a) simple present and (b) simple past verb inflections for all three verb classes.

(a) Person and number	AR (hablar) verb root	inflection	ER (comer) verb root	inflection	IR (partir) verb root	inflection
First, sing.	habl	o	com	o	part	o
Second, sing.	habl	as	com	es	part	es
Third, sing.	habl	a	com	e	part	e
First, pl.	habl	amos	com	emos	part	imos
Third, pl.	habl	an	com	en	part	en

(b) Person and number	AR verb root	inflection	ER verb root	inflection	IR verb root	inflection
First, sing.	habl	é	com	í	part	í
Second, sing.	habl	aste	com	íste	part	iste
Third, sing.	habl	ó	com	ió	part	ió
First, pl.	habl	amos	com	imos	part	imos
Third, pl.	habl	aron	com	ieron	part	ieron

Verb root changes in irregular verbs

Of the approximately 900 irregular verbs in Spanish, over 800 involve verb root irregularities (Stockwell, Bowen & Martin, 1969). In the present tense, root vowel changes occur in the form of diphthongisation or a vowel substitution in forms in which the stress is in the changing syllable:

Person, number	Example: querer
First, sing.	quiero
Second, sing.	quieres
Third, sing.	quiere
First, pl.	queremos
Third, pl.	quieren

(Note that the change occurs only when the verb root vowel is stressed.)

There are two types of root vowel changes exhibiting diphthongisation:

(1) *e→ie* in stressed position, e.g. querer, cerrar, empezar.

(2) *o→ue* in stressed position, e.g. dormir, morir, contar.

Vowel substitution changes occur in the following manner:

e→i in stressed position, e.g. repetir, decir, seguir.

In the past tense root vowel changes occur in the form of vowel substitutions in the third person singular and plural. (See Table 4.4.) There are two types:

(1) *o→u* in the third person singular and plural, e.g. dormir, morir.

(2) *e→i* in the third person singular and plural, e.g. sentir, pedir, servir.

First, sing.	dormí
Second, sing.	dormíste
Third, sing.	durmió
First, pl.	dormimos
Third, pl.	durmieron

(Note that the change occurs only in the third persons.)

Table 4.2 (verb person) indicates that over-reliance on the infinitive and on the third person singular were prominent for all groups. In addition, over-reliance on the gerund only occurred with the primary language learners, and over-reliance on the first person singular was quite frequent for instructed adults.

Table 4.3 (verb class) indicates that although relatively few verb class errors were made, instructed second language learners made more errors in which *ir/er→ar* and non-instructed learners made more errors in which *ar→er/ir*.

Table 4.4 (verb root) indicates that for all groups from which data were collected, there were few instances in which learners changed the root of non-root-changing verbs and numerous instances where the wrong person of a root-changing verb was changed (**juegamos*) or where root-changing verbs were unchanged.

Adjective–noun gender agreement

In order to produce the correct gender marking on an adjective, the learner of Spanish must know: (1) which adjectives are marked for gender, and (2) which nouns are masculine and which are feminine. Most

TABLE 4.2 *Types of verb person errors and their proportional frequencies for all five groups of subjects*

Error-type	Instructed American children		Non-instructed American children		Instructed American adults		Non-instructed American adults		Native Spanish-speaking children	
	# errors total errors	%	# errors total errors	%	# errors total errors	%	# errors total errors	%	# errors total errors	%
Toward infinitive	12/34	35	28/101	28	4/20	20	12/37	32	28/51	55
Toward 3rd sing.	5/34	15	32/101	32	6/20	30	9/37	24	2/51	4
Toward gerund	0/34	0	3/101	3	0/20	0	2/37	5	19/51	37
Toward 3rd pl.	5/34	15	12/101	12	0/20	0	4/37	11	2/51	4
Toward 1st sing.	5/34	15	10/101	10	10/20	50	6/37	16	0/51	0
Toward other	7/34	20	15/101	15	0/20	0	3/37	8	0/51	0
Total wrong Total answer	34/80	43	101/287	35	20/461	4	37/313	12	51/306	17

gender-marked adjectives end in -*o* in the masculine and -*a* in the feminine. The appropriate marking depends on the gender of the modified noun. Roughly half the frequently used adjectives in Spanish are not marked for gender; they are not particularly difficult to recognise, however, as virtually all of them end with a consonant or an *e*. Examples are: *verde* (green), *feliz* (happy), *pobre* (poor).

Noun gender in Spanish is usually, but not always, marked by the final vowel, -*o* marking masculine and -*a* feminine. Nouns not ending in *o* or *a* were not considered in this study. While nouns referring to people or animals are generally inflected according to sex associations, nouns referring to things are not. Hence, nouns such as 'beard' and 'tie' may be feminine although they are more pertinent to men, and nouns such as 'dress', 'necklace' and 'brassière' may be masculine although they are associated with women.

Table 4.5 indicates that all groups made more agreement errors in which feminine adjectives became masculine than vice versa. Table 4.6 indicates that only second language learners made noun gender errors, and they made substantially more errors in situations where the gender of the noun differed from that of its referent, as in *el vestido*, a masculine noun meaning 'dress'.

Use of the copula: ser and estar

In Spanish the words *ser* and *estar* correspond to the English 'be'.

Ser

There are basically five uses for *ser*. The following two will be examined in this study:

(1) With a locative when the subject is an event, e.g.

El concierto	es	en el Lincoln Center
(The concert	is	in Lincoln Center)
EVENT +	*SER*	+ LOCATIVE

(2) With an adjective when the speaker considers that the adjective describes an intrinsic unchanging property of the subject, e.g.

Carlos	es	flaco.
(Carlos	is	skinny.)
	SER +	ADJ

TABLE 4.3 *Verb class errors and their proportional frequencies for all five groups of subjects*

	Instructed American children (/)	(%)	Non-instructed American children (/)	(%)	Instructed American adults (/)	(%)	Non-instructed American adults (/)	(%)	Monolingual children (/)	(%)
ar → er/ir tot. ar ans.	2/22	9	7/48	15	8/99	8	8/54	15	0/49	0
er/ir → ar tot. er/ir ans.	4/28	14	9/88	10	39/231	17	14/104	13	0/117	0

TABLE 4.4 Verb root errors and their proportional frequencies for all five groups of subjects

	Instructed American children (l)	(%)	Non-instructed American children (l)	(%)	*Instructed American adults (l)	(%)	Non-instructed American adults (l)	(%)	Monolingual children (l)	(%)
Type 1 errors Type 1 answered	No data	No data	23/42	55	49/94	52	15/24	28	16/47	34
Type 2 errors Type 2 answered	No data	No data	20/41	49	41/82	50	15/45	33	29/58	50
Type 3 errors Type 3 answered	No data	No data	1/87	1	8/174	5	2/99	2	3/101	3

*High denominators are due to higher number of subjects in this group.
Type 1 error = *juga (juega)   Type 2 error = *juegamos (jugamos)   Type 3 error = *cuerto (corto)

TABLE 4.5 *Adjective–noun gender agreement errors and their proportional frequencies for all five groups of subjects*

Error-type	Instructed American children (/)	(%)	Non-instructed American children (/)	(%)	*Instructed American adults (/)	(%)	Non-instructed American adults (/)	(%)	Monolingual children (/)	(%)
f adj. + m. tot. mkd. & unmkd. f adj. ans.	61/100	61	64/98	65	51/153	33	29/953	31	12/102	12
m. adj. + f. tot. mkd. & unmkd. mas. ans.	6/44	14	4/34	12	16/64	25	7/43	16	2/38	5

*High denominators are due to higher number of subjects in this group.

TABLE 4.6 *Noun gender errors and their proportional frequencies for all five groups of subjects*

	Instructed American children (/)	(%)	Non-instructed American children (/)	(%)	*Instructed American adults (/)	(%)	Non-instructed American adults (/)	(%)	Monolingual children (/)	(%)
Noun errors/ gender/ref. total of these nouns answer	16/78	21	11/70	16	24/118	20	9/75	12	0/80	0
Noun errors/ no gender associations or gend. = ref. total of these nouns answered	9/90	10	0/105	0	3/133	2	3/98	3	0/110	0

*High denominators are due to higher number of subjects in this group.

Estar

There are two basic uses for *estar*:

(1) With a locative when the subject is a person or thing, e.g.

Mi hermano	esta	en Boston
(My brother	is	in Boston)
PERSON +	*ESTAR*	+ LOCATIVE

(2) With an adjective when the speaker considers the subject to be in the temporary state indicated by the adjective, e.g.

El agua de la ducha	esta	fria
(The shower	is	cold)
EVENT +	*ESTAR* +	ADJ

Comparison of Ser and Estar

Note the following examples contrasting the uses of each verb.

(1) Mi hermano   esta   en Boston, but
    (My brother)

    La conferencia   es   en Boston.
    (The lecture)

(2) Mis amigos   estan   callados, but
    (My friends   are   silent [aren't talking]).

    Mis amigos   son   callados.
    (My friends   are   quiet [timid]).

Table 4.7 illustrates that while for most groups over-reliance on *ser* and *estar* occurred in specific situations (e.g. in only locative or only adjectival situations), instructed children incorrectly used *ser* consistently across all environments. In locative environments, all groups (save the instructed children) over-relied on *estar* more than *ser*. In the adjectival environment, both instructed groups relied substantially more on *ser* than *estar* (although the instructed children always relied on *ser*).

Discussion

The variable of native language was examined by comparing the errors of first and second language learners. The data reported in this study could not clearly support or refute a case for interference. Although second language learners made more determiner errors where English and Spanish were non-congruent, so did first language learners. While we cannot negate the possibility that the second language learners are relying on first language transfer, the fact that the monolingual Spanish-speaking children made errors on almost half of the determiner items in which English and Spanish were non-equivalent and on hardly any determiner items in which Spanish and English were equivalent, leads one to suspect that there is something inherently more difficult for all learners of Spanish in the former situation. The case for transfer is further weakened by the fact that two of the four groups learning Spanish as a second language made a substantial number of determiner errors in situations where English and Spanish were equivalent. If the learners had been relying on native language patterns, this would not have occurred.

The variable of age was explored by comparing the errors of child and adult second language learners. Table 4.1 shows that both child and older learners made more determiner errors in situations where English and Spanish were non-equivalent than in situations where they were equivalent. Moreover, while the proportion for each error of the non-instructed children is very close to the proportions of the non-instructed older learners, the proportions for the child versus older learners in instructed groups are dissimilar. If the determiner errors in situations where English and Spanish are non-equivalent are the result of first language interference, perhaps the instructed American children made more errors in this situation (72% of the time as opposed to the adults 46% of the time) because the instructed children's proficiency level was lower, and they relied on transfer as a strategy more than the second language learners with a higher proficiency. In this study of language learning strategies of elementary and intermediate level ESL students, Taylor (1974: 2) found that 'the elementary subjects' reliance on the transfer strategy was found to be significantly higher than that of the intermediate subjects'.

An examination of the verb person errors presented in Table 4.2 reveals that both child and older learners of Spanish incorrectly over-rely on the infinitive between 20% and 30% of the time. Although the differences in the proportions of different verb person errors vary a good deal between child and adult learners. This variation is especially wide when comparing the two instructed groups. The reason for this may be related to the differences in proficiency level between the two groups (the instructed American children seemed to have the lowest proficiency in Spanish of all the groups as they had more difficulty in understanding and answering the questions in our oral interview than did the other

TABLE 4.7 *Errors in Ser and Estar and their proportional frequencies for all five groups of subjects*

Error-type	Instructed American children (I)	(%)	Non-instructed American children (I)	(%)	*Instructed American adults (I)	(%)	Non-instructed American adults (I)	(%)	Monolingual children (I)	(%)	
ser (loc) → estar tot. ser (loc) ans.	1/46	2	28/45	62	39/71	55	37/44	84	15/39	38	ser estar
estar (loc) → ser tot. estar (loc) ans.	41/48	85	8/47	17	31/73	42	7/56	13	0/40	0	(loc)
ser (adj) → estar tot. ser (adj) ans.	0/16	0	5/15	33	2/24	8	6/15	40	1/16	6	ser estar
estar (adj) → ser tot. estar (adj) ans.	25/32	78	14/30	47	14/48	29	7/30	23	2/30	6	(adj)

*High denominators are due to higher number of subjects in this group.

groups), or with differences in curriculum and/or attitude between the two groups. (The non-instructed groups are obviously presented with the same 'curriculum' — the natural environment.) For example, the instructed American older learners relied on the infinitive less than any of the other groups. While interviewing them, the investigator noticed that these subjects monitored their answers more carefully than the other subjects. That is, despite attempts to create a natural speech situation, this group appeared to be more concerned with form and less concerned with meaning than the others; consequently, they made more of an effort to conjugate than the others. This is most likely due to the fact that secondary foreign language classrooms in the USA typically emphasise grammatical correctness and a student's grade is dependent upon this. Another example of how curriculum may influence the errors and strategies between groups of instructed second language learners can be seen in the instructed older students' strong over-reliance on the first person singular. When visiting the instructed adults' classes, the investigator noticed that the students' only opportunity to communicate in the second language consisted of the teacher asking them questions about themselves (e.g. 'How are you?', 'What is your name?') to which the students had to answer using a complete sentence. Consequently, all 'communication' for these learners was in the first person singular, a form on which they incorrectly over-relied 50% of the time in our interview. The effects of instruction on second language acquisitions will be further explored in the discussion of environment.

When comparing the instructed American children with the instructed American older students, Table 4.3 indicates that for both groups there were more verb class errors in which *er/ir→ar* than errors in which *ar→er/ir*, a fact which puts a critical period for language learning in doubt. In addition, when comparing the non-instructed children with the non-instructed older students, we see that both of these groups made slightly more errors in which *ar→er/ir* than errors in which *er/ir→ar*. Although this latter comparison is in disagreement with the first comparison, it nevertheless strengthens the idea that age does not seem to be a variable.

When comparing verb root errors of child versus adult second language learners, Table 4.4 indicates that both child and older non-instructed learners of Spanish made substantially more verb root errors in irregular than regular verbs, and the number of type 1 errors (i.e. *juega→*juga*) was approximately equal to the number of type 2 errors (i.e. *jugamos→*juegamos*). (It was not possible to compare the results of the two instructed groups because the instructed children had not yet covered root-changing verbs in their Spanish class.)

Table 4.5 illustrates the fact that both child and older learners of Spanish made more agreement errors in which the feminine adjective became masculine than vice versa. The proportions of error between the children and the older students vary substantially and consistently. While the instructed children made agreement errors such that the feminine adjective became masculine 61% of the time, the instructed older students made this error only 33% of the time. Similarly, the non-instructed children made this error 65% of the time and the non-instructed adults made it 31% of the time. In addition, both groups of children made substantially more agreement errors in general than the adult groups. There is no reason to believe that this phenomenon is associated with proficiency level since, although proficiency level varies between the child and older instructed learners, it does not vary much between the child and adult non-instructed learners. While age appears to be a factor, how or why it does so remains unclear.

Table 4.6 illustrates types of noun gender errors made by child and adult second language learners of Spanish. It reveals that both groups of learners make more noun gender errors of the noun's referent than noun gender errors in nouns which have no gender associations or nouns whose gender matches the referent. Age appeared to have no influence, with all second language learners seeming to rely on a noun's meaning when assigning it an inflectional marking for gender.

The data presented in Table 4.7 reveal that non-instructed American children and non-instructed American adults incorrectly over-relied on *estar* when the complement of the sentence is a locative, a great deal more than they incorrectly over-relied on *ser*. However, in situations where the complement of the sentence is an adjective, the two groups behaved differently with the children over-relying more on *ser* and the adults on *estar*. It was difficult to compare the results of the two instructed groups since the instructed children virtually never used *estar* (they had been taught how to use both verbs but could not verbalise the rules for *ser* and *estar* use to the investigator). In sum, the idea that age is not a factor in second language learning strategies is supported by the complement = locative part of the *ser/estar* investigation, but the results of the complement = adjective part are too ambiguous to shed any clear light on the question. The complement = adjective results seem to indicate that most learners are aware that both *ser* and *estar* are used before adjectives, but that they are not yet sure of when it is appropriate to use each. This is perhaps what Richards refers to as 'incomplete knowledge of a rule'.

The variable of environment was examined by comparing the errors of instructed and non-instructed second language learners. Table 4.1 illustrates that while it is true that both instructed and non-instructed learners made more determiner errors where English and Spanish were non-equivalent than where the two languages were equivalent, both groups of instructed learners made substantially more determiner errors when English = Spanish than did the non-instructed groups. When conducting a pilot study for the present research, the investigator noticed that American college students studying Spanish often incorrectly inserted a Spanish definite article where none would even exist in English. The following are among the sentences taken from their compositions:

*El fuma los cigarrillos.	(He smokes cigarettes.)
*Vamos a la nuestra casa.	(Let's go to our house.)
*Quiero dos botellas del vino.	(I want two bottles of wine.)

Since this was a pilot study from one class, we assumed this phenomenon was the result of something peculiar to that particular class. However, Table 4.1 indicates that this phenomenon occurs a good deal in other Spanish classes and hardly at all among non-instructed learners. Perhaps in their efforts to make the language learning task simpler for students, teachers and textbooks oversimplify the rules in their presentations; or perhaps because instructed learners rarely come into real contact with the language, they do not get to hear or consequently assimilate many meaningful examples of the rules which they are explicitly taught in their classroom.

The results of the verb person investigation, presented in Table 4.2, provided little concerning the role of environment. The verb class errors, presented in Table 4.3, indicate that while both groups of instructed learners made more verb class errors in which *er/ir→ar* than errors in which *ar→er/ir*, both non-instructed groups made more *ar→er/ir* than *er/ir→ar* errors, a fact which suggests that the environment influences errors and strategies. Although the reason for this is not entirely clear, we do know that Spanish textbooks introduce *ar*-ending verbs before *er*- and *ir*-ending verbs and that instructed students may remember best what they have learned first. However, it is also true that there are more *ar*-ending verbs in the language, which should make the non-instructed learners also over-rely more on this class.

Table 4.4 illustrates the verb root errors made by the subjects of this study. On the basis of this table, we can see that both instructed and non-instructed adults made more verb root errors in irregular than regular verbs and each group made an approximately equal number of type 1 (*juga*) and type 2 (*juegamos*) errors. It should be noted, however, that although each of the two adult groups made an approximately equal proportion of type 1 and type 2 errors, the non-instructed adults had a much lower proportion of errors than the instructed adults. It was not possible to compare the results of the two groups of American children because, as previously noted, the instructed children had not yet learned about irregular verbs.

Table 4.5 shows a high degree of similarity between the types of gender agreement oversimplification and the proportions by which they took place. Both instructed and non-instructed subjects made many more agreement errors in which the feminine-marked adjective was incorrectly marked as masculine than vice versa. These results are not surprising in that the masculine form is considered to be the unmarked form for gender-marked adjectives and nouns.

Table 4.6 indicates that both instructed and non-instructed groups made more noun gender errors in situations where the gender of the noun does not agree with that of its referent than noun gender errors where the referent has no gender or has a gender which matches that of the noun.

The results of the *ser* and *estar* study, presented in Table 4.7, cannot clearly address question 3. It was difficult to compare the two groups of children as the instructed children seemed to have a strategy all of their own, that of relying solely on *ser* in situations where the complement is either an adjective or a locative. When comparing the instructed and non-instructed adults, we can see that while both groups incorrectly over-relied on *estar* more than *ser* in locative situations, the instructed adults over-relied on *ser* more than *estar* when the complement was an adjective while the non-instructed adults over-relied more on *estar* than *ser* in this situation.

Conclusions

The results of this study show clearly the difficulty in attempting to categorise errors as being the result of interference or overgeneralisation. While some errors unequivocally appear to be the result of interference, the appearance of the same error among monolingual primary language learners puts this conclusion in question.

Findings also provide no evidence that child and adult learners differ greatly in their errors and their approaches to learning a second language. The results show that child and adult learners made the same kinds of determiner errors, verb class and verb root errors, gender agreement and noun gender errors, and *ser* and *estar* errors. While it is true that there were differences in the numbers of errors made by children and adults, it was nevertheless clear that their oversimplifications were of the same nature. These findings oppose a critical period theory which suggests that adults and children must rely on different strategies for learning language. This study was not designed to compare proficiency levels or rates between child and adult learners, which has been the basis for most behavioural evidence. We suggest, however, that other variables such as motivation and learning situation account for the differences we so often see between child and adult language learners. The only way to truly investigate the variable of age would be to examine child and adult second language learners while attempting to control for equal types of motivation, equal language learning situation and equal amounts of time in the language learning situation.

To determine the role of learning environment in second language learning, this study compared the errors of classroom (foreign) language learners with free (second) language learners. The findings show about an equal number of similarities and differences in the types of errors made by instructed and non-instructed learners. Similarities in error types occurred in verb root, gender agreement and noun gender errors. Differences in errors occurred in determiners, verb class, and in *ser* and *estar* use. Based on similar data from our pilot study, we believe that the exceptionally high number of determiner errors (in situations where English and Spanish are congruent) among only the instructed learners is related to how teachers and/or textbooks are presenting this aspect of Spanish grammar. Other data from this study also suggest that formal instruction affects learners' errors and strategies. We found, for example, that instructed learners relied less on the infinitive form when marking verb person than did non-instructed learners, and we believe that this is due to the instructed learners' preoccupation with grammatical correctness (thus, they tried to conjugate more) and to the non-instructed learners' preoccupation with getting a message across. In addition, we found that the instructed adults had an exceptionally high over-reliance on the first person singular verb inflection. We again propose that this is related to the classroom since all of their opportunities to communicate in Spanish occurred in the classroom and consisted of their answering questions posed by the teacher about themselves. Since students had to answer using a complete sentence, they practised the first singular more than any other form.

Several implications concerning second and foreign language teaching and research can be drawn from this study. First, because so many of the errors made by second/foreign language learners represent oversimplifications which could be predicted, foreign language teachers should demonstrate these potential trouble areas to students much as they demonstrate trouble areas based on contrastive differences.

Secondly, children learning their native language make overgeneralis-ation errors which show that they are actively involved in the learning of their language despite the fact that many of their grammatical rules are applied inappropriately. With time, children 'outgrow' these errors without the 'benefit' of language drills. Children begin to apply rules appropriately as they communicate more and more. Because second language learners seem to overgeneralise much in the way first language learners do, language teachers should allow their students to freely communicate in the classroom for significant portions of the class time. It appears that getting more involved with language use will give learners an opportunity to modify their hypotheses about the grammar, practise the grammar until it eventually becomes subconscious, and to express their feelings and emotions — something which is usually absent in teacher-centred foreign language classrooms.

Third, foreign language teachers should be more careful not to induce their students to make errors by oversimplifying rules to the point of inaccuracy, by forcing students to answer questions using only complete sentences, or by designing drills which force students to use one verb or gender form more than another.

With regard to research, it was illustrated several times that researchers' criteria for classifying an error as first language interference or second language simplification are often vague and inaccurate. The decision has traditionally been based on simply the appearance of the error. Although the present research went a step further by comparing second language and first language errors, error classifications were nevertheless inadequate. While future researchers should continue to examine the appearance of second language errors, they should, at the same time, examine second language errors of learners from several language backgrounds, some of which are equivalent and some non-equivalent to the grammar aspects focused on in the second language. In addition, researchers should ask the second language learner why she/he made a particular error. It is surprising how many learners are consciously aware of why they do what they do.

Another research implication to come out of this study is that it is unrealistic to attempt to discuss percentages of first language interference and second language simplification errors. It appears that interference and overgeneralisation occur in different aspects of the grammar. It would seem more important then to report on where each seems to occur in the language instead of how much each of the two error sources occur.

The last implication which can be drawn is that there is a need to develop a means for measuring proficiency level among the subjects of a group. This becomes even more challenging when we are examining non-instructed learners. Unlike with instructed learners, free learners vary more as a group as there is virtually no control over how much or how little they come into contact with the second language. We suggest that future researchers devise some sort of oral interview which will place subjects into specific levels of proficiency. If instructed and non-instructed subjects are being compared, subjects from both groups should be given the same interview so that data will be comparable.

References

AHUKANNA, JOSHUA, LUND, NANCY and GENTILE, J. ROLAND 1981, Inter- and intra-lingual interference effects in learning a third language. *Modern Language Journal* 65, 281–7.

DULAY, H. and BURT, M. 1974a, Errors and strategies in child second language acquisition. *TESOL Quarterly*, 7(2), 129–36.

— 1974b, You can't learn without goofing: An analysis of children's second language errors. In J. RICHARDS (ed.) *Error Analysis*. London: Longman.

DUSKOVA, LIBUSE 1969, On sources of errors in foreign language learning. *International Review of Applied Linguistics* 7(1), 11–36.

FATHMAN, A. and PRECUP, L. 1983, Influences of age and setting on second language acquisition. In M. BAILEY, M. LONG and S. PECK (eds) *Second Language Acquisition Studies*. Rowley, MA: Newbury House.

GASS, SUSAN 1984, A review of interlanguage syntax: Language transfer and language universals. *Language Learning* 34(2), 115–31.

HARRIS, Z. 1954, Transfer grammar. *IRAL* 20, 259.

HILL, JANE H. 1970, Foreign accents, language acquisition, and cerebral dominance revisited. *Language Learning* 20, 237–48.

JAIN, M.P. 1974, Error analysis: Source, cause, and significance. In J. RICHARDS (ed.) *Error Analysis*. London: Longman.

KRASHEN, STEPHEN 1976, Formal and informal linguistic environments in language acquisition and language learning. *TESOL Quarterly* 10(2), 157–68.

— 1982, *Principles and Practice in Second Language Acquisition*. Oxford: Pergamon Press.

LE COMPAGNON, BETTY 1984, Interference and overgeneralization in second language learning: The acquisition of English dative verbs by native speakers of French. *Language Learning* 34(3), 39–57.

LENNEBERG, ERIC H. 1967, *Biological Foundations of Language*. New York: Wiley.

MACNAMARA, JOHN 1973, Cognitive strategies on language learning. In J. OLLER and J. RICHARDS (eds) *Focus on the Learner*. Rowley, MA: Newbury House.

RICHARDS, JACK 1974a, A non-contrastive approach to Error Analysis. In J. RICHARDS (ed.) *Error Analysis*. London: Longman.

— 1974b, Error analysis and second language strategies. In J. SCHUMANN and N. STENSON (eds) *New Frontiers in Second Language Learning*. Rowley, MA: Newbury House.

— 1976, Second language learning. In R. WARDHAUGH and H. D. BROWN (eds) *A Survey of Applied Linguistics*. Ann Arbor, MI: University of Michigan Press.

SCHUMANN, J. 1976, Second language acquisition research: Getting a more global look at the learner. In H.D. BROWN (ed.) *Papers in Second Language Acquisition*. Ann Arbor, MI: University of Michigan Press.

STOCKWELL, R.P., BOWEN, J.D., and MARTIN, N. 1969, *The Grammatical Structures of English and Spanish*. Chicago: University of Chicago Press.

TAYLOR, B. 1974, Overgeneralization and transfer as learning strategies in second language acquisition. Unpublished doctoral dissertation, University of Michigan.

WOLFE, D. 1967, Some theoretical aspects of language learning and language teaching. *Language Learning* 17(3, 4), 173–188.

YORIO, C. 1976, Discussion of: Explaining sequences and variation in second language acquisition. In H.D. BROWN (ed.) *Papers in Second Language Acquisition*. Ann Arbor, MI: University of Michigan Press.

5   Processing Profiles of Low Grade 3 Filipino Readers in English and Pilipino

ERLINDA REYES and WILLIAM T. FAGAN

Introduction

Children in the Philippines encounter two languages in school. The Philippines National Board of Education in 1974 instituted a policy whereby English would be the medium of instruction for science and mathematics while all the other subjects would be taught in Pilipino. Except perhaps for children from affluent homes in Metro Manila, there is no contact with English in spoken form prior to school entrance. In addition, Pilipino (the standard language based on Tagalog) is spoken by little over one-half the population. While Pilipino is similar in phonology, morphology, lexicon, and syntax to other regional languages, it is not mutually intelligible with all of them. Nevertheless, as Gonzalez & Raphael (1981) point out, 'it is relatively easy for a non-Tagalog (speaker) to learn Tagalog-based Pilipino' (p. 282).

Low readers, by definition, find it difficult to process one language. How do they manage when they are confronted with two, often unfamiliar languages? The purpose of the study reported here was to describe the processing profiles of low-achieving readers in Pilipino and English.

Related literature

Studies which have compared reading processing across languages have generally based their analyses on the work of Goodman & Burke (1972) who devised an elaborate system for investigating miscues (unexpected responses) which occur during reading. These miscues are interpreted within three cueing systems: graphophonic, syntactic, and semantic (Goodman, 1970).

Studies by Romatowski (1981) of reading in English and Polish, and by Mott (1981) of English and German showed that the subjects generally attempted to use more graphic input in the language that was most unfamiliar to them. There tended to be less variation in the use of syntactic and semantic information. However, studies of English and Spanish (Barrera, 1981; Hudelson, 1981), English and Yiddish (Hodes, 1981), and English and French (Malicky, Fagan & Norman, 1987) indicated more similarities than differences in the use of graphophonic, syntactic, and semantic information. Kendall, Chmilar, Shapson & Shapson (1984), who studied the reading performance of French immersion and English instructed children reading in English, found that the children transferred some of their knowledge of their first language (English) to the second. This knowledge was either common to both languages, or facilitated or interfered with the learning of the second.

Within the Pilipino language there is almost an ideal correspondence between graphemes and phonemes. This, of course, is not so in English. Likewise Pilipino differs from English in its use of syntactic markers. Past tense of verbs, for example, is indicated in Pilipino by attaching a prefix (*nag*) to the root word, while for the future tense, the first syllable of the verb is attached as a prefix so that '*laro*' (play) becomes '*lalaro*'. Plurality is not marked within the noun stem but by the addition of the word '*mga*', so that 'the book' is '*ang anklat*' while 'books' is '*ang mga anklat*'. Within the semantic component one obvious difference is that there are not as many synonyms in Pilipino as in English. The concepts in English that would be expressed by the words 'want', 'like' and 'need' would be represented by a single label '*gusto*' in Pilipino. These types of language differences could possibly result in differentiated processing for beginning readers of both languages.

Sample

From three third-grade classes of 140 students in Manila, 15 students were designated by their teachers as being about one year behind in terms of their reading ability in Pilipino. The achievement level was confirmed by the subjects' performance on the passages administered in the study, which indicated that passages at the primary level were too difficult for them. The average number of miscues in English and Pilipino was 18 and 15 miscues per 100 words, respectively. There were five boys and 10 girls in the group; their mean chronological age was 9 years 2 months. One child was designated as high socio-economic status, two as low, and the remainder as middle socio-economic status.

Procedures

Within March of their grade 3 year each subject was seen individually by a researcher at the Philippines Normal College Graduate School and read passages orally in English and Pilipino and gave a free recall. An easy Pilipino passage was given first to help the children understand what was expected of them. The passages for the study were administered alternately in order to avoid a learning effect. All sessions were tape-recorded and later transcribed for analysis.

The reading passages were taken from an informal reading inventory by Cronin (1982) and were devised as part of her doctoral dissertation. There were four comparable forms of passages that ranged from first to sixth grade levels. Passages were varied in difficulty across grade levels, and equivalence was established across forms by writing each passage according to a set of criteria based on words, average T-unit length. The passages were narrative in structure, and the topics were animals (Forms A, B) and sports (Forms C, D). The placement of passages at particular grade levels was made through comparing the word usage and sentence structure with other informal reading inventories, and recommended reading materials for grade 1 through 6. Difficulty was also determined by the Fog Index of readability (Gunning, 1968).

Form B was translated into Pilipino and the translation was edited by the chairman of the Graduate Specialisation in Pilipino at the Philippines Normal College and director of the Language Study Center. Form A was administered in English. The following information was obtained from the children's reading. The percentage of agreement by two independent raters for assigning information to categories was 95.

Graphophonic similarity

(1) High graphophonic similarity: two out of three word parts (initial, medial, final) were used in the child's response.
(2) Attention to initial, medial, and final cues: the percentage of miscues accessed from the initial, medial, and final parts of the text words.

Syntactic semantic similarity

(1) Syntactic acceptability — sentence level: the percentage of miscues

that were syntactically compatible within a sentence unit.

(2) Syntactic acceptability — part sentence level: the percentage of miscues that were syntactically acceptable within a unit smaller than a sentence.

(3) Semantic acceptability — sentence level: the percentage of miscues that were semantically congruent within a sentence unit.

(4) Semantic acceptability — part sentence level: the percentage of miscues that were semantically acceptable within a unit less than a sentence.

Meaning generation

(1) Major meaning change: the percentage of miscues that interfered with meaning across sentences or involved one of the key concepts of the passage. (Two independent raters were asked to delete one-third of the least important concepts; then one-half of the least important remaining concepts. The one-third left were considered the key concepts. The percentage of agreement was 93.)

(2) No meaning change: the percentage of substitutions, or additions, or omissions by the reader that did not change the meaning intended by the author.

(3) Minor meaning change: the percentage of miscues that resulted in a change in meaning that was confined to a single sentence and did not interfere with meaning beyond that sentence, or involve any key concepts.

Recalls

A modified form of the comprehension recall categories of Drum & Lantaff (1977) and Fagan (1985) was used.

(1) Text exact: recall information was identical to that of the text.

(2) Text specific: a unit of recall information (here a clause) was a paraphrase or a re-ordering of a particular unit from the text.

(3) Text entailed: the recall unit represented a combination or synthesis of text information.

(4) Text experiential: the recall included inferences or elaborations on the text data.

(5) Text erroneous: the recall was erroneous in terms of the text data.

Results

Hotelling t^2 tests were used to compare profiles for each of the four groups of analyses. When overall differences occurred, univariate analyses were used to identify the particular source of the difference. The means and variances are reported in Table 5.1.

The readers differed significantly across languages in terms of the nature of the graphophonic information accessed ($F(4,25)$ = 14.71, $p < 0.001$). This difference was attributed to the degree to which the readers attended to final letter cues as they read orally ($F(4,25)$ = 9.47, $p < 0.001$). Readers did not differ on the degree to which their responses were highly graphically similar to the text word, nor on their selection of cues from initial and medial positions. For both languages, however, the initial part of the words was most dominant in terms of cue selection. When reading in Pilipino, the final word part was selected about equally as often as was the initial part of the word in generating a response.

TABLE 5.1 *Means and variances for grade 3 readers in Pilipino and English (variances are in parentheses)*

	English	Pilipino
Graphophonic		
High similarity	0.36 (0.008)	0.41 (0.015)
Initial	0.89 (0.013)	0.83 (0.035)
Medial	0.77 (0.025)	0.58 (0.023)
Final	0.41 (0.088)	0.81 (0.040)
Syntactic/semantic		
Syntactic: sentence	0.61 (0.015)	0.58 (0.051)
Syntactic: part sentence	0.83 (0.049)	0.86 (0.041)
Semantic: sentence	0.61 (0.020)	0.55 (0.057)
Semantic: part sentence	0.87 (0.013)	0.86 (0.042)
Meaning generation		
No change	0.16 (0.003)	0.24 (0.022)
Minor change	0.58 (0.006)	0.67 (0.019)
Major change	0.26 (0.009)	0.09 (0.008)
Recall data		
Exact	0.14 (0.032)	0.12 (0.008)
Specific	0.26 (0.038)	0.39 (0.033)
Entailed	0.08 (0.004)	0.15 (0.006)
Experiential	0.20 (0.029)	0.20 (0.016)
Erroneous	0.32 (0.047)	0.14 (0.017)

There were no differences across languages in the use of syntactic and semantic information. The children were less able to utilise cues from these information systems at a sentence level as opposed to a part sentence level.

In generating meaning, the particular language being read did make a difference ($F(3,260) = 8.24$, $p < 0.0001$) and the source of this difference lay with miscues that resulted in major meaning change ($F(3,26) = 8.14$, $p < 0.001$). The children were inclined to make more significant changes in English than Pilipino. Likewise there were overall significant differences in the nature of the recalls ($F(5,24) = 18.82$, $p > 0.02$) although this difference was not strong enough to be detected for specific categories. The means indicate that the majority of recalls were either exact recall or very specific in terms of the text. In both languages the readers engaged in inferencing and elaborating one-fifth of the time. The source of greatest discrepancy was in the amount of error in the recalls: while 14% of the recall data was erroneous when the children read in Pilipino, this percentage rose to 32 when passages were read in English.

Discussion and Conclusions

On three of the four analyses there were significant differences between subjects reading in English and in Pilipino; thus differences exist in the processing of these languages. When reading in Pilipino, the children attended more to the final part of the word in selecting graphophonic cues. This could be due to the fact that the word structure of Pilipino and English differs. In Pilipino all vowels and consonants (except *h*) occur in final position. Since the range of graphemes that occur in final position in English words is limited and constrained by previous letters, it is understandable why in Pilipino, with a greater range of grapheme expectancies, the subjects would be inclined to attend more. Although not statistically significant, it is interesting that the children attended more to the medial part of the English words. For English words, cues from the initial and medial parts are often strong indicators as to the identity of the word. There were no significant language differences on responses in terms of their high degree of graphophonic similarity to the text words. This finding is consistent with that of Barrera (1981) who investigated the reading of Spanish-speaking grade 3 children when reading Spanish and English. However, in Barrera's study the means for high graphophonic cue usage were much higher than in the present study (approximately 0.60 versus 0.40). This discrepancy could be due to the fact that the readers of this study were low achievers.

In spite of many syntactic differences between Pilipino and English, the children performed similarly in their use of syntax across languages. A similar result was noted by Romatowski (1981) for Polish and English and by Malicky, Fagan & Norman (1987) for French and English. The high syntactic similarity across languages for this study and that by Malicky, Fagan & Norman could be explained by the low-level passages that were used and within which the syntax was rather simple. The Romatowski study, on the other hand, involved much higher level passages.

While the readers did not differ in the degree to which they used semantic cues, they did differ in terms of how they generated meaning in relation to the author's meaning framework. While the substitution of 'rooster' for 'hamster' in the sentence 'John has a pet hamster' makes sense, it changes the author's meaning framework. This tendency to substitute words that were personally meaningful was also discovered by Malicky, Fagan & Norman. Variation from the author's meaning may be due to the relative inexperience of the subjects with the target language in either a spoken or a written form. Perfetti (1975) showed that children's ability to read a word was as much influenced by their past auditory experiences with the word as by their having seen and heard it before. Possessing a limited lexicon at an oral level would be likely to result in an individual's interaction with the environment through that language being impoverished (Cummins, 1978–79) and would limit a reader in accessing the word, thus resulting in substitutions, some of which would change the author's meaning. While the overall differences in recall cannot be related to a particular category, the large discrepancy between the amount of erroneous data in the recalls corresponds to the results of the Malicky, Fagan & Norman study. In that study this category difference did reach significance, which may be due to their larger sample size. A large amount of erroneous recall in English is consistent with the significant difference in meaning generation at the time of input processing. Since there was greater variation from the author's meaning when reading English, it might be assumed that as the readers tried to organise this information for recall, discrepancies and inconsistencies would result.

In spite of the differences, there were also a number of similarities across processing in both languages. The readers tended to process graphophonic information similarly from initial and medial positions of a word; they were similar in terms of how they used semantic and syntactic information cues as they read. The percentage of miscues which did not change meaning or changed meaning slightly did not differ. Except for the amount of erroneous recall, the profiles of the nature of the information used were similar across languages. This supports Hodes' (1981) contention that language processing is a general phenomenon and is not always language-specific. Genesee (1979) pointed out that once underlying processes have been learned in one language, they may be applied in the processing of another. The degree to which processing in one language may transfer to another may depend on the learners' threshold of competence for, as Cummins (1978–79) states, a particular threshold of competence must be attained if the learner is 'to avoid cognitive disadvantages and to allow the potential benefits of becoming bilingual to influence . . . cognitive growth' (p. 42). The subjects of this study were relatively low in their competence with both Pilipino and English which, according to Cummins, will limit their interactions with the environment (through reading in this case) in both languages.

In summary, while the results of this study indicated that language processing transcends languages, there was also evidence that the subjects were sensitive to nuances within languages and adjusted their processing accordingly.

Implications

Since word identification in reading is much influenced by the oral language proficiency of the readers, it is important that they are subjected to a programme that has a large oral language component in relation to the written language. In this way they can interact meaningfully with their environments at an oral level while continuing to amass an increased lexicon which may be applied to comprehending the language of print. The language experience approach to generating text, in which the teacher acts as a scribe and comments on language features as the children contribute information for transcription, would provide opportunities for oral language interaction and for noting the transition from the oral to the written mode.

The commonality of processes across languages suggests that it is not necessary to teach processes independently in different languages. Focusing upon a process in one language should provide a base for the utilisation of that process in another language. However, some processing is influenced by differences within the language structures: thus children should be taught to monitor in both languages. (There were no corrections for the sample of this study in either Pilipino or English.) Thus as children become more versed in the languages, similar and contrastive features of the languages may be pointed out to them, which may be used to heighten their awareness (or meta-awareness) of the languages that they are expected to learn.

Acknowledgements

The data for this study were collected by Ms Elisa Banan, faculty member, PNC Graduate School, and researcher, PNC Research Center. The translation was edited by Dr Alejandro Q. Perez, chairman of graduate specialization in Pilipino at the PNC Graduate School, and director of the Language Study Center.

References

BARRERA, R. 1981, Reading in Spanish: Insights from children's miscues. In R.W. SHUY (ed.) *Linguistics and Literacy Series 1: Learning to Read in Different Languages*. Washington, DC: Center for Applied Linguistics.

CRONIN, M.C. 1982, Construct validity and the measurement of reading process. Unpublished doctoral dissertation, The University of Alberta, Edmonton, AB.

CUMMINS, J. 1978–79, Bilingualism and educational development in anglophone and minority francophone groups in Canada. *Interchange* 9, 40–51.

DRUM, P.A. and LANTAFF, R.E. 1977, Scoring categories for protocols. Paper presented at the Second Annual Language Conference, Boston.

FAGAN, W.T. 1985, Comprehension categories for protocol analysis. In W.T. FAGAN, J.M. JENSEN and C.R. COOPER (eds) *Measures for Research and Evaluation in the English Language Arts*. Urbana, IL: ERIC:RCS and NCTE.

GENESEE, F. 1979, Acquisition of reading skills in immersion programs. *Foreign Language Annals* 12, 71–7.

GONZALEZ, A. and RAPHAEL, T.C. 1981, Transitional reading problems in English in a Philippine bilingual setting. *Reading Teacher* 35, 281–6.

GOODMAN, K. 1970, Behind the eye: What happens in reading? In K.S. GOODMAN and O.S. NILES, *Reading Process and Program*. Urbana, IL: National Council of Teachers of English.

GOODMAN, K.S. and BURKE, C.L. 1972, *Reading Miscue Inventory*. New York: Macmillan.

GUNNING, R. 1968, *The Technique of Clear Writing*. New York: McGraw-Hill.

HODES, P. 1981, Reading: A universal process — a study of Yiddish and English bilingual readers. In R.W. SHUY (ed.) *Linguistics and Literacy Series 1: Learning to Read in Different Languages*. Washington, DC: Center for Applied Linguistics.

HUDELSON, S. 1981, An investigation of the oral reading behavior of native speakers reading in Spanish. In R.W. SHUY (ed.) *Linguistics and Literacy Series 1: Learning to Read in Different Languages*. Washington, DC: Center for Applied Linguistics.

KENDALL, J.R., CHMILAR, P., SHAPSON, L.R. and SHAPSON, S.M. 1984, English reading skills of kindergarten and grade one immersion students. Paper presented at the Colloquium on Research in Reading and Language Arts in Canada, Lethbridge, Alberta.

MALICKY, G., FAGAN, W. and NORMAN, C. 1987, Reading processes of French immersion children reading in French and English. *Canadian Journal of Education*.

MOTT, B.W. 1981, A miscue analysis of German speakers reading in German and English. In R.W. SHUY (ed.) *Linguistics and Literacy Series 1: Learning to Read in Different Languages*. Washington, DC: Center for Applied Linguistics.

PERFETTI, C.A. 1975, Language comprehension and fast decoding: Some psycholinguistic prerequisites for skilled reading comprehension. Paper presented to the Development of Reading Comprehension Seminar of the International Reading Association, Newark, DL.

ROMATOWSKI, J.A. 1981, A study of oral reading in Polish and English: A psycholinguistic perspective. In R.W. SHUY (ed.) *Linguistics and Literacy Series 1: Learning to Read in Different Languages*. Washington, DC: Center for Applied Linguistics.

Part II:
Language and Culture

6 Culture and Meaning in French Immersion Kindergarten

SANDRA WEBER and CLAUDETTE TARDIF

The young child beginning a second language immersion programme in kindergarten must cope not only with the new experience of formal schooling, but also with a second language environment, one in which the teacher does not speak often in the more comfortable words of the child's first language. Yet, although kindergarten is for many children their first encounter with a second language, the research literature of French immersion education has almost totally ignored classroom processes and the child's experience at this grade level. What is the child's first experience of French immersion schooling? What aspects of classroom life are relevant to understanding second language acquisition and how are they relevant? What is the nature of communication in immersion classrooms? How is meaning constructed within the school context? These are some of the fundamental and difficult questions with which we must periodically come to grips in order to develop more comprehensive theories of immersion teaching and learning within the school context.

This study reports some of the findings of an ethnographic investigation into the child's experience of French immersion kindergarten. After discussing the primacy of culture as a major determinant of meaning in the classroom, we shall explore three layers of culture and suggest how they structure the child's experience of kindergarten, influencing the routines, rituals, and ultimately, the meaning constructed in immersion classrooms.

Research Perspectives and Procedures

The methodological framework for our research stems from the ethnographic and phenomenological traditions of grounded theory in educational research as articulated or exemplified by such researchers as

Edwards & Furlong (1978), Barritt (1984), Spindler (1982) and Delamont (1983). The focus of these approaches is on describing and understanding experience in context, and on discerning both the implicit and the explicit meaning of situations to the people living them. Following Geertz (1973) and McLaren (1986), this study attempts to connect action to its sense rather than link behaviour to its determinants. The ultimate aim is a grounded theory (Glaser & Strauss, 1967, 1978) whose concepts emerge from analysis of concrete experiential data to describe the particular in such a way as to point, also, to the more general. This is made possible, in part, through rigorous methods of analysis that include constant comparison and cross-checking across categories, searching for negating examples, category saturation, and accounting for all the data (following Barrit, 1984 and Turner, 1981). In contrast to the product orientation of much of the research in French immersion education, the emphasis of our research method is on description, on process, on meaning structures, and on prolonged observations in the natural setting as the source of data.

Two French immersion half-day kindergarten classes (combined enrolment of 39) were followed on a continuous basis throughout an entire school year (1985–86), and subsequently on an intermittent basis the following year in grade 1. Situated in a middle-class professional neighbourhood in Edmonton, the kindergartens were taught by the same teacher in a 'dual-tracked' public school that offers both French immersion and 'regular' (unilingual English) programmes at the elementary levels in addition to a 'regular' junior high programme. The criteria used for selecting the kindergartens were:

— a teacher with at least two years prior experience in immersion kindergarten;
— a teacher willing and able to act as a collaborative researcher by taking journal and observation notes;
— a teacher who spoke to the children exclusively in French for at least 90% of the school day;
— kindergartens judged by two experienced supervisors to have an established immersion programme and clientele fairly typical of Alberta.

We used a variety of data-gathering techniques: extensive classroom observations and field notes, audio- and video-recordings, note-keeping by the teacher, and both semi-structured and open-ended interviewing of parents and children, including interviews with the children that incorporated the use of a shy, three-and-a-half year old puppet as 'co-interviewer' to encourage the children to discuss their views candidly. The researchers independently and sometimes jointly observed each class of children two days a week during strategically selected four-week blocks interspersed throughout the 1985–86 school year. Our observations focused on recording as much as possible of the children's actions, expressions and words. Field notes included descriptions of the context, setting and classroom procedures as well as formulations of initial questions and/or interpretations (in separate columns) for further investigation. Significant key incidents (incidents that seemed important or unusual to the children) were written up using Erickson & Shultz's (1977) work as a guideline.

The observers and a video camera were present in the classroom on the very first day of school in order to witness the children's initial contact with immersion schooling. Thereafter, the video camera was in each class once a week for an hour from the beginning of September until the end of April, providing a continuous record even when the researchers were not there. The videotapes have proved to be of particular methodological significance, providing pertinent information on social context, shared meaning, and the paralanguage dimensions (Pennycook, 1985) of sense-making.

Throughout two years, the classroom teacher acted as a research participant, keeping a journal and participating in the collection of the data. The use of three observers (including the teacher) assures an exchange of viewpoints and a more complete observation, providing one of the methodological advantages of the project.

The guiding questions for data collection were always: 'What is the child's experience? What is the content and nature of classroom interaction?' and 'How does the child make sense of her/his experience? What does what is going on mean to the child?' However, in keeping with ethnographic and phenomenological research strategies, we did not go into the classroom with preconceived categories for observation or with rigidly defined data collection procedures, but rather adapted and refined our procedures as new questions emerged in the light of data already collected. As an example, we had initially centred our classroom observations on the teacher-directed 'circle time' and the children's subsequent spontaneous interaction in the various play centres. As our knowledge of the situation grew, we realised the additional importance of observing the children as they got dressed to go outside and whenever they lined up to go anywhere in the school. These were moments when the children commented freely on their perceptions and understanding of their experience. As well, it soon became evident that what the children did or thought was often related to the teacher's behaviour and perceptions and vice versa.

The interviews pertinent to this paper were 'led' by a shy puppet who had never been to school before, and centred on the following lines of enquiry: What is kindergarten? What do you do in kindergarten? How come the puppet can't understand the teacher? What could the puppet do if he doesn't understand the teacher? How do you come to understand the teacher? Is it OK not to understand? How do you know what to do? Later on, the children were asked to help the puppet by translating or explaining certain key French phrases that, from our classroom observations, we knew to be familiar and important components of the teacher's communication.

In addition to the two classes indicated, two other French immersion kindergarten classrooms and two regular English (first language) kindergartens were observed and video-recorded over a six-week period in order to provide additional data, insight, and perspectives for a more valid interpretation of the main corpus. Both of the additional immersion classrooms and one of the English kindergartens were from slightly lower socio-economic status (SES) neighbourhoods and included several immigrant children. One of these classes was from the Separate (Catholic) School Board. The bulk of the observations and videotaping in these classrooms occurred during the beginning days and months of two consecutive school years. Including the two immersion kindergartens that were followed intensively for a longer period, we have thus gathered detailed portraits of how six kindergartens began a school year.

A preliminary analysis and interpretation of a large portion of the data is now complete. The majority of the video and audio tapes have been transcribed and selected samples have been analysed. The process of analysis and interpretation has included detailed descriptions of 'key incidents' (Erickson, 1981), category saturation and cross-checking (Turner, 1981), discourse analysis (Halliday, 1975; Mehan, 1979), phenomenological analysis (Barritt, 1984; Van Manen, 1984), and consultation of the pertinent work of other scholars. This chapter reports only some of the many findings of our study, focusing on a general description of the nature and the meaning of classroom experience, with special emphasis on culture and ritual.

The Primacy of Culture in Classroom Life

The primacy of the cultural aspects of life in schools has been well documented in other settings (e.g. Jackson, 1968; Getzels, 1974; LeCompte, 1978) and is readily observed in the teachers' attempts to organise classroom life and in the children's reactions to those attempts. Drawing on the work of anthropologists such as Goodenough (1971) and Pelto (1970), we use the word 'culture' to refer to both (a) shared patterns of beliefs and knowledge by which people order their perceptions and experiences and in terms of which they act, and (b) customary patterns and organisation of behaviours and symbolic manifestations or expressions of these patterns. A thematic content analysis of our observation notes and of the transcripts of classroom interaction revealed three layers or categories of culture that seem important to understanding immersion kindergartens. We found that all excerpts or units from our field notes and the transcripts could be understood in terms of one or more of these categories. Ordered from the more general to the specific, these categories are: (a) the North American culture of childhood associated with L1, (b) the culture of schooling, and (c) the culture of French immersion kindergarten teaching, a subculture of (b).

(A) The culture of childhood

Although there is some evidence for universals in the culture of childhood, especially concerning elements of play (e.g. Lundy Dobbert, 1985), the culture of childhood may also be viewed as an adult construct (Skolnick, 1975), a series of images and normative expectations held by a particular adult group regarding what a child is, how children act and feel, what they need and want. Children themselves have little choice but to become involved in the prevailing culture, taking up some of it as their own and rejecting other aspects of it. Particularly if the teacher and children share the same social class, the culture of childhood can be a meeting ground of common experience or subject of negotiation for both adult and child (Delamont, 1983; Edwards & Furlong, 1978). Research in contexts where the culture of childhood of the teacher differs from that of the students (e.g. Philips, 1983) illustrates the importance of this element to the children's classroom experience.

Although there are many important differences, there are also many commonalities between the French and English Canadian cultures of childhood that seemed in the context of this study to facilitate the children's gradual adaptation to L2 culture. The analysis of our data suggests that one of the ways in which the children and teachers succeeded in their collective negotiation of meaning in the immersion classroom was by drawing initially on shared elements of the culture of childhood. The immersion teachers, for example, often drew on the children's prior experience and knowledge of such universal children's games as hide-and-seek or peek-a-boo to introduce French vocabulary. Similarly, the teachers often read (in French) fairy tales already familiar to most children in English, thereby superimposing new words on what Bruner (1975) calls the 'cognitive maps' the children brought to the situation. The children responded actively, questioning and guessing and using all their prior knowledge to make sense of the second language experience. When, before turning the page of the book, the teacher asked (in French) 'What is going to happen next?', the children usually hypothesised appropriately with enthusiasm, seeming to relish being able to participate competently, as if taking pride in showing 'I know'. It is thus convenient, and perhaps ironic, that many of the fairy tales so deeply ingrained in English Canadian culture are in fact adaptations of the French originals. In a similar fashion, many of the songs used at the beginning of the year in the immersion kindergartens had L2 words set to melodies from L1 songs already familiar to the children. The children thus did not have to concentrate on learning the melody and they delighted in recognising the tunes as familiar friends.

In North American society, the cultural artifacts of childhood include a vast array of consumer fads, toys that are so widely distributed and advertised that almost all children have them or know about them — a constant and changing parade of Transformers, Cabbage Patch dolls, He-Men, Wrinkle Pets, etc. Although many educators (e.g. Postman, 1982) and parents question the values reflected by these toys and condemn the marketing strategies used to sell them, the fact remains that the children almost inevitably bring these cultural artifacts to school, often for 'show and tell'. These shared symbols help create a 'we-ness' or cohesiveness as the children try to initiate conversations about them. The teachers we observed often used these occasions to speak in French about something in which the children were interested, asking the children questions in French about their favourite toys, etc. Increasingly linked with consumer products and toys, the pervasive influence of television (Postman, 1982) among all social classes and the widespread availability of such programmes as 'Sesame Street' and the Saturday morning cartoon shows provide a similar shared core of experience that, for better or worse, the children bring to the classroom.

Yet another aspect of childhood culture was reflected in the choice of play centres so common to kindergartens and day-cares: the old familiar sandbox, the block corner, the lego toys, the dress-up corner, the doll's house, the plasticine, the crayons, etc. These centres reflect many of the things children do in our society and ways in which they are expected to learn to play together. Once more, the transition between the familiar world of early childhood and the strange environment of school and a second language is made a little easier because of the incorporation of the familiar in the strange.

Certain holidays such as Halloween and Christmas figure prominently in the North American culture of childhood, especially for children from middle and upper socio-economic backgrounds. For example, the ritual of dressing up in a costume and going out trick or treating is a signpost for many children: it means they are 'big enough to go out on Halloween'. The teachers made much of the familiar holidays, bringing in the symbols associated with these occasions and clarifying and extending their meaning in French.

There were also holidays celebrated in the French immersion classrooms that were not known by most of the children, holidays that are specific to the culture of childhood of the second language but not the first. The children's reactions, for example, to the teachers' attempts to explain the French Canadian festivals of 'La fête de la Sainte Catherine' or 'Le Carnaval du Québec' were very different from the familiar and easy way they understood Valentine's Day or Easter celebrations. The L2 holidays did, however, evoke lots of questions and attention from the children who obviously enjoyed them. There is as much to be said for novelty as for comfortable familiarity in terms of classroom motivation. The contrast between the children's reactions to familiar and unfamiliar holidays highlights the potential importance of both L1 and L2 cultures of childhood to the construction and organisation of meaning within the classroom. The teachers we observed often utilised the L1 culture in planning their L2 school programmes in order to capitalise on shared understandings as a useful base for meaningful L2 dialogue, especially at the beginning of the year. As the year progressed, however, the teachers introduced more and more elements specifically related to the second language culture of childhood, adding more and more unfamiliar content and challenging the children to figure things out. For less homogeneous classes (e.g. classes for immigrant children), the common elements of childhood culture shared by the children or shared by both L1 and L2 cultures might be few, posing a different challenge to the teacher. In some contexts, there may be great disparity between the culture of childhood associated with L1 and that of the school's L2, particularly in the subtleties of how children are expected to behave. More case studies need to be carried out in diverse settings to broaden our knowledge of the different challenges and possibilities that exist in immersion schooling.

(B) The culture of schooling

According to Gracey (1972), 'Kindergarten is the place where children begin to learn the pupil role. At the core of this learning is a set of classroom routines which the teacher introduces and then trains the children to follow' (p. 163). Our data suggests that Gracey's findings hold for the immersion setting as well.

A content analysis of the videotapes and observation notes revealed that much of what occurred in the classrooms is implicitly, and often explicitly, related to what researchers such as Jackson (1968) refer to as the culture of schooling. Although we know from our conversations with the teachers that they often extensively and consciously focused on the teaching of French vocabulary and phrases, for the children, the meaning of much of the activity of the first weeks of immersion kindergarten centred on adapting to the peculiar characteristics of school life. Their talk, questions and actions centred on:

— getting used to the school-specific organisation of people: e.g. lining up, sitting in a circle, doing things in a large group and in small groups, choosing partners, girls as a distinct group from boys, how to choose a play centre; adapting to physical space and materials, e.g. how story corner works, the playground, going to the washrooms, how to put the blocks away, how to use the centres, where to go;

— internalising the time structure of school: e.g. the concept of recess — going outside but not going home, you have to come back inside the classroom; the sequence of school-specific activities: first we do the calendar routine, then we do the weather routine, then we sing; a dividing up of the day into a familiar pattern of time blocks, each block symbolised or announced by a 'meaning-marker' such as a specific song or phrase or gesture;

— learning the interaction rules and power relations of school: e.g. not to talk while teacher is talking, look at teacher for directives on what to do, ask permission to go to the bathroom, wait for your turn to do things, learn to read subtle clues concerning when it seems all right to comment aloud in the group context, etc.

The major, although perhaps 'hidden' or implicit, curriculum of the French immersion kindergartens we observed is learning how to behave in school and learning what school is about. Moreover, our observations in the English kindergartens (which were similar in many respects to the immersion kindergartens), lead us to hypothesise that, in many important ways, immersion kindergartens are not very different from other classrooms. Jackson (1971) defines the hidden curriculum in classroom life as 'the curriculum of rules, regulations and routines, of things teachers and students must learn if they are to make their way with minimum pain in the social institution called "the school"' (p. 20). Edwards & Furlong (1978) point out that the organisation of classroom talk is inseparable from the management of classroom meaning in a context set up primarily for 'the control of knowledge by the patterning of communication' (p. 11).

The culture of schooling will be illustrated further below in a section focusing on routine, patterns and rituals.

(C) The culture of French immersion teaching

Like most kindergarten contexts, immersion and otherwise, the classrooms we observed included structured circle time, play centres, dress up corners, fine motor tasks, art activities, logic games, problem solving situations, music, and movement activities. These activities provide opportunities for children to explore, to initiate, to act on their environment, and to develop through concrete experiences. However, while in many ways very similar to English first language kindergartens, the French immersion kindergartens we observed had their own distinctive features. For example, as a result of not being able to rely solely on linguistic cues to communicate with the children, the immersion teachers were particularly attentive to other communicative strategies which permit them to impart meaning to a situation. As we discuss elsewhere (Weber & Tardif, 1988), much use is made of gesture, tone of voice, visual aids, and of careful structuring of the environment. Indeed, one of the things that seems to help the children make sense of the 'strange' linguistic stimuli impinging upon them is the fact that they experience the situation simultaneously in very diverse and concrete ways. For the children, the second language seems to be integrated into their total experience and understanding of the situation, but not necessarily in a word-by-word or a word-to-concept fashion. For example, when asked by the puppet to explain the meaning of certain familiar French phrases that the teacher had been systematically using, the children almost always answered in terms of their personal experience of the situation rather than providing an exact translation. Thus, the frequent and comical explanation for the French phrase meaning 'What is the weather like today?' was, 'It means to look outside the window', reflecting part of the experienced classroom routine relating to the weather, where the teacher always looked towards the window when asking questions.

The daily songs sung in all the French immersion kindergartens visited are another example of the culture of French immersion teaching. Even on the first day, the children were able to participate in some fashion in the song routines by carefully watching the teacher and each other, by imitating gestures, and by mouthing words or trying to approximate in some way the appropriate sounds. Songs appear to play a very important role as signals or cues, marking off neatly the end of one activity and the beginning of another, carving up the day into familiar sequences of time and function. In a sense, the songs seem to say to the children (i.e. mean to the children): 'Stop this', or 'Come here', or 'Now it's time for —'. Although some of them are adaptations of French words to English melodies, many of the songs have a French origin and become part of the culture specific to teaching French immersion kindergarten. Most of the songs are accompanied by meaningful body movements and provide outlets for emotional expression. Singing might also serve to cement the child's sense of belonging to a group through collective participation in a shared event, cultivating a sense of 'we-ness' and a commonly shared base of classroom culture. The songs serve as important vehicles of communication concerning classroom activity long before the literal meaning of their words is clearly understood.

As we have already discussed in the section on the first language culture of childhood, the holidays and other cultural events related to the second language are prominent examples of the culture of immersion teaching. Through analysis of provincial curriculum guides and through conversations with teachers at national conventions, we learned that many of these L2 French Canadian festivities become so firmly embedded in the culture of French immersion teaching that, from British Columbia to Newfoundland, immersion students celebrate the Quebec winter carnival even if there is no snow, and they attend imitation 'cabanes à sucre' even if there are no sugar maples around for a thousand miles. Whether or not these festivities really constitute French Canadian culture as it is lived in each province is another matter entirely. Indeed, we might even hypothesise that the culture of French immersion teaching does not always reflect the subtleties, variations and depth of French Canadian culture. It is important to distinguish between L2 culture itself and the culture of L2 teaching, since the two are not necessarily synonymous.

The next section describes how routines and rituals constituted an essential part of immersion classroom culture.

Routines, Rituals, and the Construction of Meaning

The children quickly learned the participation structures (Erickson & Schultz, 1977) of characteristic activities in all the classrooms we observed. Events in the classroom almost immediately came to have a predictable order and sequence involving characteristic routines, some of which took on the complexity and symbolic meaning of rituals. As Moore & Myerhoff (1977) write: 'Rituals . . . frame, punctuate and bracket the flow of social life, thereby assigning meaning to events' (p. 19). Moreover, as Turner (1982) asserts, 'rituals do more than simply inscribe or display symbolic meanings or states of affairs but instrumentally bring states of affairs into being'. We agree with McLaren (1986) that rituals are related more to the construction rather than merely to the reflection of human reality. Our analysis of the content of circle time lessons and the children's reactions to those lessons revealed that routines often constituted the major portion of the lesson and heavily influenced the meaning the children attributed to their classroom experience.

At the beginning of the year, the children watched the teacher and each other attentively, carefully imitating and gradually finding pleasure in their ability to participate in the many rituals that structure classroom life. The 'bonjour' ritual, for example, is the first thing the children do in every French immersion kindergarten the authors have visited. With much motioning of the hands, or pointing to a taped circle on the carpet, the teacher (speaking in French without a word in English) manages to make the children understand that they are to sit in a circle around her. Then after relying on such things as the well-understood 'Shh' with hands to lips to quiet the children, the teacher begins the bonjour song, 'Bonjour, les amis, bonjour', to be replaced later on in the year with 'Bonjour, bonjour, comment ça va?' As we later found out from other teachers, these same songs are sung in countless classrooms across Canada, part of a largely undocumented culture of immersion kindergarten teaching. Next, the teacher points to herself and says her own name, and then says 'Bonjour' to each child by name. She then makes a small circular motion with her hand in front of her mouth to indicate that each child is expected to respond by repeating what the teacher models in French ('Bonjour, Madame L.'). Gradually, as she continues around the circle, the teacher only prompts when necessary.

The bonjour ritual was quickly followed by the calendar ritual, with the children counting the days in unison as Teacher points to the numbers and leads the chorus (gradually, as the year progresses, the children do it without any verbal cues). Next, Teacher looks out of the window and asks, 'Quel temps fait-il aujourd'hui?' (trans. 'What is the weather like today?'), thereby immediately cueing a song about the weather and then having the children move hands on a weather clock to the appropriate images (windy, cloudy, sunny, etc.) to indicate the weather. And so the rituals succeed each other, their familiar sequence helping the children anticipate what comes next, and key gestures, words, and melodies acting as clues or meaning markers which help the children attribute appropriate meaning to the situation. Each situation seems to have what could be called its inherent meaning structure or potential for meaning. There are only so many semantic options in any situation, and in the classrooms we observed, the situation was often carefully orchestrated to narrow the range of potential meanings.

Meaning in the immersion classroom

The teacher-initiated rituals of the kindergarten classroom pervasively structured the children's experience and expectations. From the moment the children set foot in the classroom, the implicit (and often explicit) question guiding much of their individual and collective actions seemed to be, 'What does she want of me? What am I supposed to do? What did she say?' Especially at the beginning of the year, the children's expressed focus was not on learning French *per se*, but rather on understanding what was expected of them and what they could in turn expect. Although the fact that the teacher is speaking a language that the children cannot understand would seem a priori to be a major source of frustration and difficulty, contrary to our expectations, the second language element seemed to play only a minor, albeit significant, role in classroom communication. The video-recordings and interviews clearly show that the children were able to construct much meaning from the immersion situation even at the beginning of the year. They responded appropriately and did not exhibit inordinate confusion. Meaning in the classroom did not seem to reside in words as much as in context and in the paralanguage elements of communication. We use the term 'paralanguage' in its broadest sense, to incorporate the kinesic (gestural) and the proxemic (spatial) in addition to the paraverbal. Meaning in the classroom appeared to be situationally embedded and for the children, words often seemed to be 'words-as-acts' (Edwards & Furlong, 1978). As an example, when asked the meaning of nouns such as 'recréation' (trans. recess), the children often answered in terms of their own actions and feelings, saying things like, 'It means to go outside and play on the monkey bars'. Analysis of the meaning of the children's language suggests that their concepts and their interpretations of the world are very much what Merleau-Ponty (1962) refers to as 'embodied' meanings.

Meaning is continually being interpreted and negotiated within the social context of the classroom: between individual children and the teacher, between small groups of children, and among the larger group. The teacher and students individually and collectively are engaged in defining the situation and in conferring meaning on their experience. The teachers in this study did not ask the children to say everything in French. They were quite willing to have the children initiate conversation and make comments in English. The teachers reacted to what was being said by the child by responding in French. It would appear that children do not need to understand every word spoken by the teacher; there seemed to be a 'scaffolding of meaning' (Bruner, 1975) constructed around the second language situation with gestures, body movement, intonation, concrete materials, pictures, and rituals. The children appeared to have a tolerance for linguistic ambiguity which allowed them to draw on the total context for their clues to meaning rather than relying solely on the linguistic information that was provided.

Discussion

There has been concern expressed by some educators that beginning an immersion programme at the kindergarten level may cause undue cognitive and emotional difficulty for children. The research to date has not adequately addressed this issue nor has it provided a general understanding of how the young child actually reacts and adapts to the second language kindergarten experience.

The second language proved to be much less of a barrier than we had anticipated. During the first days of school, we carefully observed the children with some of these concerns in mind, half expecting tears and visible discomfort as signs of the stress of beginning immersion. We were very surprised at just how easily the children adapted to the situation — with very few tears, very little fuss, and with lots of smiles and enthusiasm despite an obvious initial shyness in some of the children. In fact, it is often the parents and the teachers rather than the children who seem to be the most challenged. If anything, it was the school-specific rather than the language-specific aspects of the classroom experience that seemed in a sense to be the 'foreign' culture. The fact that not understanding the teacher seemed to be only a minor nuisance to the children may be indicative of the fact that children are more tolerant of ambiguity than are adults. Even in their first language, young children are used to not understanding everything adults say. They do not feel as socially awkward about not understanding as adults might in a similar situation, nor are they as reluctant to ask for help. Not knowing everything, relying on adults, and asking lots of questions are part of the socially accepted role of being a child.

Our findings suggest that the culture of schooling and its concomitant subculture of French immersion teaching persistently influenced and shaped the meaning of the kindergarten experience for the children. The construction of meaning in the immersion classroom is not only an individual process but also is simultaneously a group process. The children are 'in the same boat' of not understanding French together and school is very much a group-oriented institution. The children come to understand the situation by attending not only to linguistic cues but also by interpreting the paralinguistic clues as well as the routines and rituals of school culture, of childhood culture and of the second language context. Because our study highlights the importance and the pervasiveness of at least three layers of culture in the classroom, it would be interesting to analyse them further to see how variations in L1 culture (e.g. immigrants from diverse L1 cultures, or programmes for minority L1 children) affect the children's experience of immersion education. Perhaps, for example, teachers need to take the L1 culture into more consideration, assessing in detail the 'fit' between L1 culture, L2 culture, and the culture of schooling and of second language teaching. In the French immersion classrooms we have visited, this fit seems quite comfortable for most of the children, although as educators we question the values of many aspects of the culture of schooling. Description and analysis of specific classroom cultures could help assess the use and purpose of many immersion teaching practices, perhaps calling into question some of the routines that are taken so much for granted that their inherent value is never questioned. Our description of prevailing classroom norms and practice does not constitute a blanket endorsement but rather reflects our conviction that in order to determine what should be, we need to examine what is.

Although we have found many commonalities in the limited number of classrooms we have observed, we are not asserting that all French immersion teachers share exactly the same culture of teaching. As Feiman-Nemser & Floden (1986) point out, important cultural differences amongst teachers may be associated with age, experience, teaching philosophy, gender, social class, school norms, location, subject matter and grade level. The first and second language history and ethnic identity of the teacher may also be important factors. Researchers have barely begun to explore the diversity of teaching cultures. Our work makes a modest beginning by looking at the specific context of French immersion kindergarten and by identifying some possible elements important to understanding that context.

Acknowledgements

We gratefully acknowledge the financial support of this project by the Central Research Fund (SSHRC) and by the Small Faculties Committee for the Support and Advancement of Scholarship of the University of Alberta.

We would also like to acknowledge the considerable contribution of Barbara Lavallee (one of the kindergarten teachers) to this study. Her enthusiastic support and her assistance in collecting the data was invaluable.

References

BARRITT, L. 1984, Analyzing phenomenological descriptions. *Phenomenology and Pedagogy* 2(1), 1–10.
BRUNER, J. 1975, The ontogenesis of speech acts. *Journal of Child Language* 2(1), 1–20.
DELAMONT, S. 1983, *Interaction in the Classroom* (2nd edn). London: Methuen.
EDWARDS, A. and FURLONG, V. 1978, *The Language of Teaching. Meaning in Classroom Interaction*. London: Heinemann Educational Books.
ERICKSON, F. and SHULTZ, J. 1977, When is a context? Some issues and methods

in the analysis of social competence. *Quarterly Newsletter of the Institute for Comparative Human Development* 1(2), 5–110.

FEIMAN-NEMSER, S. and FLODEN, R. 1986, The cultures of teaching. In M. WITTROCK (ed.) *Handbook of Research on Teaching* (3rd edn). New York: Macmillan.

GEERTZ, C. 1973, *The Interpretation of Cultures*. New York: Basic Books.

GETZELS, J.W. 1974, Socialization and education. *Teachers College Record* 76(2), 218–25.

GLASER, B. and STRAUSS, A. 1967, *The Discovery of Grounded Theory: Strategies for Qualitative Research*. Chicago: Aldine.

— 1978, *Advances in the Methodology of Grounded Theory: Theoretical Sensitivity*. Mill Valley, CA: The Sociology Press.

GOODENOUGH, W. 1971, *Culture, Language, and Society*. Reading, MA: Addison-Wesley.

GRACEY, H. 1972, *Curriculum or Craftsmanship*. Chicago: University of Chicago Press.

HALLIDAY, M. 1975. *Learning How To Mean: Explorations in the Development of Language*. London: Edward Arnold.

JACKSON, P.W. 1968, *Life in Classrooms*. New York: Holt, Rinehart and Winston.

— 1971, The students' world. In M. SILBERMAN (ed.) *The Experience of Schooling* (pp. 148–64). New York: Holt, Rinehart and Winston.

LeCOMPTE, M.P. 1978, Learning to work: The hidden curriculum of the classroom. *Anthropology and Education Quarterly* 9(1), 22–37.

LUNDY DOBBERT, M. 1985, Play is not monkey business: A holistic biocultural perspective on the role of play in learning. *Educational Horizons*, Summer, 158–63.

McLAREN, P. 1986, *Schooling as a Ritual Performance*. Boston: Routledge & Kegan Paul.

MEHAN, H. 1979, *Learning Lessons*. Cambridge, MA: Harvard University Press.

MERLEAU-PONTY, M. 1962, *Phenomenology of Perception* (Trans. Colin Smith). London: Routledge & Kegan Paul.

MOORE, S.F. and MYERHOFF, B. 1977, *Secular Ritual* (pp. 3–24). Amsterdam: Royal Van Gorcum.

PELTO, P. 1970, *Anthropological Research: The Structure of Inquiry*. New York: Harper and Row.

PENNYCOOK, A. 1985, Actions speak louder than words: Paralanguage communication and education. *TESOL Quarterly* 19(2), 259–82.

PHILIPS, S.U. 1983, *The Invisible Culture: Communication in the Classroom and Community on the Warm Springs Indian Reserve*. New York: Longman.

POSTMAN, N. 1982, *The Disappearance of Childhood*. New York: Dell Publishing.

SKOLNICK, A. 1975, The limits of childhood: Conceptions of child development and social context. *Law and Contemporary Problems* 39(3), Summer, 38–77.

SPINDLER, G. (ed.) 1982, *Doing the Ethnography of Schooling: Educational Anthropology in Action*. New York: Holt, Rinehart and Winston.

TURNER, B. 1981, Some practical aspects of qualitative data analysis: One way of organizing the cognitive processes associated with the generation of grounded theory. *Quality and Quantity* 15, 225–47.

TURNER, V. 1982, *From Ritual to Theatre: The Human Seriousness of Play*. New York: Performing Arts Journal Publications.

VAN MANEN, M. 1984, Doing phenomenological research and writing: An introduction. *Phenomenology and Pedagogy* 2(1), 36–69.

WEBER, S. and TARDIF, C. 1988, An ethnography of French immersion kindergarten: Sense-making strategies in second language classrooms. Paper presented at the Annual Second Language Research Forum, University of Hawaii at Manoa.

7 Bilingualism: Exploring Language and Culture

ALVINO E. FANTINI

Language as World View

> Mamá, ¿por qué yo nací como nene?
> ¿Por qué no nací como Dios?
> ¿O como el sol . . . como una bola de fuego?
>
> Mamá, why was I born a little boy?
> Why wasn't I born like God?
> Or like the sun . . . like a ball of fire?
>
> (Mario, age 5)

At a very early age, the human child is already capable of expressing abstractions, creating metaphors, and pondering philosophical issues like the one above (Fantini, 1985). Yet, we don't usually think about our ability to speak. Most of us simply take language for granted, that is, unless we find ourselves in a situation where we don't share a common tongue. However, second language development and intercultural contact are increasingly commonplace experiences for many people around the world. The result is that numerous issues are being raised related to functioning with dual languages and cultures and the insights which derive from bilingual use.

For the monolingual individual, lack of awareness of one's own language use is probably due to the fact that as we master our native tongue, it in turn masters us. This is because acquisition of a mother tongue provides more than an expressive medium for communicating, one which is far from being a 'neutral' system. Rather, language is a medium (or paradigm) which directly influences our entire lives (Chilton Pearce, 1971). In linguistic terms, this notion is known as 'language determinism and relativity'. In other words, the mother tongue acquired

110

in infancy influences the way we construct our vision of the world (hence, language determinism). For the developing bilingual, then, use of two different languages provides access to differing visions of that same world (language relativity). Furthermore, the ability to function in more than one language also provides a way of 'stepping outside of' one paradigm and of being able to compare and contrast one view with the other.

Considering the words within each language system helps to understand what this means. For example, English, Chinese or Arabic words do not equate directly in meaning; rather they represent different systems for classifying, segmenting and categorising our experiences. The existence of a set of words which organise experience in a particular way implies more than learning lists of vocabulary, but just as importantly, perceiving the characteristics of those phenomena important to the speakers of a particular language.

Let us consider an example from Italian language-culture. 'Pasta' is the generic or superordinate term for a whole class of experiences which includes 'maccheroni' (or macaroni) but not 'poodles'. In other words, acquisition of the word 'pasta' presupposes recognition of phenomena in the world which differ in some aspect (such as maccheroni and poodles) while recognising those which are similar (hence, pasta, maccheroni and linguini). Although the second example illustrates words of the same class, they are hierarchically arranged — from general to more specific. For example, pasta subdivides at the next level into about four categories, depending on mode of preparation: pasta *asciutta*, pasta *ripiena*, pasta *al brodo* and pasta *al forno* (dry and covered with a sauce, stuffed, in broths and in the oven). Each category further subdivides into varieties, depending on additional characteristics. Hence, pasta asciutta, for example, includes a long list of experiences like: tagliatelle, fusilli, capellini, fedelini, spaghetti, spaghettini, zite, zitoni, mezzane, perciatelli, and many others. Although our pasta example may seem trivial to non-Italians, it is obviously of significance to Italian speakers, hence the elaborate list of words.

In each of our languages, the words we use reflect the way we categorise experiences just as they also reinforce a particular categorisation. Furthermore, to apply the words appropriately to an experience presupposes that recognition of characteristics of phenomena may go unnoticed by the speakers of another language-culture, whether those traits be shape, size, mode of preparation, texture, colour, etc., as in the pasta example, or other aspects of experience. Therein lies one link between structuring experience in a particular way (culture) and encoding experiences into words (language).

The language we acquire leads us to categorise the world in a particular way just as the way we categorise is reflected in the language we use. In these ways (and in others), languages orient their users to particular ways of knowing and viewing the world. This notion is the basis for the determinism and relativity hypothesis formulated many years ago by the linguist Benjamin L. Whorf (1956), still debated today. Although many people do not accept Whorf's idea entirely, it cannot be wholly dismissed either. How each language influences a speaker's perception and cognition remains an intriguing question.

Language — A Two-Edged Sword

Already by five years of age, children demonstrate the ability to use language not only to communicate, but also to formulate profound questions. Unaware of their own amazing feat — mastery of complex patterns of sounds, forms and grammar — children acquire their native tongue almost unthinkingly. Its acquisition is almost incidental to their efforts to explore, to question, to communicate (Fantini, 1985).

Moreover, language appears to be species-specific. In fact, many believe that words are what make the anthropoid human. This may explain the Biblical statement: '. . . in the beginning was the Word'. Yet, language has also been termed original sin — a lie — since word creations substitute for the thing signified. Indeed, as we master words we sometimes fail to differentiate between verbal symbols and the reality for which they stand. However, words serve only to evoke what is meant conceptually, thereby providing vicarious experiences for both speaker and hearer. Once acquired, words exert a powerful influence throughout our entire lives, mediating all that we think, say and do.

While languages mediate, they also liberate. That is to say, our ability to symbolise permits us to 'move' conceptually through time and space. We recall and tell of things past, or move ahead into the future, merely by pronouncing different words. So great in fact is our faith in words that we may even feel viscerally the 'reality' of being in the past or future described. Yet, obviously we can neither retrieve the past nor insure the future, but only symbolise about them. Physically, we always remain in the present moment and space, while we experience the illusion through words of being liberated from these dimensions.

Children learn of the power of language early on. This is evidenced, for example, in the child of three who recounts an unfortunate event at the nursery, and cries. The same is true of the child of four who speaks of dinosaurs with obvious delight even though he or she only really 'knows' of dinosaurs through language, preserver of our collective human memory. Since language aids the imagination, the make-believe, the child can put into words wild fantasies, such as when describing in exquisite detail an encounter with a wicked witch. Real or imagined, language brings into 'existence' even that which may not exist at all! (Fantini, 1985).

Language not only aids thought, but at times constrains it, even contradicting our experiences. Two examples may help to illustrate this. In the first, a child taking a cognitive test in kindergarten is asked to point to one of four pictures which best depicts the concept 'fastest'. Confronted with choices of a donkey, an elephant, a car and an aeroplane, the child points unhesitatingly to the elephant. He describes their great speed which he has observed in Tarzan movies on television, and then shows with his hand how slowly aeroplanes move across the sky. Through language, he will eventually 'learn' to invert notions derived from his own direct perceptions. In an opposite case, the child panics when taken aboard an aeroplane, screaming, kicking and crying. No attempts to ease his fears calm him, until moments later he ceases abruptly, noting that he has not become tiny nor disappeared as he has so often observed of others who boarded planes and flew off into the sky. In each case, language was used to 'explain' (or contradict) perceptions (Fantini, 1985).

So much of learning throughout life is accomplished through language, augmenting — and sometimes constraining — the possibilities of what we can understand. Through language we can consider the impossible and explore the unknowable as revealed by the comments of the five-year-old quoted at the beginning of this article, pondering death and yearning for immortality, transcending life itself.

Since language is with us from our earliest years, it is difficult to imagine what our lives might be like without this ability to symbolise and to communicate with others. It is little wonder that accounts of wild and feral children, reared apart from society, have so intrigued linguists concerned with this question (Brown, 1958; Singh & Zingg, 1966; Lane, 1976; and Curtiss, 1977).

Communicative Competence and Intercultural Contact

Language is more than an ability to articulate; it is all that is involved in communicating with others: (1) a linguistic dimension (the sounds, forms and grammar of language); (2) a paralinguistic dimension (the tone, pitch, volume, speed and other affective aspects of how we say things); (3) an extra-linguistic component (all the non-verbal dimensions — gestures, movements, grimaces, etc.), and (4) a sociolinguistic dimension — the different ways or styles used to express ourselves in each new situation, each style dependent on social factors such as age, role, sex, relationship, and the topic and setting of the speech event, among others. Every individual learns and masters all of these dimensions as part of his or her communicative competence. By the age of five, in fact, most children are so proficient in all areas that they can easily judge the correctness or nativeness of other speakers. Moreover, children exposed to two or more languages early on display their ability to master and use two or more systems appropriately.

It would seem, therefore, that individuals exposed to a second language must develop a differing or an expanded vision of the world. This development is affected by the different constructs of the world inherent in each language system, as well as by the differing interactional strategies used by speakers of each system. Beyond that, knowing more than one language also allows participation with individuals of different cultural groups, expanding social possibilities while enlarging psychological ones.

A simple graph may help to place the bits and pieces forming a world view, into a cohesive whole (see Figure 7.1). Interaction among these components (generally referred to as form, meaning and function by linguists), then, are the basis for a world view. Moreover, each of these components varies from culture to culture, accounting for the

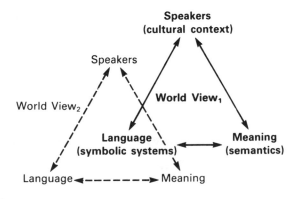

FIGURE 7.1

differing visions of the world held by each society. This notion may help to explain why the process of developing a second language (or becoming bilingual) is more than mastery of a tool. In fact, it is precisely for these reasons that significant development in a second language often effects changes in the components and a reconfiguring of their interrelationships (note the dotted lines). In other words, it results in a paradigm shift, a change in world view, or to put it metaphorically, a 'crack in the cosmic egg' (Chilton Pearce, 1971).

Intercultural experiences are similarly valuable, providing exposure to another language-culture. Contact with individuals of other ethnic backgrounds and speakers of other languages not only opens a door to exploring another world view, but also provokes questions about one's own values and assumptions — an often disquieting experience. Hence, intercultural exposure provides opportunities to gain new perspectives on oneself while also learning about others. It affords an excellent way to understand language and culture as mediators of our 'knowing'. Keenly aware of this, Don Juan, the Yaqui sorcerer, frequently challenged Castaneda, his apprentice, with the words: 'Who do you think you are to say the world is thus and so just because you think it is? Who in hell gave you the authority? The world is a strange place . . . full of mystery and awe' (Castaneda, 1973).

Teaching Language and Culture

Most language teachers, intercultural trainers and bilingual educators acknowledge that language and culture are interrelated, yet they often lack explicit understanding of this interrelationship. The lack of a clear concept of this interrelationship explains why there is a general dearth of appropriate techniques to teach language-culture, except through often trivial activities. A common example is the Spanish teacher who shows slides of a bullfight in an attempt to introduce 'culture', or the intercultural expert who investigates general cross-cultural communication processes, but fails to acknowledge how a specific language mediates those processes. For the language teacher, the real challenge is how to teach language within a constant cultural context of which it is an expression. To state the problem another way, the task is not simply to teach new ways to say old things (i.e. new symbols for old thoughts) but rather to aid students in the discovery that a new language system leads to new ways of perceiving, of classifying and categorising, of interacting, new ways of 'seeing' and 'knowing' the world. For the intercultural expert, the challenge is to integrate language as a pervasive aspect of intercultural orientation, not merely as 'tool', but as the paradigm which best reflects and affects culture.

For the bilingual educator, understanding the interrelationship of language and culture provides new incentives for a commitment towards developing and maintaining bilingualism not only for limited-English-speakers (i.e. maintenance bilingual education), but for *all* children, especially the monolingual ones. Monolingual children indeed are most in need of dual language education to ensure that they too benefit from participating in dual visions of the world and to preclude the 'smug narrowness and the narrow smugness' of the ethnocentric being (Fishman, 1976).

The psycholinguistic distinction of compound and co-ordinate bilingualism touches on this point (Jakobovits, 1970). The first type is that which typically develops in classrooms where the target language is learned with and through constant reference to one's native tongue. The student learns new 'equivalents' for saying what he or she has always said. Co-ordinate bilingualism, on the other hand, results from acquiring each language directly, in separate contexts, and with no reference to the other (as with most bilinguals who acquire their languages in naturalistic settings). For the co-ordinate bilingual, each language provides different guides to perception, different configurations of the world, and two distinct modes for communicating about it.

Classroom language learners, however, are not always limited to compound functioning, nor are co-ordinate bilinguals forever constrained to separate functioning. Increased use of a second language with native speakers in their own cultural context will move the classroom learner towards co-ordinate functioning. The types of classroom activities selected by the teacher may either further or hamper this goal. Likewise, analytical study of language will cause a co-ordinate bilingual to become increasingly aware of connections across two formerly unrelated codes.

For language teachers and other educators, awareness of the interrelatedness of language and culture is only a beginning. Once this is understood, their goal might be to move students towards increasing co-ordinate ability. This requires knowing ways to present all aspects of communicative competence to the extent possible despite the artificiality of the classroom situation — beyond recitations, memory exercises, verb paradigms and grammar translations, towards real language use. Students need not only to produce correct linguistic utterances, but appropriate ones, delivered with the proper accompanying voice, tones, gestures, and other interactional behaviour. In fact, it is well known that linguistic accuracy is less critical to effective communication in a second language than the accompanying paralinguistic and extra-linguistic aspects. Native speakers are much more likely to overlook grammatical errors than to excuse 'inappropriateness' of interactional style and behaviour. All of this requires increased attention to language as used within its cultural context. Work towards this goal ensures that the learner will not only develop proficiency in Spanish or English, but do so in a manner acceptable to native speakers.

The teacher must also acknowledge that he or she is only a single speaker, a single model — male or female, with a fixed role and relationship to his/her students. The teacher's speech, therefore, is only one idiolectic sampling from among whole communities of speakers. At best, a classroom will always be an artificial construct in which input is severely limited, distinct from naturalistic settings. Once these distinctions between classroom learning and field language acquisition are acknowledged, however, we can begin to consider ways to make the classroom a richer simulation of the field situation.

We can also create situations to introduce learners to other varieties of speech. For example, if we accept the importance of diverse input, we can partially remedy this through taped recordings, radio and movie or videotapes when teaching foreign languages. Audio-visuals assume new importance; no longer are they merely 'supplementary aids' but rather important means of providing exposure to different speech samples. Simulation and role playing become techniques for altering the social situation to avoid a static classroom setting. Creation of a bus station or a cocktail party requires participants to assume roles as well as to practise speech and behaviour appropriate to each circumstance. Such techniques are indispensable when we realise the significance of exploring and practising diverse styles. Once teachers understand more explicitly the links between language and culture, they will understand the need to go beyond the limitations of most language classrooms. They will also realise the need to provide cultural and interactional experiences appropriate to the speakers of the language under study and to be wary of artificial methods which, although effective for teaching language structures, create their own 'methodological' cultures, concealing what is truly important for developing co-ordinate bilingualism. Methods such as Audio-lingual, Silent Way, Suggestopedia, Counselling-Learning, and the like, serve as examples of this possibility if not balanced by opportunities for learning appropriate cultural interaction as designated and accepted by native speakers of the target language.

For some, second language learning may always be strictly an intellectual endeavour. However, for those who want a second language in order to interact and communicate, it can lead to much more. Acquisition of another language and entry into another culture offer the possibility of going beyond the limitations of one's own world view. 'If you want to know about water, don't ask a goldfish,' someone once said. Those who have never learned a second language nor entered another culture are like the goldfish, taking for granted the milieu in which it has always existed. As educators — whether interested in foreign languages, intercultural communication, bilingual education, or international and global education — then, we recognise the importance of helping our students towards increased bilingualism and biculturalism. To be effective, however, we need a clearer concept of how language and culture are interrelated, an understanding of implications for developing bilingualism, as well as better techniques for providing classroom experiences which support both.

Entry into another world view, hopefully, will help individuals develop an appreciation for the diversity and richness of human beings. This shift in perspective is the kind Ferguson (1980) described as 'the greatest revolution in the world — one which occurs with the head, within the mind'. As educators, we may indeed have a significant role in this revolution — one which leads to greater tolerance, respect and understanding. For this to happen, we require the attitudes, awareness, knowledge and skills which will make us each a better global citizen, able to empathise and understand other persons on their own terms. Exposure to more than one language and one culture, *in a positive context*, offers such a promise. Hence our commitment to bilingualism and biculturalism — both by preserving the home language-cultures of so many of our children, and by teaching a second language-culture to those who have none.

References

BROWN, ROGER 1958, *Words and Things*. New York: The Free Press.
CASTANEDA, CARLOS 1973, *A Separate Reality*. New York: Pocket Books.
CHILTON PEARCE, JOSEPH 1971, *The Crack in the Cosmic Egg*. New York: Washington Square Press.
CURTISS, SUSAN 1977, *Genie: A Psycholinguistic Study of a Modern-Day 'Wild Child'*. New York: Academic Press.
FANTINI, ALVINO E. 1985, *Language Acquisition of a Bilingual Child: A Sociolinguistic Perspective*. Clevedon, England: Multilingual Matters (also (1982) *La adquisición del lenguaje en un niño bilingüe*. Barcelona, Spain: Editorial Herder).
FERGUSON, MARILYN 1980, *The Aquarian Conspiracy*. Los Angeles: J.P. Tarcher.

FISHMAN, JOSHUA 1976, Bilingual education: An international sociological perspective. Speech delivered to the National Association of Bilingual Educators, San Antonio, Texas.

JAKOBOVITS, LEON A. 1970, *Foreign Language Learning: A Psycholinguistic Analysis of the Issues*. Rowley, MA: Newbury House.

LANE, HARLAN 1976, *The Wild Boy of Aveyron*. Cambridge, MA: Harvard University Press.

SINGH, J.A.L. and ROBERT M. ZINGG 1966, *Wolf-Children and Feral Man*. New York: Archon Books, Inc.

WHORF, BENJAMIN L. 1956, *Language, Thought and Reality*. Cambridge, MA: MIT Press.

Related works

ADLER, PETER S. 1976, Beyond Cultural Identity. In L.A. SAMOVAR and R.E. PORTER (eds) *Intercultural Communication* (2nd edn). Belmont, CA: Wadsworth Publishing Co.

BAETENS-BEARDSMORE, HUGO 1982, *Bilingualism: Basic Principles*. Clevedon, England: Multilingual Matters.

FANTINI, ALVINO E. 1978, Bilingual behavior and social cues. In M. PARADIS (ed.) *Aspects of Bilingualism*. Colombia, SC: Hornbeam Press.

GROSJEAN, FRANÇOIS 1982, *Life with Two Languages: An Introduction to Bilingualism*. Cambridge, MA: Harvard University Press.

HAKUTA, KENJI 1986, *Mirror of Language: The Debate on Bilingualism*. New York: Basic Books.

NINE-CURT, CARMEN JUDITH 1976, *Teacher Training Pack for a Course on Cultural Awareness*. Cambridge, MA: National Assessment and Dissemination Center.

SAVIGNON, SANDRA J. 1983, *Communicative Competence: Theory and Classroom Practice*. Reading, MA: Addison-Wesley.

8 Cultural Processing and Minority Language Children with Needs and Special Needs

GEORGES DUQUETTE

Introduction

Minority language children are a challenge to the unilingual English educator or human communication specialist. Difficulties exist because in spite of our advanced knowledge, excellent training programmes and competent professionals our efforts as a society are largely spent in order to meet the needs of majority language children.

This small oversight (expecting everyone to have the same cultural and linguistic background needs) has meant that much of the educational and clinical language research has been carried out with unilinguals. Very few of the studies in bilingual (first and second) language education have been introduced into the training programmes of teachers, administrators and human communication specialists, and most of the trainees themselves are unilingual speakers of English. As a result, these highly trained professionals, once certified, know little about the role and importance of the home culture and first language of children whose mother tongue is other than English.

Even though a large majority of North American children today come from minority language families, the home culture and first language of these children are usually not considered because differences in cultural and language needs fall outside the scope of competence of the unilingual language specialist or special education teacher. Services, therefore, are provided in a language familiar to the specialist, but less familiar to the minority language child. When some efforts are made to consider the child's background, existing practices will show that assessments are often done haphazardly by non-native speakers of the language through tests that have not been carefully weighed as to questions of cultural and linguistic authenticity, statistical validity and reliability.

While we now better understand that the acquisition of communicative skills depends in large measure on the development of the first language (Cummins, 1978, 1984; Genesee, 1988; Krashen & Terrell, 1983; Lambert & Tucker, 1972; Lapkin & Swain, 1982; Skutnabb-Kangas & Toukomaa, 1976), we are also finding out that there is more in the home culture that relates to language development than might at first appear. In fact, culture may be to language what language is to speech because they each involve (Duquette, 1985; Kaplan, 1966; Manolson, 1983) a process of understanding our world and expressing ourselves within that world.

The purpose of this chapter is to show the close relationship that exists between the home culture and the acquisition of (the first) language. It will clarify the notion of culture through a review of the literature, underscore elements in the home environment which contribute directly to the language acquisition process, and identify needs and special needs. (The word 'need' refers here to the average child who requires certain essentials in the course of development; the expression 'special need' also refers to essentials, but which are greater in number or degree, as in the case of developmentally handicapped. Minority children, unlike majority language children who receive services in their first language, are most often offered services by the education and clinical language sciences in a second language and culture.) Finally, it will make recommendations for increased research and improved services in the area of minority language development. The chapter intends to provide a theoretical framework for future studies on the relationship between the home culture and first/second language acquisition.

The Notion and Relevance of Culture

Culture versus context

Since the early 1970s it has been established that communicative skills are best acquired in context (Bandura, 1977; Burt & Dulay, 1981; Fishman, 1968; Hymes, 1974; Paulston, 1974; Widdowson, 1978; Wilkins, 1976). Most of these authors view contexts as situations which provide situational information for language interaction. The *Standard College Dictionary* (1963) states that context is 'something that surrounds and influences, as environment or circumstances'. Bryen (1982) adds that context provides world knowledge.

The importance of context in the language acquisition process is accepted today by most language specialists. The role and importance of culture, however, are not that easily defined. Rivers (1983), referring to Halliday's use of the word 'context', says: 'Contextual refers in this case to the inner as well as outer context, not only to situational features, but also to linguistic and emotional factors that are often strongly influenced by the attitudes and values of the speaker's cultural environment' (p. 122). Is culture different from context? The publications that attempt to grapple with the notion of culture and its relationship to the acquisition process (Dunnett, 1981; Gearing & Sangree, 1979; Hall, 1966, 1973; Linton, 1977; Luria, 1976; Morain, 1983; Papalia, 1983; Saville-Troike, 1982; Trueba et al., 1981; Valdes, 1986) generally view culture as group-determined behaviour.

If knowledge can be data-driven and concept-driven (Duchan & Katz, 1983), clearly, then, context can be understood as data-driven processing and culture as a collective form of concept-driven processing. A young child receives input during the first two years of life (Piaget, 1963), but something happens in this process: the child begins to organise the information, and through the recurrence of patterns or routines develops certain expectations. These expectations are cognitive in nature, but also cultural because the child learns not only in isolation, but also from others (Bandura, 1977) as a result of living within a family (group) unit and school community.

Minority language children also evolve this way, but because their home language is less important in our society and the social structure of daily lives, they often do not receive the same kind of reinforcement from parents, language specialists and other professionals in special education that majority language children do in fact receive (Cummins, 1984; Trueba et al., 1981).

Cognition and non-verbal development

We know that a non-verbal period of language development precedes verbal communication (Luria, 1976). This is a time when the quality of input comprehension can actually make a difference in the child's future level of performance (Krashen & Terrell, 1983). Language is rooted in those early interactions between mother and child, a stage of development commonly called the 'Motherese period' (Newport, Gleitman & Gleitman, 1977). During this time parents can make a difference in the way they interact and stimulate communication with their non-verbal child (Manolson, 1983).

As thought and (the first) language emerge and grow in parallel to one another (Vygotsky, 1962), the child discovers meaning in some contextualised behaviour and is taught to interpret that meaning in a culturally defined way. Because meaning, world knowledge and categorisation are key aspects of comprehension (Wessells, 1982) language is used as a way to vehicle thoughts and concepts of the world (Stern, 1981). If, as the cognitivists believe, language is rooted in experience and the way we actively conceptualise that experience, then the non-verbal period is a fertile 'input' phase for later language development. Krashen (1981) suggests that the acquisition of language in a communicative mode is an unconscious process as compared to the learning of language (which is more syntactic and conscious in nature). He is not alone in thinking this way (Bialystok, 1979: implicit versus explicit learning; Carroll, 1981: automatic versus conscious learning; Cummins, 1978: BICS versus CALP; McLaughlin, 1980: incidental versus intentional learning; Stern, 1975: intuitive versus rational learning; Stevick, 1980: performing versus critical self). The natural, unconscious acquisition of verbal and non-verbal language skills appears to take place in the same way we unconsciously pick up other kinds of information and skills we need in order to understand our world and function in that world.

There exists in the home environment a structured 'collective unconscious' (not the same as but not inconsistent with Jung's (1973) use of this expression) which is nothing less than an established and collectively agreed upon unconscious organisation of daily life (Gearing & Sangree, 1979). It involves routine activities, natural or codified signs for communication purposes, defined interpretations, anticipated and expected behaviours, all of which take place on a day to day basis.

Self-identity

The period of adolescence is characterised by insecurity and a search for identity (Erikson, 1980; Henson, 1981). This is the age when peer acceptance becomes important, and the self tests itself against peers within social groups and further defines itself through adjustments.

The process of identity, however, does not begin in adolescence, although that is no doubt the time when the self's identity is most obviously tested. An interesting study would be to find out how adolescents with strong home culture ties would differ in their adjustments within a 'bilingual' society from those whose home culture is weak. Studies have shown a clear relationship between one's sense of roots and self-identity

(Mead, 1963; Osterrieth, 1973). If the bonding with the home culture during the Motherese period and first six years of life is weak or there exists little in terms of sociocultural support then there could develop an alienation between the adolescent and his or her home culture as there already exists in a natural way with the second majority language culture.

Genesee (1987: 101), quoting Taylor, Barrili & Aboud (1973), says: 'Language can be an important symbol of ethnic identity. Indeed, research in Canada has shown this to be the case for English and French Canadians.' Genesee goes on to explain how bilingualism creates a 'reduction in social distance between English and French'. This tension in social distance appears beneficial if the home's cultural identity is strong, as it is for English Canadians taking French immersion. For a French Canadian living outside Quebec or a Spanish American in a heavily anglicised environment, the pull towards assimilation is strong, particularly when the child begins to leave the home, takes his or her place in society, and experiences the role-playing expectations of a majority language society. As in the case of the first language, the child's first experience of self is that provided by the home. If that experience is watered down and no clear identity is formed, assimilation will not only be swift, but the social distance of that adopted identity will (if culture is, as Gearing defines it, 'synchronized behavior') be at odds with the first home culture (Carlton, Colley & Mackinnon, 1977: 122–3). Educationally, we know that students are more resourceful and successful if they are familiar with the contexts, approaches and subject matter to which they are exposed. Success builds upon success, and transfer of learning is possible if we first enhance development in the home culture.

While adolescence is a period of insecurity because of the numerous changes taking place, an acceptance by oneself and others of one's personal cultural identity can increase that sense of security. To what degree there is a correlation between cultural identity and the sense of belonging needs to be studied further, but what is certain is that the age of adolescence, impacted as it is by majority group expectations, will lead the self to find an identity whether or not it is its own to begin with, with the results or consequences that selection may bring.

Culture, cognition and self-identity

Learning is an active process (Piaget, 1963; Wessells, 1982). As we model and adjust to the behaviours and routines of others (Gearing, 1984), we develop an identity of who we are in relation to the family and inner social groups we have identified with. This growth of self through an understanding of our world's behaviours and language is expressed through different contexts, and our successes enable us to move on into the outside world. If that world is a natural extension of the family, then the growth process simply continues. If it is different, then is the time better spent mastering the world we come from in order to be equipped to meet the challenge of living bilingually, or is it simply better to abandon the cradle of one's childhood years and devote all of one's energies to the majority language? Studies tell us about the importance of those early experiences, and the next few pages will explore some reasons why the home culture is of such importance to language development.

The Home Culture: Early Life Routines and Language Acquisition

Early in life, the child becomes part of the world through a series of varied experiences. However, with time, there emerge patterns and routines. The child learns to expect that given certain conditions there will usually follow an already experienced series of events. For instance, after supper, the child knows that when the mother takes out the pyjamas, the baby powder, the towel and face-cloth that a certain procedure which he or she has lived before will occur once again in a regular and defined way. Communication around such routines occurs, whether verbal or non-verbal. The child readily recognises the expectations of the mother, in fact participates in the behaviour surrounding these expectations, and responds to them with prior knowledge in a conceptually active way.

Here are some routines which infants and very young children may experience:

(1) The early morning routine (waking up, washing, getting dressed)
(2) Breakfast (preparation for the meal, eating, washing up)
(3) Nappy change (several times during the day)
(4) Lunch (similar to breakfast routine)
(5) Going out (preparation, getting to destination, activity, returning home)
(6) Games and activities (taking out the toys, play with parent, left alone with toys, putting toys away)
(7) Naptime
(8) Snack time
(9) Visitors (arrival, attention to baby, adult-talk, departure)

(10) Supper time (similar to breakfast/lunch routines)
(11) Bath time (preparations, bath, pyjamas)
(12) Family time (watching TV, special attention to baby)
(13) Snack time
(14) Bedtime (kissing/hugging baby, giving toy/winding music box, dimming or closing lights)

Such structural routines become the basis of behaviour not only for the child but also for all those sharing life in that particular household. Individual cognitive processing occurs, but because learning is not done alone but collectively as well, there is also some cultural learning which takes place.

In the case of a minority language child the cultural environment of the home can be quite different from that of a majority language one. If, in fact, there is some truth to the Whorfian hypothesis (Whorf, 1956; Wessells, 1982), and language has an effect on thought which helps to preserve the culture, then language and culture need to be considered together.

Meeting the Needs of Minority Language Children

Professionals, to be effective, should pay attention to the following points.

Recognition of the child's home culture

The home environment is where the young child is first exposed to contextualised language interactions. It is also in the home that the child learns to interpret and organise the world in a culturally coherent way, structure a way of life, develop expectations, and find the most appropriate behaviours to help him or her meet personal needs. This recognition of expected routine structures and encoding of 'appropriate' responses is developed early in life, and any professional coming into contact with children, including minority language children, should first recognise their needs in terms of the context and the culture of the home environment.

Many professionals feel helpless in knowing how to cope with the scenario in which they find themselves, or choose to disregard the importance of the home culture of these children. So, what they do is select what they feel is the next best alternative. If they cannot meet the needs of the child, it appears logical to at least provide expert services in a culture and language which are familiar to them and hope it doesn't make much difference in the long run. The consequences of such decisions can be very serious, and it is the responsibility of the profession to ensure that *all* children's needs are met.

Distinction between 'need' and 'problem'

Some years ago, children who experienced some perceived degree of difficulty in their learning or were at variance with the norm in their behaviour or performance were considered to have 'problems'. A glance at the literature in special education shows how pervasive the approach actually was. Many of the children who were considered to have problems came from minority language homes; these perceptions of 'problems' were often not founded (Cummins, 1984) since they came about as a result of attitudes and norms found in the majority language culture.

Today, although there are some subtle currents of change and inspiration in the air, the trend continues. The reason appears to lie in the scientific approach which has trained professionals to view issues to be resolved as problems. The 'problem' refrain comes from a teacher/professional-centred perspective which acknowledges the existence of a need in a student, but a need which becomes a problem for the professional who does not know how to meet that need. There is, nevertheless, a new perspective that tries desperately to be heard. Ever since Carl Rogers (1969, 1983), Abraham Maslow (1970), and the Humanist School of education, many educators have been uncomfortable with the term 'problem' and now prefer using the word 'need', since it better represents the perspective of the student — a perspective that is child- and not teacher/professional-centred. Children with needs and special needs from minority language homes are no exception to this rule.

Children need to be understood and to express themselves (in the same positive light experienced by other children) in their own first language (Cummins, 1984; Manolson, 1983; Trueba, this volume), home context and culture. Their minority language background brings out the limitations not of the children, but of the professionals who are asked to respond to their needs.

Encouragement of the participation of parents

Turn-taking and the quality of mother–child interaction also has an effect on acquisition (Manolson, 1983). The emotional bond is vital because it provides the child with a sense of belonging (Osterrieth, 1973); so also is the understanding between parent and child as to their shared interpretations of the world and the reinforcements of these interpretations that take place. Professionals should work closely with parents and even closer with minority language parents because of the differences in cultural background.

Encouragement of further contact with peer and adult models in the same cultural group

The importance of modelling should not be underestimated (Bandura, 1977). Under specific circumstances, certain behaviours are expected; children pick up those behaviours if they wish to be effective in their communicative behaviour. This means that modelling involves the structuring of one's behaviour to suit the anticipations of others under specifically defined circumstances. Children learn to shape their behaviours in order to meet these expectations, and thus become successful communicators.

Promotion of the experience of success in the home environment

A factor which is often overlooked and which is crucial to both cultural and language processing is the experience of success. When parents delight in their children's behaviours and frown upon others, they have an effect upon the shaping of those behaviours and the parenting of successful experiences for children. To change the cultural environment is very often to change the way people perceive behaviour and their interpretation of success.

Assessment and development of programmes which are consistent with the home culture and first language of children

The literature in the field (Cummins, 1984; Garcia, 1981; Genishi & Dyson, 1984; Hall et al., 1981; Flores & Riley, 1982; Lidtz, 1982) urges professionals to carry out more statistically valid assessment procedures with minority language children and to focus upon their home culture and first language background. It is the responsibility of the Profession to ensure that their members are in step with the research and are guided by these studies, instead of by their own personal prejudices. It is a serious matter when a Profession allows its members to meet the needs of only the majority language population.

Particular attention to minority language children with special needs

Some children are more in need of help than others. It is particularly important that special education children receive the proper services from the outset if they are going to be provided with any possible chance of developing a system of communication. Professionals who insist that cognitive and linguistic assessment procedures and language development programmes be carried out in the majority language and not the first language of the child are (in light of current studies) limiting further the child's chances of success. While their procedures may be better adapted to the cultural and language needs of professionals (language of self, tests, existing programmes, etc.), they do not respond to the particular needs of the minority children.

A child with special needs can spend eight to twelve years or more without uttering a single word. If language is a rule-governed symbol system that is capable of representing one's understanding of the world (Bryen, 1982: 7), then a child who learns to communicate non-verbally concepts that reflect an understanding of the world has in fact developed the capabilities of language, even though communication is at a non-verbal level. That is true because the child is familiar with the cultural world in which he or she has become a part over the years and is able to understand that world and express feelings about it through that particular 'home culture' perspective.

Practical Recommendations

Concentration of efforts

Of course, we cannot expect an entire profession to be instantly retrained, to become experts in bilingual education, to have native-like proficiency in a second language, to develop and administer culturally authentic assessment materials, or to create overnight national educational programmes in keeping with minority children's home language and culture. However, we can at least begin by implementing the following two recommendations:

(1) There should be established in each province or state a language assessment and development centre serving the needs and special needs of minority language children. Each centre would combine specialists in the areas of both language development and bilingual education. In addition to providing services, these centres would offer expert advice to the language professionals who in the performance of their duty try to meet the needs and special needs of minority language children.

(2) There should also co-exist a graduate level university programme in bilingual education and special education which would train professionals to provide the kind of advice that is so desperately needed in our society. These specialists could be trained as educators specialising in bilingual (first and second language) education and special education, counselling, administration, and even combine this expertise with studies in speech pathology, language assessment, therapy, and so on.

Other recommendations

To parents:

(1) Maintain the home language and culture, and continue to communicate with the child in the language which is most natural to the entire family.

(2) Establish routines at school which are consistent with the home environment and stimulate non-verbal communication around routines recognised and understood by the child.

(3) Select language specialists who by their background and training are not only open to, but can appreciate the importance of emphasising the child's home culture and language in developing his or her communication skills.

(4) Insist that cognitive and language assessment and the communication programme of the child is first carried out in the family's home language.

(5) Double-check to be sure that the assessment and educational programme is not just a watered-down version and/or translation of the English programme.

(6) Ask whether or not the testing instruments have the same statistical

reliability and the tests the same kind of validity as the English tests. In addition, test materials should be 'authentic' to the culture of the child. (An operational definition of 'authentic materials' is materials produced by native speakers for native speakers: Bégin, 1982.)

(7) Ensure that the language specialists are aware of the child's routines in the home.

(8) Ensure that the language specialists have the necessary cultural and linguistic competence in the background to understand fully and appreciate how and why these routines exist, so that such routines can be incorporated into a communication programme (Miller, 1984).

(9) Make sure that those professionals doing the assessment are not only fluent in the child's first language, but can synchronise with the child's home culture. Otherwise, how can the results be considered valid? It is quite unacceptable in this day and age that a language assessment should be carried out by a specialist who is not competent in the first language of the child whose language is to be assessed.

(10) Ask to play a major role in the development of their child's communication system (Manolson, 1983). Ask that the key component of the communication programme be in the home since communication builds upon the Motherese period (Bryen, 1982).

To members of the community:

(1) In bilingual communities and where the numbers warrant, schools for students with special needs should provide the necessary language expertise for minority language students.

(2) At school, in more monolingual communities where minority language children are fewer, there should be at least one (or more) staff members of the community who belongs to the minority language group. Such members from the home culture offer in their contact with the child a natural link and familiarity with the home environment.

(3) Any parent(s) with a developmentally handicapped child needs a good support system. Groups such as the Association for the Mentally Retarded should be well informed as to the needs of their parent members who are culturally and linguistically different. They should know that the services such parents seek on behalf of their children's needs are not always available.

To educators and language professionals:

The personal opinion of a professional is not a professional opinion. It is essential that the teacher or language specialist recognise the strengths as well as the limits of his or her training. The most highly trained professional today is not necessarily trained to meet the needs and special needs of minority language children. This is especially true when assessment and educational language development programmes are involved.

To training institutions:

Given our pluralistic society, there is a need to inform new teachers and language professionals of current findings in bilingual education. They need to know the most effective means for achieving success with minority language students. New courses should be developed in concert with faculties of education so that these pertinent issues relevant to cognitive and language development may be addressed.

To researchers:

There needs to be more research with minority language children with special needs. Is the success experienced with other minority children transferable to those with special needs? A comparison of minority groups with majority language groups gives us an idea, but other variables (socio-economic status, culture and language status, etc.) also need to be considered. More studies also need to be carried out on the relationship between the home culture and first language acquisition in a bilingual environment.

To governments:

(1) The Municipal Government:
School board trustees or officials, organisations, families and friends can have an impact upon the hiring of professional staff to provide the specialised services required by a culturally different member of the community. Parents have much to say as to the education and services which their children receive.
(2) The Provincial or State Government:
    (a) Usually, the primary responsibility for education lies with the provincial or state government. Parents should ask whether their child is guaranteed the necessary special education services under the law. Parents need to know their rights in order to have their child receive competent professional services (which to be effective have to be consistent with the cultural and linguistic home

environment) so that suitable language assessment and development programmes can be implemented.

(b) The province or state can also have an impact upon the training of language specialists and professionals so that greater emphasis can be placed upon meeting the needs of children from minority groups.

(3) The Federal Government:

Where there exists a high concentration of minority language families and when bilingual and multicultural education is promoted, very often federal representatives themselves can by their advice or contacts with the province or state assist the individual family in obtaining the services so necessary to a child's development.

Conclusion

Language is a tool of communication picked up and used in context; it develops along shared conceptual frameworks, structured behaviours and social expectations. Both the context and the culture of the home environment provide the clues which facilitate the acquisition of comprehensible input and emergence of successful communication skills.

To expect minority language children with needs and special needs, assessed as they are in a second language and asked to perform in a culture and language which is not their own, to achieve as well as majority children is an unrealistic and unfair expectation. Minority language children are at a disadvantage in so far as parents and the learned professions do not acknowledge the importance of their home culture and first language. When they do, these children's performance should compare very well with the performance of majority language children.

Studies clearly indicate that to encourage the development of the first language prepares children for greater success in the first and second language, while to minimise that exposure is to invite difficulties in both the first and second language. However, there is more to language development than the rudiments of speech; there is a whole system of understanding, conceptualising and behaviour that needs to be considered. The home context and culture are vital to the emergence of comprehension and communication skills.

References

BANDURA, A. 1977, *Social Learning Theory*. Englewood Cliffs, NJ: Prentice-Hall.

BÉGIN, G. 1982, L'authenticité dans l'enseignement des langues. *Bulletin de l'association canadienne de linguistique appliquée* 4(1), 53–63.

BIALYSTOK, E. 1979, An analytical view of second language competence: A model and some evidence. *Modern Language Journal* 63.

BRYEN, D.N. 1982, *Inquiries into Child Language*. Boston: Allyn and Bacon.

BURT, M. and DULAY, H. 1981, Optimal language environments. In J.E. ALATIS, H.B. ALTMAN and P.M. ALATIS (eds) *The Second Language Classroom*. NewYork: Oxford University Press.

CARLETON, R.A., COLLEY, L.A. and MACKINNON, N.J. 1977, *Education, Change, and Society*. Toronto: Gage.

CARROLL, J.B. 1981, Conscious and automatic processes in language learning. *The Canadian Modern Language Review/La Revue canadienne des langues vivantes* 37, 462–74.

CUMMINS, J. 1978, Education implications of mother tongue maintenance in minority language groups. *The Canadian Modern Language Review* 34, 395–416.

— 1980, The construct of language proficiency in bilingual education. Paper presented at the Georgetown Round Table on Languages and Linguistics.

— 1981, *Bilingualism and Minority Language Children*. Toronto: OISE Press.

— 1984, *Bilingualism and Special Education: Issues in Assessment and Pedagogy*. Clevedon, England: Multilingual Matters 6.

CUMMINS, J. and SWAIN, M. 1986, *Bilingualism in Education*. London: Longman.

DUCHAN, J. and KATZ, J. 1983, Language and auditory processing: Top down plus bottom up. In N. LASKY and J. KATZ (eds) *Central Auditory Processing Disorders*. Baltimore: University Park Press.

DUNNETT, S.C. 1981, English language teaching from an intercultural perspective. In G. ALTHEN (ed.) *Learning Across Cultures*. Washington, DC: NAFSA.

DUQUETTE, G. 1985, Do cultural perceptions facilitate language acquisition? *The Canadian Modern Language Review* 41(2), 524–33.

ERIKSON, E. 1980, *Identity and the Life Cycle*. New York: Norton.

FISHMAN, J. 1968, *Readings in the Sociology of Language*. The Hague: Mouton.

FLORES, A.R. and RILEY, M.T. 1982, The why, what, and how of a bilingual approach for young children and el porque, el cual y el como de un enfoque bilingue para niños preescolares. Dallas: Department of Health and Human Services.

GARCIA, E. 1981, Bilingual development and the assessment of language impairment. Paper presented at the Council for Exceptional Children Conference on the Exceptional Child, New Orleans.

GEARING, F. 1984, Notes on Israel. Unpublished manuscript.

GEARING, F. and SANGREE, L. (eds) 1979, *Toward a Cultural Theory of Education and Schooling*. New York: Mouton.

GENESEE, F. 1987, *Learning Through Two Languages*. Rowley, MA: Newbury House.

GENISHI, C. and DYSON, A.H. 1984, *Language Assessment in the Early Years*. Norwood, NJ: Ablex.

HALL, E.T. 1966, *The Hidden Dimension*. New York: Doubleday.

— 1973, *The Silent Language*. New York: Anchor Books.

HALL, W.S. *et al.* 1981, *Situational Variables in the Use of Internal Stage Words*. Washington, DC: National Institute of Education.

HENSON, K.T. 1981, *Secondary Teaching Methods*. Toronto: D.C. Heath.
HYMES, D. 1974, *Foundations in Sociolinguistics: An Ethnographic Approach*. Philadelphia: University of Pennsylvania Press.
JUNG, C.G. 1973, *Memories, Dreams, Recollections* (revised edn). New York: Pantheon.
KAPLAN, R.B. 1966, Cultural patterns and intercultural education. *Language Learning* 16, 1–20.
KRASHEN, S.D. 1981, *Second Language Acquisition and Second Language Learning*. New York: Pergamon.
KRASHEN, S.D. and TERRELL, T.D. 1983, *The Natural Approach: Language Acquisition in the Classroom*. New York: Pergamon.
LAMBERT, W.E. and TUCKER, G.R. 1972, *Bilingual Education of Children: The St. Lambert Experiment*. Rowley, MA: Newbury House.
LAPKIN, S. and SWAIN, M. 1982, *Evaluating Bilingual Education: A Canadian Case Study*. Clevedon, England: Multilingual Matters 2.
LIDTZ, C.S. 1982, Psychological assessment of the preschool disadvantaged child. Paper presented at the Council for Exceptional Children, Houston.
LINTON, R. 1977, *Le fondement culturel de la personnalité*. Paris: Dunod.
LURIA, A.R. 1976, The directive function of speech in development and dissolution. In R. WARDHOUGH (ed.) *The Contexts of Language*. Rowley, MA: Newbury House.
MANOLSON, A. 1983, *It Takes Two to Talk*. Toronto: Hanen Early Language Resource Centre.
MASLOW, A.H. 1970, *Motivation and Personality* (2nd edn). New York: Harper & Row.
McLAUGHLIN, B. 1980, Theory and research in second language learning: An emerging paradigm. *Language Learning* 30, 331–49.
MEAD, M. 1963, Our educational emphases in primitive perspective. In G.D. SPINDLER (ed.) *Education and Culture*. New York: Holt, Rinehart & Winston.
MILLER, N. (ed.) 1984, *Bilingualism and Language Disability: Assessment and Remediation*. San Diego: College Hill Press.
MORAIN, G. 1983, Commitment to the teaching of foreign culture. *Modern Language Journal* 67(4), 403–12.
NEWPORT, E.L., GLEITMAN, L.R. and GLEITMAN, H. 1977, Mother, I'd rather do it myself: Some effects and non-effects of maternal speech style. In C. SNOW and C. FERGUSON (eds) *Talking to Children*. New York: Cambridge University Press.
OSTERRIETH, P. 1973, *Introduction à la psychologie de l'enfant*. Paris: Presses universitaires de France.
PAPALIA, A. 1983, *A Practical Guide for Developing Communicative Proficiency and Cultural Understanding in Secondary School Education Programs*. New York: New York State Association of Foreign Language Teachers.
PAULSTON, C.B. 1974, Linguistics and communicative competence. *TESOL Quarterly* 8(4), 347–62.
PIAGET, J. 1963, *La construction du réel chez l'enfant*. Paris: Neuchatel, Delachaux et Nestlé.
RIVERS, W.M. 1983, *Communicating Naturally in a Second Language*. New York: Cambridge University Press.
ROGERS, C.R. 1969, *Freedom to Learn*. Columbus, OH: C.E. Merrill.

— 1983, *Freedom to Learn for the 80s*. Columbus, OH: C.E. Merrill.

SAVILLE-TROIKE, M. 1982, *The Ethnography of Communication*. Oxford: Basil Blackwell & Mott.

SKUTNABB-KANGAS, T. and TOUKOMAA, P. 1976, Teaching migrant children's mother tongue and learning the language of the host country in the context of the socio-cultural situation of the migrant family. *University of Tampere Research Reports*, 19.

Standard College Dictionary, 1963, Toronto: Funk & Wagnallis Company.

STERN, H.H. 1975, What can we learn from the good language learner? *Canadian Modern Language Review* 31, 304–18.

— 1981, Communicative language teaching in learning: Toward a synthesis. In J.E. ALATIS, H.B. ALTMAN and P.M. ALATIS (eds) *The Second Language Classroom*. New York: Oxford University Press.

STEVICK, E. 1980, *A Way and Ways*. Rowley, MA: Newbury House.

TAYLOR, D.M., BASSILI, I. and ABOUD, F. 1973, Dimensions of ethnic identity: An example from Quebec. *Journal of Social Psychology* 89, 185–92.

TRUEBA, H. *et al.* (eds) 1981, *Culture and the Bilingual Classroom*. Rowley, MA: Newbury House.

VALDES, J.M. 1986, *Culture Bound*. Cambridge: Cambridge University Press.

VYGOTSKY, L.S. 1962, *Thought and Language*. Cambridge, MA: MIT Press.

WESSELLS, M. 1982, *Cognitive Psychology*. New York: Harper & Row.

WHORF, B. 1956, Science and linguistics. In J.B. CARROLL (ed.) *Language, Thought, and Vitality: Selected Writings of Benjamin Lee Whorf*. New York: Wiley.

WIDDOWSON, H.G. 1978, *Teaching Language as Communication*. Oxford: Oxford University Press.

WILKINS, D.A. 1976, *National Syllabuses*. Oxford: Oxford University Press.

9 Learning Needs of Minority Children: Contributions of Ethnography to Educational Research

HENRY T. TRUEBA

Ethnographic research, if conducted according to the criteria for a good ethnography established by G. and L. Spindler (1987a: 18–23), is indeed one of the most powerful instruments for understanding the role of culture in knowledge acquisition and the diverse needs of cultural minority students. Ethnography, in the Spindlers' tradition, is a rigorous scientific inquiry conducted systematically, comparatively, with full recognition of the social, economic and cultural contexts of behaviour, and in conjunction with other available data from other sources — ethnohistorical, quantitative, survey, and linguistic, but without extending the evidence beyond its inferential limits.

Ethnography focused on minority students has a unique potential in educational research. With the rapid demographic changes in the Western world, the importance of understanding the needs of minorities is becoming the most crucial issue of contemporary educational research. The fact is that the minorities are rapidly becoming the majority. Several American states have a school-age minority population of over 50% (California, Texas, New Mexico), and some of the largest cities have between 70 and 90% minority student populations — Detroit, Chicago, New York, Los Angeles, Baltimore, Dallas, Philadelphia and many others (US Bureau of the Census, 1984).

An additional reason for the selection of the ethnographic approach in the study of the educational needs of minority children is that not only are these needs poorly understood, but the tragic fact today is that in the USA there are 13 million children — most of them from ethnic and linguistic minority families — living in poverty (40% of all the poor are

children, the largest percentage since the 1950s, according to the advance
reports on population statistics of the US Dept of Commerce, Bureau of
the Census, 1987). There is a Southeast–Southwest belt which encompasses
the largest concentration of ethnic children living in poverty, with the
largest density of population, a population which is both the youngest in
age and the lowest in academic achievement. The mean age of White
Anglo-Saxon persons is 31 years of age, of Blacks is 24, and for Hispanics
is 21. There are 2.9 million White (non-Hispanic) people over 85 years
of age (and 36,000 over 100 years of age), and as many as 10% of the
poor are over 65 years of age. Indeed, the hope of the future seems to
be in the large minority populations who begin to constitute the core of
the labour force. By 1985, 82% of the labour force was already composed
of minority, immigrant and female populations; this reflects a rapid
change in the labour force traditionally constituted by non-Hispanic White
males.

The presence of about 35 million linguistic minority persons in the
USA is reported in the 1980 Census of Population (US Bureau of the
Census, 1984). Of them, 10.5 million are under the age of 17, and
19.5 million are not fluent in English. Almost half of this linguistic
minority population, that is, 15.5 million (45%), is Hispanic; French,
German and Italian language speakers follow, totalling 8.4 million (24.2%
of the linguistic minority population with approximately 8.5% each). The
Hispanic linguistic minority population is highly concentrated in the
Southwestern states of California (6.9 million), Arizona (727,000), New
Mexico (618,000), Colorado (475,000) and Texas (3.8 million), and in
New York (4.5 million). The relative concentration of linguistic minorities
in the Southwestern states is over 25%, and in California is estimated
near 30%. Young and undocumented workers, particularly Hispanic, will
continue to arrive by the thousands as poverty and political instability
threaten Mexico and Latin American countries.

The Hispanic population, according to the 1986 and 1987 Advance
Population Report (issued by US Department of Commerce, Bureau of
the Census, in August 1987) constitute a population of 18.8 million and
increased 30% between 1980 and March of 1987 (in contrast with the
non-Hispanic population that increased 6% in the same period). The
total population increase was of 4.3 million in that period of time. While
there is some improvement in the education of Hispanics, their school
attainment lags behind that of non-Hispanics. The same is true for their
economic condition: they have the largest families and the lowest income.
Between 1981 and 1986 there were 25% more Hispanic families living
below the poverty level. In 1986 approximately 1.1 million Hispanics

lived in families with incomes below the poverty level, and half of these families had single mothers as heads of households. In the same year, 62% of the Hispanic household members living below the poverty level never completed high school. Hispanic families — much younger than non-Hispanic ones — will continue to increase in size (US Department of Commerce, Bureau of the Census, 1987: 1–5).

The prospects for the future are bleak and invite reflection. Over 70% of all Hispanic students attend segregated schools (up 15% since 1983), and 63% of Blacks continue to attend segregated schools (down 13% from 1983). Only 2% of all Hispanics ever reach college, and only about 1% graduate from college or enter graduate school. Dropout rates for Blacks and Hispanics are the highest in the country, and range from 40 to 75% of entering high school students. Yet, the democratic fabric of American society and its long tradition of success is based on the reservoir of energy and commitment to achieve. Much of the success of minority and immigrant children is attributed to schooling. Waves of immigrants and refugees enter the USA joining other minorities in their quest for a better life. Their children's overall speedy adjustment, and ultimate success or failure in mainstreaming, seems to be determined by previous family experiences and by their ability to handle cultural conflict (G. Spindler, 1977; G. Spindler & L. Spindler, 1983, 1987a, 1987b; McDermott, 1987a; Trueba & Delgado-Gaitan, 1988; Trueba, 1983, 1987a, 1987b, 1989; DeVos, 1984).

One of the main concerns of educational ethnographers is the understanding of English literacy by speakers of other languages. Literacy in English plays a very important role in the immigrant, refugee and other minority children's ability to communicate and to demonstrate competence in learning. Schools are in a difficult position; they have been viewed as the social institution whose primary responsibility is to mainstream minorities. Yet, the rapid and unexpected increase in the flow of diverse minority populations can be overwhelming. This is precisely the case of La Playa, the school in which the study reported here was conducted. To complicate matters, often school administrators, teachers, psychologists and educational researchers pay little attention to cultural factors affecting learning (Trueba, 1987a; Goldman & Trueba, 1987).

Problems of achievement and emotional adjustment in schools are related to literacy in English. The classification (or misclassification) of minorities as 'learning disabled students' and their over-representation in school attrition rates are problems to literacy in English (Rueda, 1987).

Ethnographic studies of English literacy acquisition have shown that there is a significant relationship between cultural congruency and effective learning (Au & Jordan, 1981; Duran, 1983; Diaz, Moll & Mehan, 1986; Erickson, 1986; Tharp & Gallimore, in press). However, cultural incongruencies and language differences alone do not fully explain the academic failure of most minority students. There are additional social structural constraints, such as prejudice and poverty, which place serious obstacles to their achievement and upward mobility (Ogbu, 1974, 1978, 1981, 1982, 1987; Ogbu & Matute-Bianchi, 1986; Suarez-Orozco, 1987, 1989). Finally, there may also be serious and unresolved cultural conflicts and discontinuities in the transition from the home to the school culture (G. Spindler, 1974, 1982; G. Spindler & L. Spindler, 1983, 1987a, 1987b) that determine the low level of English literacy in minority children (Trueba, 1987a, 1987b, in press). (See Table 9.1.)

The importance placed on educational attainment by recent studies of the Rand Corporation would suggest that we must pay attention to the educational needs of linguistic minorities, especially in the process of literacy acquisition (McCarthy & Burciaga Valdez, 1985, 1986). While Rand researchers find progress and upper mobility within Hispanic groups, and specifically document improvement in education, higher levels of English proficiency and better jobs among second- and third-generation Hispanics (McCarthy & Burciaga Valdez, 1986: 60–5), they also warn us about the rapid increase in this population and the need to accelerate our efforts.

Although we do not have advance population reports for the state of California, in 1980 some 28.8%, or 6.3 million, of its total population of some 22 million people of five years of age and older were linguistic minorities, Hispanics accounting for 15% (1980 Census, US Bureau of the Census, 1984). Hispanics also formed (and most likely still do some years later) the largest 'minority' student population in California, also holding the highest high school dropout rate of any group (45% between the 10th and the 12th grades, and 40% before the 10th grade), and the largest representation among 'learning disabled' students (Rueda, 1987). In California there were fewer than 200,000 'Limited English Proficiency' (LEP) students in 1970, but LEP students increased to half a million by 1985.

Study of Four Children in La Playa

Several ethnographic research projects, essentially without any substantive funding, mostly in the form of doctoral dissertations and field

TABLE 9.1 *From cultural differences to learning handicaps*

	Initial encounters	*Transitional* *Attempts at mainstreaming*	*Stages* *Classification, redefinition & outcomes*
Society	Pre-arrival, relocation, traumas, separation and losses. 'Critical degradation incidents', ethnic identity crises, 'passing for' ethnic community and peer group responses	Immigrants' relationship with sponsors, public service officers, etc. Seeking employment, discrimination experiences as 'degradation incidents'.	Minority status and 'vicarious' experiences as a member of ethnic group. First experiences in mastering the social system in limited arenas, through home and peer group socialisation. Understanding public institutions: school, banks, hospitals, welfare office, etc.
School	Early informal assessment linguistic and cultural differences. 'Getting acquainted' period. Confusion and stress.	Formal testing and classification of children. Process of 'construction of consensus' among school personnel. Dilemmas placing 'disabled' children.	Difficulties entering the 'Zone of Proximal Development' due to lack of contextual information, time fragmentation and traumatic communicative exchanges. Cycle of poor performance, stress and distress leading to long-term decrease in cognitive and communicative skills
Home	Survival priorities, early readjustment to local environment. Differential perception of new culture and early redefinition of roles within family.	Economic, emotional and cultural crises. Increased cultural and linguistic distance from adults.	Increased alienation from home culture, language loss and peer influence. Selective acculturation, overall tension between home values and dominant society values. Lack of home support for academic tasks and achievement.
Self	High stress and anxiety. Confusion about self-identity, and early manifestation of anticipatory anxiety about culture shock and conflict.	Identity crisis and impact of 'degradation incidents' on personality structure. Coping with stress, fear and anxiety.	Depression, confusion and inability to cope with stress. Extended withdrawals, angry participation, or anxious attempts to engage, without significant rewards. *Overall inability to build a learning relationship with teachers and more informed peers.*

studies as part of requirements associated with courses in ethnographic research methods, have been conducted at the La Playa School in California since 1981.

Research team, setting and design

This study, which is part of a larger one, reports on the findings obtained from data gathered and analysed by request of the school. The larger study attempted answering questions that arose during several years of fieldwork activities regarding school personnel's perceptions about children's incompetence to deal with cognitive tasks. The study was conceived as a focused ethnographic study along the lines of previous work by Trueba and associates (see Trueba, 1983, 1987a, 1987b), the work by Mohatt & Erickson (1981), Au & Jordan (1981), Moll & Diaz (1987), and Trueba (1983, 1989). The team of researchers included two doctoral students and this author. We visited the school and community regularly, spending an average of 12 hours per week per person between September of 1984 and June of 1986, either making observations, conducting interviews, or collecting data through other methodologies. Data analysis and reporting is not yet finished. We are in the process of following up certain students to high school, or to schools elsewhere in central west California.

The larger study was intended to document the learning problems of 40 students classified as 'learning disabled' in the La Playa Elementary School (pseudonym). A second study concentrated on 12 minority children considered to be the most severe cases among the 'learning disabled' minority children. This study is focused on four children, a subsample of the latter study, for the purpose of examining in closer detail the profile and interactional strategies of teachers and children in the hope of understanding better the educational needs of linguistic minority students. The four children were: Richard, an 11-year-old Sudanese child who spoke fluent English (with a British accent, as well as Dinka and Aràbic), placed in a 5–6 grade combination class; two Laotian children, Douang, an 11-year-old girl, and Vilaph, a 12-year-old boy literate in French (though this fact was ignored by teachers), both placed in 5th grade; and Carlos, a 9-year-old Mexican boy repeating 3rd grade.

Thus, this chapter examines part of the corpus of data collected through systematic observations, interviews and tape recordings conducted over a two-year period. The research questions were at the beginning rather general and common-sensical:

(1) What is the nature of learning disabilities?
(2) What is the nature of classroom instruction and what are the patterns of student participation?
(3) What is the level of English literacy of the children?
(4) What types of instructional activities seem to maximise children's learning potential?

One of the underlying concerns was that perhaps stress and trauma levels prevented these students from participating meaningfully in the daily academic and social activities, and that their cognitive development may have been slowed down during the process of second language acquisition and the acquisition of English literacy. Furthermore, we were concerned, as the research progressed, that the social and psychological isolation of these children would hinder their overall long-term cultural adjustment.

Within walking distance from a major California university, the La Playa Elementary School forms part of a beach community composed largely of Indo-Chinese and Hispanic immigrants, transients, students and low income persons. Consequently it attracts non-mainstream children. In 1986 La Playa served 591 students, half of whom spoke as a first language one of the following 25 languages: Spanish (101), Hmong (77), Lao (31), Vietnamese (28), Chinese (12: 7 Chinese proper, 3 Mandarin, and 2 Cantonese), Portuguese (7), Japanese (6), Hebrew (6), Arabic (5), Korean (5), Danish (3), Hindi (3), Croatian (2), Hungarian (2), Indonesian (2), and eight other language groups each represented by a single student, Bengali, Dinka, French, Ilocano, Tagalog, Malaysian, Polish, and Punjabi. Our main concern was with the first four groups, not only because they were the most numerous, 237 out of the 298 Limited English Proficiency (LEP) students, i.e. 82% of the LEPs, but also because they presented the most acute adjustment and achievement problems.

Findings: Richard, Douang, Vilaph and Carlos

Obviously we found much of what we had expected to find regarding levels of participation and academic competence. But beyond the general findings, we gained a deeper understanding of why and how these children become more and more incompetent and isolated, and how these problems affect their transition from the home culture to that of the school.

The most general findings were that there was:

(1) Lack of meaningful participation in class activities, especially in contexts where activities were conducted by the entire group.

(2) Less scholarly productivity if compared with mainstream children or
    with minority children who had acquired fluency in English. This was
    reflected in academic activities at home and in school .
(3) Pervasive anxiety or fear, and confusion, particularly associated with
    public performances. The signs of emotional problems during inter-
    ethnic interaction had decreased for many other minority children,
    but remained very high for the four children under study.

In order to visualise our observations, I will give some examples.

Richard

Richard, the 11-year-old Black Sudanese who speaks perfect British
English, is the son of a doctoral student, middle-aged African, head of
a polygamous family, and high ranking member of the diplomatic service
in Sudan. Richard's mother, the first wife of the diplomat, was left in
Sudan, while his stepmother (a younger Black woman) was chosen by
her husband to come to America. Richard was referred to the psychologist
because he expressed anger in public, engaged in fist fights and refused
to participate in classroom activities. Otherwise, he seemed to be alert
and intellectually aggressive. One day the reading lesson covered American
rivers. It is Richard's turn. The teacher asks: 'Richard, where is the
Mississippi? Point to it on the map.' Richard remains silent, and just
before the teacher gives the floor to another student, Richard starts: 'It
is indeed the largest American river, but I know the Nile, and it is bigger
. . .' Then Richard surprises the whole class with a detailed description
of what the Nile is like, and how people depend on it for their subsistence.
The teacher presses on the matter of American rivers, and Richard
ignores him.

Another day, the teacher made a casual comment about American
politics, and Richard began to recite by heart the names of Presidents of
the USA and made comments on other politicians, such as Tip O'Neil
and Senator Kennedy. Yet, Richard's academic performance, his tests,
his homework, and his actual participation in the maths and reading
lessons continued to be marginal or absent. He would refuse to follow
instructions and do some operations when he was in disagreement with
the teacher: 'Is not that way [he'd say], you do it this way.' His aggressivity
and classroom attitude (perceived as arrogance by his peers) resulted in
further isolation and lower academic performance. His father, annoyed
by teacher reports and complaints, came over to school to confront the
teachers: 'If you cannot discipline, I will; if you don't want to hit him,
tell him and I will.'

Douang

Douang, the 11-year-old Laotian girl, was placed in 5th grade, in spite of the fact that she could hardly read at the 2nd grade level. Douang was deeply traumatised and would never speak in English, or even in Lao, in front of the teacher. She would whisper in Lao in her friend's ear once in a while. One day, the ESL teacher announced in the coffee lounge, as an important event, that Douang had pronounced a complete sentence, though not very clearly. 'Her expressive language is still very weak,' the teacher added. Nobody complained about Douang. Her 5th grade classroom teacher said, 'Her attitude and attentiveness are good.' She knew Douang was trying. Our observations of the entire class group during the reading lesson indicate that when instruction emphasised taxonomies, or word classes, Douang would get lost and lower her head as if she wanted to avoid eye contact or to disengage from an activity. 'Children,' the teacher would say, 'here is the list of words you need to read your lesson: fuss, snooze, separate, rock garden, marigold, and zinnia. What is snooze?' Douang would immediately become restless (moving her feet under the table) and attempt to remain inconspicuous. After a period of reading silently the first paragraph, the teacher would ask, 'Did you *all* finish?' The teacher read quickly through the passage and began to discuss vocabulary. The lesson goes on like that while Douang was continuously moving her feet and shaking all over. She seemed to be terrified of being asked another question. At the end of the painful exercise, she would return to her friend's side seeking some relief.

Douang wrote the following:

When I am 18 I plan to get an car I am going to ride to school I will learn more I think I would go to college or UC I will learn and if I learn college I will graduate. When I am 22 I will found a work to do or learn more english again or I will ask my brother to found me some work to do.

After several days of painful work Douang presented this composition:

At my house we have 13 people in the house and we have three bed room [bedroom] my brother my brothe [brother's] wife sleep in one bed room [bedroom] my brother have a lot of cloth and my bed room [bedroom] is environment [spacious] because we have 7 people in my bedroom and we have lot of cloth to and other bed room have 4 peope [people] sleep in my house is environment.

The compositions from Douang show determination to succeed, regardless of the serious problems she was facing in school.

Vilaph

Vilaph, the 12-year-old Laotian boy who had been at the school for two and a half years, was deeply troubled, but sociable. He has a hot temper and is constantly moving his feet, hands, and his eyes. His restlessness increases during forced performance in large groups, for example in the teaching of reading. His teacher knows that Vilaph refuses and kicks the bench in anger. 'He is very low in maths, even counting beans and trading for 10 sticks is hard for him,' says his teacher; 'he learns words by rote, but has no consonants or other phonic skills.' Vilaph's friends say that his older siblings yell at him all the time, and hit him often. The main teacher's monthly report read: 'Poor Vilaph, he didn't have a clue . . ., but he tried so hard with the less difficult materials I gave him; it was sad . . . Excellent artist and superior motor skills, but something is not attached right.' Here is an example of one of his compositions. He wrote this on Halloween:

> I Buy A pumpkin and I Drow [draw] my punkin [pumpkin] face is gross: — One boy came and trick or treat at my hous [house] and the punkin [pumpkin] (is took) [?] The boy ran and throw the candy and the punkin [pumpkin] laugh. — The boy cry and go homes and tell his mother. Boy come [The boy came] trick or treat, can you give some candy and the pumpking said no and I will give the boy candy to you. They boy wan . . . [?]

The ESL teacher wrote:

> He tries to read, but cannot understand. He is bored. Does not pay attention to directions any more, and he says, 'I want to be in Laos. No. I don't want to be anywhere.' Then he tells Carlos, (a child in the same class) 'fuck you,' and they get into an argument. Vilaph's face is red and the veins are clearly protruding. He cannot talk out of anger. Goes out of class and comes back shortly. He apologizes to Carlos, and says to the teacher, 'We're friends now.'

Carlos

Carlos was born in the Central west coast from a Mexican couple, and at the time of the study he was 11 years old, in 3rd grade. His father, a divorced and disabled ex-policeman, had a history of emotional problems, and was the only one living at home. Carlos' older brother, now living elsewhere, had been classified as 'communicatively handicapped', as was Carlos himself during pre-school. This classification was removed at the request of his father in the 2nd grade. He was placed in a bilingual 2nd grade classroom and did very well. Then he was transferred to all-English 3rd grade and both his attendance and his achievement went down. For several months he was missing 50% of the school days. A new teacher referral for special education classes came with the teacher statement: 'Cannot follow oral directions. Needs a great deal of help. Is easily distracted. He is depressed.' My observations showed that Carlos could not concentrate on a task for more than a few seconds. I collected his work for a month and discovered that he was doing exercises from the year before, and that his writing (in content, productivity and structure) was superior the year before. For example: he was repeating 3rd grade, and the year before had produced a composition about three pictures describing spacecraft on the surface of the earth. The first year he wrote:

> The earth was going to is explod the world. And they made a spceship. And they had all ready gone to the other planet. They land already. They planted flowers and trees. And the trees grow with fod and they build ahose [a house]. And they went back to see oh [?] the plant is but it was not thir [there] so they went back home and it was already night so they all went buck [back] to sleep. And it was moring [morning] now und [and] it was breakfast now. And they ate oranges and corn flakes and they drank orang [orange] juice and grape and mil. And they all played a game called steal the bake.

The composition a year later was turned back empty. He said he did not know what to write. I called him and asked him to see his work from the year before, and he looked surprised. There were serious family and personal problems which may explain Carlos' behaviour, but the overall productivity was clearly down. The interview with his father (which I found extremely difficult, because he pretended not to understand English first, and when I talked to him in Spanish pretended not to understand Spanish) revealed that the father would justify keeping Carlos at home 'just in case I need some water or something'. The man was physically able to walk two miles every day, and he seemed to intimidate the child with veiled threats. There were some suspicions of child abuse. But even in the previous year's composition there was some fragmentation and Carlos' composition was not as good as that of his peers.

Analysis of Findings

These examples show the problems faced by these children as they attempt to participate meaningfully, and the way that school personnel handle these children. Children's participation patterns can be reduced to these three types (see Trueba, 1983):

(1) Under-participation or minimum effective participation, primarily related to children's inability to make sense of either the content or the activity (text content, rules of interaction, and expected outcomes), manifested in extreme attempts to become inconspicuous. I have called this pattern *hypo-participation*.
(2) Over-participation or exaggerated attempts at imitating the moves of effective participants, without being able to achieve competence in the task. Often this pattern is manifested in superficial and unproductive replicas of reading or writing movements, without the child being able to actually read or write. I have called this pattern *hyper-participation*.
(3) Selective participation, often under protest, is manifested by students who have achieved a certain level of competence, but perceive the activity as difficult and unrewarding. Exercises in reading, writing, or in maths are viewed as too difficult, or boring, or risky. The risk of failing is high, and the loss of self-face is viewed as painful. I have called this pattern *hostile participation*.

The four students described classroom activities as too difficult, confusing and boring. Richard would sit, yawn and say quietly: 'I don't want to do it.' Carlos would just smile, look around, get up and, if the teacher was looking at him, pretend to write. If the teacher came closer to examine his work, he'd say, 'I don't know what to write.' Douang would remain quiet, but next morning she would come with several handwritten pages, copied from the dictionary under parental pressure.

During the research period children's performance deteriorated significantly in two ways: (1) The quantity and quality of written exercises diminished; the problems of fragmentation and meaning became more severe. (2) Actual attempts to participate in classroom activities become less frequent and assertive, perhaps as the fear of public embarrassment increased.

Douang, however, more recently showed courage to talk to the ESL teacher. She said: 'Mrs X [the maths teacher] never speaks to me. I have lots of time with nothing to do.' One day she came and said to the ESL teacher, 'I don't want to be nothing when I grow up . . . I loved my horses in Laos. We had a brown and a white one. Love my animals.' From that time to the end of the year, Douang just sat, copied simple sentences and turned in assignments with the same errors. And Vilaph was more emphatic stating, 'I don't want to be anywhere but in Laos'. Carlos has continued to miss school frequently, and still smiles, as if he could not find any other way of coping with the world around him.

Cognitive taxonomies and cultural knowledge

Children's many experiences, objects, and thoughts, with their corresponding taxonomies, as well as the organisation of these experiences, objects and taxonomies, appear to be far removed from those of teachers. In turn, teachers are culturally unfamiliar with the children's world at home and in their ethnic community. Communication between teachers and children is defective and superficial, even on activities which seem 'obvious' to the teachers, for example related to Christmas, Halloween or Thanksgiving or other celebrations. These celebrations evoke different symbols and meaning in different children.

There is clear quantitative evidence of limited productivity on the part of these four children if compared with their peers. Classroom tasks and homework assignments are either incomplete or never presented. Furthermore, the quality (both penmanship and structural organisation) of the compositions is clearly much lower. Their work tended to be typically fragmented, with syntactic problems (as shown in the above compositions), and the researchers had evidence that in many instances children could not grasp the central meaning, or even the intent as presented by the teacher. In some extreme cases, there was no attempt at participating; the student would just keep his/her head down for the entire period, or just sat quietly, daydreaming as if they had given up entirely any attempts to understand the world around them. There was one important exception, however: during small group sessions with the ESL and special education teachers, and only when children were given the opportunity and encouragement to select the content and the process of the activity. Vilaph, Carlos and to a lesser extent Douang and Richard, engaged willingly (although for a short time) in academic tasks and presented (albeit full of grammatical errors) wonderful descriptions of their fantasies or experiences relevant to their home countries.

Emotional turmoil

There is some evidence that these and other children observed were going through cycles of deep depression and mental isolation to a state of panic. This was shown in sudden changes from hyperactivity (hyper-participation) to decreasing efforts to participate or respond to questions (hypo-participation). Even children's willingness or ability to focus on simple directives seems lacking. At the same time, under certain unexpected stimuli (a loud command from the teacher or the voice of the principal, for example) we observed signs of fear in the form of physical restlessness, unfocused changing gaze, uncontrolled feet and hand movements, frequent need to go to the bathroom, and other expressions of emotional turmoil. This high stress increased during times of performance in front of large groups, and was at times associated with manifest serious embarrassment and attempts to hide on the part of the children, especially if they were reprimanded. Vilaph and Richard show their anger, and refuse to answer more questoins with 'I don't know', that discourages the teacher from asking again. Carlos and Douang lower their heads and show a forced smile.

Language and logic

With respect to the control of the English language, these children cannot distinguish semantic ranges in the use of words, identify incorrect syntactic forms (verb tenses, or word order), and cannot articulate orally accurate descriptions of events. Most importantly, they cannot comprehend, separate, or generate concepts that are taxonomically or contextually related. They have not had the opportunity to internalise domains and relationships of related concepts, of different classes of objects (types of flowers, foods, personnel, institutions, etc.) and activities associated with American holidays (Christmas and Halloween). The reason is that those domains and concepts are culturally defined and can only be learned in appropriate social and cultural contexts, not in the classroom. Their knowledge of the language and academic subjects remained as superficial and approximate as their understanding of cultural domains. In general, these children cannot communicate in English for academic purposes in ways that would demonstrate competences in establishing logical relationships (cause–effect versus simple association in time or space, for example) through specific language structures. Does it mean that these children cannot express those concepts or relationships in other languages? We know they are quite competent in other languages.

Their lower English skills stand in contrast to the fact that all four of them are fluent in other languges (Richard speaks Dinka, Arabic and perfect Oxford English; Vilaph and Douang know French, Lao and probably other local dialects; Carlos is fluent in Spanish).

The problems in adjustment and communication in English as a foreign language are also related to their social distance from mainstream America and lack of the cultural knowledge available to mainstream teachers and children. No wonder these children are ready to give up all efforts to catch up in school, and blame themselves for their failure, thus internalising their 'learning disabilities' as a personal attribute, rather than as a result of factors extrinsic to their mental abilities. Instruction in a language and through a culture which are not understandable becomes a source of cultural conflict, especially when high school instructional strategies are supported by a strong social value placed on 'success' and 'failure' as measured through tests.

To the documentation of resistance to literacy (Erickson, 1984, 1986, 1987), recent studies have added a discussion of the appropriate conditions to maximise the acquisition of English literacy by injecting into the instructional system linguistically and culturally congruent strategies that smooth the transition from the home to the school learning environments. For example, the work of K. Au & C. Jordan (1981), and R. Tharp & R. Gallimore (1988) in Hawaii and Southern California, fall in this category. Also the work of C. Delgado-Gaitan with Mexican families in Carpinteria, California (as well as her previous work: see, for example, Delgado-Gaitan, 1987), and the study conducted by Trueba, Jacobs & Kirton (1988) among the Hmong people of Santa Barbara, would fall in this category. Finally, the work by Julia Richards (1987) among the Mayan children of Guatemala, of Naney Hornberger (1988) among the Quechua children of Peru, of Jose Macias (1987) among the Papago, and Donna Deyhle (1987) among the Navaho should be included. All these studies are now in press, or recently published. What is significant about these studies is that they show the intimate relationship between language and culture in the process of cultural adjustment to the schools, as well as students' need to internalise school cultural values in order to achieve academically.

Mariko Fujita and Toshiyuki Sano (1988) have compared and contrasted American and Japanese day-care centres, using the Spindlers' reflective 'cross-cultural interviews'. They have elicited videotape analysed by Japanese and American teachers of each other's centres. This study has permitted us to reflect on the socialisation for 'independence' or for 'nurturing tolerance and co-operation' characterising American and Japanese teachers respectively. Following also the work of Spindler, S. Borish (1988) used Spindler's model of 'compression and decompression' cycles focusing on the socialisation of high school Kibbutz youngsters who endure intense adult-like working experiences 'in their winter of their discontent', while getting ready to enter the armed forces. The functions of schooling and the youngsters' relationships with their teachers as friends leave no room for 'dropouts'.

There are a number of additional theoretical developments in anthropologically inspired field-based studies dealing with effective interventions by social scientists in schools, or after school hours, with minority children. These interventions were guided theoretically by the work of Vygotsky (1962, 1978) and Neo-Vygotskians (Cole & D'Andrade, 1982; Cole & Scribner, 1974; Cole & Griffin, 1983; Diaz, Moll & Mehan, 1986; Moll, 1986; Wertsch, 1981, 1985; Boggs, 1985; Tharp & Gallimore, 1988). The interventions were implemented and analysed according to the models developed by M. Cole, J. Wertsch, P. Griffin, D. Newman, L. Moll, H. Mehan and others from the Laboratory of Comparative Human Cognition (LCHC), and those of the Kamehameha Early Education Program (KEEP).

We need to understand better the educational needs of linguistic minority children, and to build an adequate learning environment for them at home and in schools. These children need assistance and support during their difficult social and cultural transition. Instruction should be tailored to children's cultural knowledge and experiences, and it should be conducted within a flexible organisational structure in which teachers have a great deal more control of the instructional strategies and activities, the use of particular materials, and of the school instructional resources (tutors, translators, parental groups, audio-visual, computer and other technological packages, etc.)

Within a socially based theory of school achievement, academic failure and/or success are not a personal attribute of the student, but the direct result of structural and psychological contextual factors that permit a child to grow intellectually. Indeed, learning successfully occurs always if a child is given the opportunity to engage in socially meaningful interactions within the Zone of Proximal Development, that is in contextually meaningful activity settings, through 'assisted performance' (with the help of others — those in the same social unit). Vygotsky describes assisted performance as the crossroads between learning and cognitive development, whereby 'the child performs, through assistance and cooperation activity, at developmental levels quite beyond the individual level of achievement' (Tharp & Gallimore, 1988). Students' commitment to engage in learning occurs during the transition from assisted to independent performance, which can be anticipated by the teacher.

How can teachers obtain a more effective communication with minority children? How can they develop a close working relationship with them, and most importantly, how can teachers help children internalise the short-term and long-term academic goals and the cultural values in which these goals are anchored? These are the concerns that surface with a close ethnographic analysis of children's 'learning disabilities'. The disabilities are the school's. Children's seeming 'unpreparedness' for mainstream schooling is only a measure of the rigidity and ignorance of our school system which creates a handicap out of social and cultural differences.

According to Vygotsky, success in social interactional contexts has powerful implications for success in academic contexts, including the strictly cognitive. Even partial social successes can help children acquire personality integration and positive self-concept during the difficult transitional period from the home to the school culture.

McDermott offers an interesting insight that should make us reflect on the current status of social science research on the failure of minority students:

> Now I am trying to move beyond the problem of school failure that has grown into a small industry involving millions of people measuring, documenting, remediating, and explaining the habits, values, and skills of minority groups that contribute so heavily to their ranks of school failure. There is a preoccupation among us: Because we claim to offer good education to all and because many minority people seem to reject, we are plagued with the questions of 'What is with them anyway?' or 'What is their situation that school seems to go so badly?' Their situation! . . . The breakthrough comes when we realize that their situation is not theirs alone; it is ours as well. We help to make failure possible by our successes . . . Failure is a culturally necessary part of the American scene. We do not need to explain. We need to confront it . . . ; explaining it will only keep it at a distance, making us its slaves. (McDermott, 1987b: 361–3)

Within the culturally based theory of academic achievement, which recognises the intimate relationship between language, culture and cognition (Vygotsky, 1962, 1978; Wertsch, 1985; Scribner & Cole, 1981; Diaz, Moll & Mehan, 1986), a number of important issues are related to the present study:

(1) How is the relationship between language and cognition mediated by the culture, and what is the role of culture in the adjustment of minority children? What is a culturally congruent learning environment? How much is the child (and his/her family) to change, and how much is the school to change?

(2) If we are to take McDermott's remarks and confront the structural necessity of academic success and failure, can we retain some hope and plan intervention strategies? Of if we accept Ogbu's taxonomy of caste-like minorities, is there room for school reform to accommodate the special needs of culturally different children?

(3) What kind of organisation of instructional activities in school would minimise failure and maximise success in culturally different children?

In all the above issues we must face the significant role that language plays in instruction and in socialisation for academic success. Language and effective teacher–student communication are essential to foster cognitive growth in children. The literacy problems faced by LEP children are related to school personnel's inability to capitalise on children's different experiences, cultural knowledge, and values. Obviously, without knowing the children's language, the teacher cannot bridge the instructional gap and adapt instructional design for culturally different children.

Concluding Thoughts

The English-Only philosophy reflects the political clouds that have obscured the discussion of important pedagogical principles applicable to all children. The principles have been spelled out by Cummins (1986) who emphatically states that cognitive skills (the ability to structure knowledge and to approach learning tasks effectively) can be best acquired through the native language and then easily transferred to a second language. Use of native language is best because critical thinking skills and cognitive structuring are conditioned by linguistic and cultural knowledge and experiences that children usually obtain in the home and bring with them to school.

Some general recommendations are in order:

(1) Place students in learning environments in which there are opportunities to evaluate and analyse failure and embarrassing (degradation) incidents related to academic performance.

(2) Identify the learning skills and levels of students in specific subjects and domains, using their mother tongue, or the language in which they were instructed.
(3) Construct learning experiences which are meaningful to children and congruent with their cultural and linguistic knowledge, and in which they play an important role negotiating the content and level of instruction.
(4) Sensitise the school personnel to develop culturally based instructional models effective for minorities.

Unfortunately, schools with high concentrations of minority children are unprepared to meet the needs of minority students. This fact, however, understandable as it is, deprives many children of using their cultural knowledge and experience. Yet, this happens beyond children's control of social institutions in which they are socialised; it is not their fault.

References

AU, K. and JORDAN, C. 1981, Teaching reading to Hawaiian children: Finding a culturally appropriate solution. In H. TRUEBA, G. GUTHRIE and K. AU (eds) *Culture and the Bilingual Classroom: Studies in Classroom Ethnography* (pp. 139–52). Rowley, MA: Newbury House.

BOGGS, S.T. 1985, *Speaking, Relating, and Learning: A Study of Hawaiian Children at Home and at School*. Norwood, NJ: Ablex.

BORISH, S. 1988, The winter of their discontent: Cultural compressions and decompressions in the life cycle of the Kibbutz adolescent. In H. TRUEBA and C. DELGADO-GAITAN (eds) *School and Society: Teaching Content Through Culture* (pp. 181–99). New York: Praeger.

COLE, M. and D'ANDRADE, R. 1982, The influence of schooling on concept formation: Some preliminary conclusions. *The Quarterly Newsletter of the Laboratory of Comparative Human Cognition* 4(2), 19–26.

COLE, M. and GRIFFIN, P. 1983, A socio-historical approach to re-mediation. *The Quarterly Newsletter of the Laboratory of Comparative Human Cognition* 5(4), 69–74.

COLE, M. and SCRIBNER, S. 1974, *Culture and Thought: A Psychological Introduction*. New York: Basic Books.

CUMMINS, J. 1986, Empowering minority students: A framework for intervention. *Harvard Educational Review* 56(1), 18–35.

DELGADO-GAITAN, C. 1987, Traditions and transitions in the learning process of Mexican children: An ethnographic view. In G. and L. SPINDLER (eds) *Interpretive Ethnography of Education: At Home and Abroad* (pp. 333–59). Hillsdale, NJ: Lawrence Erlbaum.

DEVOS, G. 1984, Ethnic persistence and role degradation: An illustration from Japan. Paper presented at the American–Soviet Symposium on Contemporary Ethnic Processes in the USSR. New Orleans, Louisiana, April.

DEYHLE, D. 1987, Learning failure. Tests as gatekeepers and the culturally different child. In H. TRUEBA (ed.) *Success or Failure? Learning and the Language Minority Student* (pp. 85–108). New York: Newbury Publishers (Harper and Row).

DIAZ, S., MOLL, L. and MEHAN, H. 1986, Sociocultural resources in instruction: A context-specific approach. In *Beyond Language: Social and Cultural Factors in Schooling Language Minority Students* (pp. 187–230). Sacramento, CA: Bilingual Education Office, California State Department of Education.

DURAN, R. 1983, *Hispanics' Education and Background: Predictors of College Achievement*. New York: College Entrance Examination Board.

ERICKSON, F. 1984, School literacy, reasoning, and civility: An anthropologist's perspective. *Review of Educational Research* 54(4), 525–44.

— 1986, Qualitative methods in research on teaching. In M.C. WITTROCK (ed.) *Handbook of Research on Teaching* (pp. 119–58). New York: Macmillan.

— 1987, Transformation and school success: The politics and culture of educational achievement. *Anthropology and Education Quarterly*, 18(4), 335–56.

FUJITA, M. and TOSHIYUKI, S. 1988, Children in American and Japanese day-care centers: Ethnography and reflective cross-cultural interviewing. In H. TRUEBA and C. DELGADO-GAITAN (eds) *School and Society: Teaching Content Through Culture* (pp. 73–97). New York: Praeger.

GOLDMAN, S. and TRUEBA, H. (eds) 1987, *Becoming Literate in English as a Second Language: Advances in Research and Theory*. Norwood, NJ: Ablex.

HORNBERGER, N. 1988, Iman Chay?: Quechua children in Peru's schools. In H. TRUEBA and C. DELGADO-GAITAN (eds) *School and Society: Teaching Content Through Culture* (pp. 99–117). New York: Praeger.

MACIAS, J. 1987, The hidden curriculum of Papago teachers: American Indian strategies for mitigating cultural discontinuity in early schooling. In G. & L. SPINDLER (eds) *Interpretive Ethnography of Education: At Home and Abroad* (pp. 363–80). Hillsdale, NJ: Lawrence Erlbaum.

McCARTHY, K.F. and BURCIAGA VALDEZ, R. 1985, *Current and Future Effects of Mexican Immigration in California: Executive Summary*. The Rand Corporation Series, R–3365/1–CR. Santa Monica, CA: Rand Corporation.

— 1986, *Current and Future Effects of Mexican Immigration in California*. The Rand Corporation Series, R–3365–CR. Santa Monica, CA: Rand Corporation.

McDERMOTT, R. 1987a, Achieving school failure: An anthropological approach to illiteracy and social stratification. In G. SPINDLER (ed.) *Education and Cultural Process: Anthropological Approaches* (2nd edn) (pp. 173–209). Prospect Heights, IL: Waveland Press.

— 1987b, The explanation of minority school failure, again. *Anthropology and Education Quarterly* 18(4), 361–4.

MOHATT, G. and ERICKSON, F. 1981, Cultural differences in teaching styles in an Odawa school: A sociolinguistic approach. In H. TRUEBA, G. GUTHRIE and K. AU (eds) *Culture and the Bilingual Classroom: Studies in Classroom Ethnography* (pp. 105–19). Rowley, MA: Newbury House.

MOLL, L. 1986, Writing as communication: Creating strategic learning environments for students. *Theory to Practice* 26(2), 102–8.

MOLL, L. and DIAZ, E. 1987, Change as the goal of educational research. *Anthropology and Education Quarterly* 18(4), 300–11.

OGBU, J. 1974, *The Next Generation: An Ethnography of Education in an Urban Neighborhood*. New York: Academic Press.

— 1978, *Minority Education and Castes: The American System in Cross-cultural Perspective*. New York: Academic Press.

— 1981, Origins of human competence: A cultural–ecological perspective. *Child Development*, 52, 413–29.

— 1982, Cultural discontinuities and schooling. *Anthropology and Education Quarterly*, 13(4), 290–307.

— 1987, Variability in minority responses to schooling: Nonimmigrants vs. immigrants. In G. SPINDLER and L. SPINDLER (eds) *Interpretive Ethnography of Education: At Home and Abroad* (pp. 255–78). Hillsdale, NJ: Lawrence Erlbaum.

OGBU, J. and MATUTE-BIANCHI, M.E. 1986, Understanding sociocultural factors: Knowledge, identity and school adjustment. In *Beyond Language: Social and Cultural Factors in Schooling Language Minority Students* (pp. 73–142). Sacramento, CA: Bilingual Education Office, California State Department of Education.

RICHARDS, J.B. 1987, Learning Spanish and classroom dynamics: School failure in a Guatemalan Maya community. In H.T. TRUEBA (ed.) *Success or Failure? Learning and the Language Minority Student* (pp. 109–30). New York: Newbury Publishers (Harper and Row).

RUEDA, R. 1987, Social and communicative aspects of language proficiency in low-achieving language minority students. In H. TRUEBA (ed.) *Success or Failure? Linguistic Minority Children at Home and in School* (pp. 185–97). New York: Harper and Row.

SCRIBNER, S. and COLE, M. 1981, *The Psychology of Literacy*. Cambridge, MA: Harvard University Press.

SPINDLER, G. 1974, Schooling in Schoenhausen: A study of cultural transmission and instrumental adaptation in an urbanizing German village. In G. SPINDLER (ed.) *Education and Cultural Process: Toward an Anthropology of Education* (pp. 230–71). Prospect Heights, IL: Waveland Press.

— 1977, Change and continuity in American core cultural values: An anthropological perspective. In G.D. DERENZO (ed.) *We the People: American Character and Social Change* (pp. 20–40). Westport: Greenwood.

— 1982, *Doing the Ethnography of Schooling: Educational Anthropology in Action*. New York: Holt, Rinehart and Winston.

SPINDLER, G. and SPINDLER, L. 1983, Anthropologists' view of American culture. *Annual Review of Anthropology* 12, 49–78.

— 1987a, *Interpretive Ethnography of Education: At Home and Abroad*. Hillsdale, NJ: Lawrence Erlbaum.

— 1987b, Cultural dialogue and schooling in Schoenhausen and Roseville: A comparative analysis. *Anthropology and Education Quarterly* 18(1), 3–16.

SUAREZ-OROZCO, M. 1987, Towards a psychosocial understanding of Hispanic adaptation to American schooling. In H. TRUEBA (ed.) *Success or Failure? Linguistic Minority Children at Home and in School* (pp. 156–68). New York: Harper and Row.

— 1989, *Central American Refugees and US High Schools*. Stanford: Stanford University Press.

THARP, R. and GALLIMORE, R. 1988, *Teaching Mind and Society: Theory and Practice of Teaching, Literacy and Schooling*.

TRUEBA, H. 1983, Adjustment problems of Mexican American children: An anthropological study. *Learning Disabilities Quarterly* 6(4), 8–15.

— 1987a, *Success or Failure? Learning and the Language Minority Student*. New York: Newbury/Harper and Row.

— 1987b, Organizing classroom instruction in specific sociocultural contexts: Teaching Mexican youth to write in English. In S. GOLDMAN and H. TRUEBA (eds) *Becoming Literate in English as a Second Language: Advances in Research and Theory*. Norwood, NJ: Ablex.

— 1989, *Raising Silent Voices: Educating the Linguistic Minorities for the 21st Century*. New York: Harper and Row.

TRUEBA, H. and DELGADO-GAITAN, C. 1988, *School and Society: Learning Content Through Culture*. New York: Praeger.

TRUEBA, H., JACOBS, L. and KIRTON, E. 1988. *Hmong Children and their Families in La Playa: Cultural Conflict and Adjustment*. University of California, Santa Barbara.

US Bureau of the Census, 1984, *1980 US Census. Current Populations Report*. Washington, DC: US Government Printing Office.

US Department of Commerce, Bureau of the Census, 1987, *The Hispanic Population in the United States: March 1986 and 1987* (Advance Report). Washington, DC: US Government Printing Office.

VYGOTSKY, L.S. 1962, *Thought and Language*. Cambridge, MA: MIT Press.

— 1978, *Mind in Society: The Development of Higher Psychological Processes*, ed. M. COLE, V. JOHN-TEINER, S. SCRIBNER and E. SOUBERMAN. Cambridge, MA: Harvard University Press.

WERTSCH, J. 1981, *The Concept of Activity in Soviet Psychology*. New York: M.E. Sharpe.

— 1985, *Vygotsky and the Social Formation of the Mind*. Cambridge, MA: Harvard University Press.

Part III:
Language Learning and Instruction

10 Language Development and Academic Learning

JIM CUMMINS

The Policy Debate: Assumptions Underlying the 'Immersion' versus 'Bilingual Education' Issue

In recent years, what has variously been called 'immersion' or 'structured immersion' has been promoted by some policy makers as a viable alternative to transitional bilingual education for language minority students (see Baker & de Kanter, 1981). Immersion programmes in this context essentially consist of all-English programmes in which minority students are 'immersed' in English with some special steps (e.g. ESL instruction) taken to help them acquire English. Immersion programmes have been strenuously opposed by proponents of bilingual education who maintain that many so-called immersion programmes are little more than 'sink-or-swim' or 'submersion' (Cohen & Swain, 1976) programmes which, in reality, provide little assistance to minority students to acquire academic competence in the language of instruction.

These arguments about the relative merits of different programmes reflect very different theoretical assumptions about the relationship between second language development and academic achievement. By a 'theoretical assumption' I mean a set of hypotheses from which predictions can be made about programme outcomes in different contexts. Two opposing theoretical assumptions have dominated the US policy debate regarding the effectiveness of bilingual education in promoting minority students' academic achievement. These assumptions are essentially hypotheses regarding the causes of minority students' academic failure, and each is associated with a particular form of educational intervention designed to reverse this failure. In support of transitional bilingual education, where some initial instruction is given in students' first language (L1), it is argued that students cannot learn in a language they do not understand; thus, a home–school language switch will almost inevitably

161

result in academic retardation unless initial content is taught through L1 while students are acquiring English. In other words, minority students' academic difficulties are attributed to a 'linguistic mismatch' between home and school.

The opposing argument is that if minority students are deficient in English, then they need as much exposure to English as possible. Students' academic difficulties are attributed to insufficient exposure to English in the home and environment. Thus, bilingual programmes which reduce this exposure to English even further appear illogical and counterproductive in that they seem to imply that less exposure to English will lead to more English achievement. The following passage from a *New York Times* editorial (10 October 1981) is typical:

> The Department of Education is analyzing new evidence that expensive bilingual education programs don't work . . . Teaching non-English speaking children in their native language during much of their school day constructs a roadblock on their journey into English. A language is best learned through immersion in it, particularly by children . . . Neither society nor its children will be well served if bilingualism continues to be used to keep thousands of children from quickly learning the one language needed to succeed in America.

Viewed as theoretical principles from which predictions regarding programme outcomes can be derived, the 'linguistic mismatch' and 'insufficient exposure' hypotheses are each patently inadequate. The linguistic mismatch assumption would predict that a home–school language switch will result in academic difficulties. This prediction is refuted by a considerable amount of research data from Canada and other countries showing that, under certain conditions, children exposed to a home–school language switch experience no academic retardation. The Canadian data involve programmes that immerse English background students in French (L2) as a means of developing a high level of bilingual and biliteracy skills. Initial academic instruction is through French, and by the end of elementary school approximately 50% of instructional time is spent through each language. Currently about 250,000 Canadian students are in various forms of French immersion programmes, which have been evaluated as highly successful in developing French proficiency at no cost to English (L1) academic skills (Swain & Lapkin, 1982). Similarly, the success of a considerable number of minority students under home–school language switch conditions refutes the linguistic mismatch hypothesis. In short, the usual rationale for bilingual education cannot fully account for the research data and thus provides an inadequate basis for policy decisions with respect to language minority students.

However, the 'insufficient exposure' hypothesis fares no better. Virtually every bilingual programme that has ever been evaluated (including French immersion programmes) shows that students instructed through a minority language for all or part of the school day perform, over time, at least as well in the majority language (e.g. English in North America) as students instructed exclusively through the majority language. In other words, the research data show either no relationship or a negative relationship between amount of exposure to English instruction in a bilingual programme and minority students' academic achievement in English.

In summary, the policy debate on bilingual programmes in the United States has not been particularly well-informed with respect to the research data. There is, however, a considerable amount of research relevant to the policy issues, and four theoretical principles that can account for the patterns of research findings are considered below. Two of these principles focus on the nature and consequences of bilingualism and bilingual education while the other two concern aspects of language proficiency and pedagogy. To reiterate, these principles can be viewed as generalisations that emerge from the research and allow policy makers to predict what the effects of different kinds of programme interventions will be.

Principles of Language Development and Bilingual Academic Achievement

The additive bilingualism enrichment principle

In the past many students from minority backgrounds have experienced difficulties in school and have performed worse than monolingual children on verbal IQ tests and on measures of literacy development. These findings led researchers in the period between 1920 and 1960 to speculate that bilingualism caused language handicaps and cognitive confusion among children. Some research studies also reported that bilingual children suffered emotional conflicts more frequently than monolingual children. Thus, in the early part of this century bilingualism acquired a doubtful reputation among educators, and many schools redoubled their efforts to eradicate minority children's first language on the grounds that this language was the source of children's academic difficulties.

However, virtually all of the early research involved minority students who were in the process of replacing their L1 with the majority language, usually with strong encouragement from the school. Many minority students in North America were physically punished for speaking their L1 in school. Thus, these students usually failed to develop adequate literacy skills in this language and many also experienced academic and emotional difficulty in school. This, however, was not because of bilingualism but rather because of the treatment they received in schools which essentially amounted to an assault on their personal identities.

More recent studies suggest that, far from being a negative force in children's personal and academic development, bilingualism can positively affect both intellectual and linguistic progress. A large number of studies have reported that bilingual children exhibit a greater sensitivity to linguistic meanings and may be more flexible in their thinking than are monolingual children (Cummins, 1984). Most of these studies have investigated aspects of children's metalinguistic development; in other words, children's explicit knowledge about the structure and functions of language itself. A problem in interpreting these studies is that the notion of 'metalinguistic development' is not yet clearly defined in the literature. Bialystok & Ryan (1985) have recently attempted to clarify this notion in terms of two underlying dimensions: namely, children's analysed knowledge of language and their control over language. They predicted that bilingualism would enhance children's control over and ability to manipulate language but not their analysed knowledge of language. These predictions regarding the likely consequences of bilingualism for metalinguistic development have generally been borne out in a number of studies (Bialystok, 1984).

In general, it is not surprising that bilingual children should be more adept at certain aspects of linguistic processing. In gaining control over two language systems, the bilingual child has had to decipher much more language input than the monolingual child who has been exposed to only one language system. Thus, the bilingual child has had considerably more practice in analysing meanings than the monolingual child.

The evidence is not conclusive as to whether this linguistic advantage transfers to more general cognitive skills; McLaughlin's review of the literature, for example, concludes that:

It seems clear that the child who has mastered two languages has a linguistic advantage over the monolingual child. Bilingual children become aware that there are two ways of saying the same thing. But does this sensitivity to the lexical and formal aspects of language generalize to cognitive functioning? There is no conclusive answer to this question — mainly because it has proven so difficult to apply the necessary controls in research. (1984: 44)

Hakuta & Diaz (1985) and Diaz (1986) have recently reported evidence that bilingualism may positively affect general cognitive abilities in addition to metalinguistic skills. Rather than examining bilingual–monolingual differences, Hakuta and Diaz employed a longitudinal within-group design in which Hispanic primary school children's developing L2 (English) skills were related to cognitive abilities with the effect of L1 abilities controlled. The sample was relatively homogeneous with respect to both socio-economic status (SES) and educational experience (all were in bilingual programmes). L2 skills were found to be significantly related to cognitive and metalinguistic abilities. The positive relationship was particularly strong for Raven's Progressive Matrices (a non-verbal intelligence test); further analyses suggested that if bilingualism and intelligence are causally related, bilingualism is most likely the causal factor.

An important characteristic of the bilingual children in the more recent studies (conducted since the early 1960s) is that, for the most part, they were developing what has been termed an additive form of bilingualism (Lambert, 1975); in other words, they were adding a second language to their repertory of skills at no cost to the development of their first language. Consequently, these children were in the process of attaining a relatively high level of both fluency and literacy in their two languages. The children in these studies tended to come either from majority language groups whose first language was strongly reinforced in the society (e.g. English-speakers in French immersion programmes) or from minority groups where L1 was strongly reinforced in the school. Minority children who lack this educational support for literacy development in L1 frequently develop a subtractive form of bilingualism in which L1 skills are replaced by L2.

This pattern of findings suggests that the level of proficiency attained by bilingual students in their two languages may be an important influence on their academic and intellectual development (Cummins, 1984). Specifically, there may be a threshold level of proficiency in both languages which students must attain in order to avoid any negative academic consequences and a second, higher, threshold necessary to reap the linguistic and intellectual benefits of bilingualism and biliteracy.

Diaz (1986) has questioned the threshold hypothesis on the grounds that the effects of bilingualism on cognitive abilities in his data were stronger for children of relatively low L2 proficiency (non-balanced bilinguals). This suggests that the positive effects are related to the initial struggles and experiences of the beginning second-language learner. This interpretation does not appear to be incompatible with the threshold hypothesis since the major point of this hypothesis is that for positive effects to manifest themselves, children must be in the process of developing both their languages; any initial positive effects are likely to be counteracted by the negative consequences of subtractive bilingualism.

In summary, the conclusion that emerges from the research on the academic, linguistic and intellectual effects of bilingualism can be stated thus. The development of additive bilingual and biliteracy skills entails no negative consequences for children's academic, linguistic, or intellectual development. On the contrary, although not conclusive, the evidence points in the direction of subtle metalinguistic, academic and intellectual benefits for bilingual children.

The linguistic interdependence principle

The fact that there is little relationship between amount of instructional time through the majority language and academic achievement in that language strongly suggests that first and second language academic skills are interdependent, i.e. manifestations of a common underlying proficiency. The interdependence principle has been stated formally as follows (Cummins, 1981: 29): 'To the extent that instruction in Lx is effective in promoting proficiency in Lx, transfer of this proficiency to Ly will occur provided there is adequate exposure to Ly (either in schools or environment) and adequate motivation to learn Ly.'

In concrete terms, what this principle means is that in, for example, a Spanish–English bilingual programme, Spanish instruction that develops Spanish reading and writing skills (for either Spanish L1 or L2 speakers) is not just developing *Spanish* skills, it is also developing a deeper conceptual and linguistic proficiency that is strongly related to the development of literacy in the majority language (English). In other words, although the surface aspects (e.g. pronunciatioin, fluency, etc.) of different languages are clearly separate, there is an underlying cognitive/academic proficiency which is common across languages. This 'common underlying proficiency' makes possible the transfer of cognitive/academic or literacy-related skills across languages. Transfer is much more likely to occur from minority to majority language because of the greater exposure to literacy in the majority language outside school and the strong social pressure to learn it. The interdependence principle is depicted in Figure 10.1.

A considerable amount of evidence supporting the interdependence principle has been reviewed by Cummins (1983, 1984) and Cummins & Swain (1986). The results of virtually all evaluations of bilingual programmes for both majority and minority students are consistent with predictions derived from the interdependence principle (see Cummins, 1983). The interdependence principle is also capable of accounting for data on immigrant students' L2 acquisition (e.g. Cummins, 1981; Hoover, Matluck & Dominguez, 1982) as well as data from studies of bilingual language use in the home (e.g. Dolson, 1985). Correlational studies also consistently reveal a strong degree of cognitive/academic interdependence across languages.

Recent studies continue to support the interdependence principle. Kemp (1984), for example, reported that Hebrew (L1) cognitive/academic abilities accounted for 48% of the variance in English (L2) academic skills among 196 7th grade Israeli students. Treger & Wong (1984) reported significant positive relationship between L1 and English reading abilities (measured by cloze tests) among both Hispanic and Chinese-background elementary school students in Boston. In other words, students above grade level in their first language reading also tended to be above grade level for English reading.

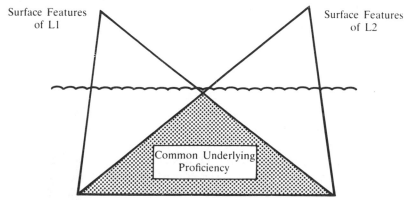

FIGURE 10.1 *The linguistic interdependence model*

Two longitudinal studies also provide strong support for the notion of linguistic interdependence. Ramirez (1985) followed 75 Hispanic elementary school students in Newark, New Jersey, enrolled in bilingual programmes for three years. It was found that Spanish and English academic language scores loaded on one single factor over the three years of data collection. Hakuta & Diaz (1985), with a similar sample of Hispanic students, found an increasing correlation between English and Spanish academic skills over time: between kindergarten and 3rd grade the correlation between English and Spanish went from 0 to 0.68. The low cross-lingual relationship at the kindergarten level is probably due to the varied length of residence of the students and their parents in the United States, which would result in varying levels of English proficiency at the start of school.

A recent study of five schools attempting to implement the Theoretical Framework developed by the California State Department of Education (1985) showed consistently higher correlations between English and Spanish reading skills (range $r = 0.60-0.74$) than between English reading and oral language skills (range $r = 0.36-0.59$) (California State Department of Education, 1985). In these analyses scores were broken down by months in the programme (1–12 months through 73–84). It was also found that the relation between L1 and L2 reading became stronger as English oral communicative skills grew stronger ($r = 0.71$, $N = 190$ for students in the highest category of English oral skills).

Finally, Cummins, Harley, Swain & Allen (1985) have reported highly significant correlations for written grammatical, discourse and sociolinguistic skills in Portuguese (L1) and English (L2) among Portuguese grade 7 students in Toronto. Cross-language correlations for oral skills were generally not significant. The same pattern of linguistic interdependence has also been reported in other recent studies (e.g. Goldman, 1985; Guerra, 1984; Katsaiti, 1983).

In conclusion, the research evidence shows consistent support for the principle of linguistic interdependence in studies investigating a variety of issues (e.g. bilingual education, memory functioning of bilinguals, age and second language learning, bilingual reading skills, etc.) and using different methodologies. The research has also been carried out in a wide variety of sociopolitical contexts. The consistency and strength of support indicated that highly reliable policy predictions can be made on the basis of this principle.

The conversational/academic language proficiency principle

A considerable amount of research from both Europe and North America suggests that minority students frequently develop fluent surface or conversation skills in the school language but their academic skills continue to lag behind grade norms (Cummins, 1984; Skutnabb-Kangas & Toukomaa, 1976). It is important for administrators to be aware of this research since failure to take account of the distinction between conversational and academic language skills can lead to prejudicial decisions regarding testing of minority students and exit from bilingual programmes into all-English programmes.

The research shows that very different time periods are required for minority students to achieve peer-appropriate levels in conversational as compared with academic second language proficiency. Specifically, conversational skills often approach native-like levels within about two years of exposure to English whereas the research suggests that for academic aspects of language proficiency, a period of five years or more may be required for minority students to achieve as well as native speakers (Cummins, 1981, 1984). This pattern can be attributed to the fact that native English speakers continue to make significant progress in English academic skills (e.g. reading and writing skills) year after year. They do not stand still waiting for the minority student to catch up. In conversational skills, on the other hand, after the first six years of life, changes tend to be more subtle. In addition, in face-to-face conversation the meaning is supported by a range of contextual cues (e.g. the concrete situation, gestures, intonation, facial expression, etc.) whereas this is seldom the case for academic uses of language (e.g. reading a text).

Cummins (1984) reported that psychologists often failed to take account of the difference between these two aspects of proficiency when they tested minority students. Because students often appeared to be fluent in English, psychologists tended to assume that they had overcome all problems in learning English and consequently that IQ tests administered in English were valid. The data clearly showed that this assumption was unfounded. Students were frequently labelled as 'learning disabled' or 'retarded' on the basis of tests administered within one or two years of the students' exposure to English in school. The data show that even students who had been instructed through English for three years in school were performing at the equivalent of 15 IQ points below the grade norm; this was a direct result of insufficient time to catch up with their native English-speaking peers.

The same logic applies to the exiting of minority students prematurely to all-English programmes. Educators frequently assume that students are ready to survive without support in an all-English classroom on the basis of the fact that they appear to be fluent in English. This surface fluency may mask significant gaps in the development of academic aspects of English with the result that the student performs considerably below grade level in the regular classroom.

In short, the research evidence suggests that although there are large individual differences between children in the rapidity with which they acquire different aspects of English proficiency, verbal psychological tests tend to underestimate minority students' academic potential until they have been learning the school language for at least five years. Another implication of these findings is that for students who have been learning the school language for less than this period, it becomes extremely problematic to attempt any diagnosis of categories such as 'learning disabilities'. However, a first step in addressing the complexities of non-discriminatory assessment and placement of minority students is to acknowledge that students' surface fluency in English cannot be taken as indicative of their overall proficiency in English.

The sufficient communicative interaction principle

Most second language theorists (e.g. Krashen, 1981; Long, 1983; Schachter, 1983; Wong Fillmore, 1983) currently endorse some form of the 'input' hypothesis which essentially states that acquisition of a second language depends not just on exposure to the language but on access to second language input which is modified in various ways to make it comprehensible. Underlying the principle of comprehensible input is the obvious fact that a central function of language use is meaningful communication; when this central function of language is ignored in classroom instruction, learning is likely to be by rote and supported only by extrinsic motivation. Wong Fillmore (1983) has clearly expressed this point:

> Wherever it is felt that points of language need to be imparted for their own sake, teachers are likely to make use of drills and exercises where these linguistic points are emphasized and repeated. And when this happens the language on which students have to base their learning is separated from its potential functions, namely those that allow language learners to make the appropriate connections between form and communicative functions. Without such connections language is simply not learnable. (1983: 170)

A limitation to the term 'comprehensible input' is that it focuses on only the receptive or 'input' aspects of interaction, whereas both receptive and expressive aspects appear to be important (Swain, 1986). Swain & Wong Fillmore (1984) have expressed the importance of meaningful interaction for second language learning by synthesising the views of leading researchers in the field in the form of an 'interactionist' theory whose major proposition is that 'interaction between learner and target language users is the major causal variable in second language acquisition' (p. 18). It is important to emphasise that meaningful interaction with text in the target language and production of text for real audiences is also included within this interactionist framework. Process writing techniques (Graves, 1983) provide an excellent means of promoting active use of written language and meaningful interaction with text among minority students.

The principle of sufficient communicative interaction also characterises first language acquisition. Young children rarely focus on *language* itself in the process of acquisition; instead, they focus on the meaning that is being communicated and they use language for a variety of functions, such as finding out about things, maintaining contact with others, and so on. In Gordon Wells' (1982) phrase, children are active 'negotiators of meaning' and they acquire language almost as a by-product of this meaningful interaction with adults.

One important link between the principle of sufficient communicative interaction and the common underlying proficiency principle is that knowledge (e.g. subject matter content, literacy skills, etc.) acquired through linguistic interaction in one language plays a major role in making input in the other language comprehensible (Cummins, 1984; Krashen, 1981). For example, an immigrant student who already has the concept of 'justice' in his or her first language will require considerably less input in the second language containing the term to acquire its meaning than will a student who does not already know the concept. In the same way the first language conceptual knowledge developed in bilingual programmes for minority students greatly facilitates the acquisition of L2 literacy and subject matter content.

Conclusion

This review of psychoeducational data regarding bilingual academic development shows that, contrary to the opinions of some researchers and educators, a theoretical basis for at least some policy decisions regarding minority students' education does exist. In other words, policy makers can predict with considerable reliability the probable effects of educational programmes for minority students implemented in very different sociopolitical contexts.

First, they can be confident that if the programme is effective in continuing to develop students' academic skills in both languages, no cognitive confusion or handicap will result; in fact, students may benefit in subtle ways from access to two linguistic systems.

Second, they can predict that, regardless of the programme, minority students are likely to take considerably longer to develop grade-appropriate levels of English academic or conceptual skills in comparison to how long it takes to acquire peer-appropriate levels of English conversational skills.

Third, they can be confident that spending instructional time through the minority language will not result in lower levels of academic performance in the majority language, provided of course that the instructional programme is effective in developing academic skills in the minority language. This is because at deeper levels of conceptual and academic functioning, there is considerable overlap or interdependence across languages. Conceptual knowledge developed in one language helps to make input in the other language comprehensible.

Finally, policy makers need to realise that conceptual and linguistic growth are dependent upon opportunities for meaningful interaction in both the target language and the L1. Exposure to the target language itself is insufficient to ensure either language acquisition or conceptual growth. Since minority students tend to experience particular problems with academic skills development in English, it is essential that literacy be taught in a meaningful interactive context. The learning problems of a considerable number of minority students are, at least in part, pedagogically induced through attempts to teach language skills in isolation from students' experience (e.g. through reliance on basal readers rather than literature, drills rather than dialogue, and ditto sheets rather than creative writing).

These psychoeducational principles open up significant possibilities for the planning of bilingual programmes by showing that, when programmes are well-implemented, students will not suffer academically either as a result of bilingualism *per se* or as a result of spending less instructional time through English. If academic development of minority students is the goal, then students must be encouraged to acquire a conceptual foundation in their L1 to facilitate the acquisition of English academic skills. Also, academic skills in both L1 and L2 should be promoted through providing opportunities for students to use written and oral language actively for meaningful communication.

For minority students experiencing academic difficulties or who are special education candidates, these principles of bilingual academic development become even more important. Too often these students are expected to acquire academic skills on the basis of a frugal diet of meaningless and impoverished language and are actively discouraged by educators from developing L1 academic skills. Administrators have a crucial leadership role to play in communicating to special educators and other professionals an understanding of the principles that explain language development and academic achievement among minority students.

References

BAKER, K.A. and DE KANTER, A.A. 1981, *Effectiveness of Bilingual Education: A Review of the Literature.* Washington, DC: Office of Planning and Budget, US Department of Education.

BIALYSTOK, E. 1984, Influences of bilingualism on metalinguistic development. Paper presented at the symposium 'Language awareness/reading development: Cause? Effect? Concomitance?' at the National Reading Conference Meeting, St Petersburg, Florida.

BIALYSTOK, E. and RYAN, E.B. 1985, Metacognitive framework for the development of first and second language skills. In D.L. FORREST-PRESSLEY, G.E. MACKINNON and T.G. WALLER (eds) *Meta-cognition, Cognition, and Human Performance.* New York: Academic Press.

California State Department of Education, 1985, *Case Studies in Bilingual Education: First Year Report.* Federal Grant #G008303723.

COHEN, A.D. and SWAIN, M. 1976, Bilingual education: The immersion model in the North American context. In J.E. ALATIS and K. TWADDELL (eds) *English as a Second Language in Bilingual Education.* Washington, DC: TESOL.

CUMMINS, J. 1981, Age on arrival and immigrant second language learning in Canada: A reassessment. *Applied Linguistics* 2, 132–49.

— 1983, *Heritage Language Education: A Literature Review.* Toronto: Ministry of Education, Ontario.

— 1984, *Bilingualism and Special Education: Issues in Assessment and Pedagogy.* Clevedon, England: Multilingual Matters (Co-published in the United States by College Hill Press, San Diego).

CUMMINS, J., HARLEY, B., SWAIN, M. and ALLEN, P. 1990, Social and individual factors in the development of bilingual proficiency. In B. HARLEY, P. ALLEN, J. CUMMINS and M. SWAIN (eds) *The Development of Second Language Proficiency.* Cambridge: Cambridge University Press.

CUMMINS, J. and SWAIN, M. 1986, *Bilingualism in Education: Aspects of Theory, Research and Practice.* London: Longman.

DIAZ, R.M. 1986, Bilingual cognitive development: Addressing three gaps in current research. *Child Development* 56, 1376–88.

DOLSON, D. 1985, The effects of Spanish home language use on the scholastic performance of Hispanic pupils. *Journal of Multilingual and Multicultural Development* 6, 135–56.

GOLDMAN, S.R. 1985, *Utilization of Knowledge Acquired Through the First Language in Comprehending a Second Language: Narrative Composition by Spanish-English speakers.* Report submitted to the US Department of Education.

GRAVES, D. 1983, *Writing: Children and Teachers at Work.* Exeter, NH: Heinemann.

GUERRA, V. 1984, Predictors of second language learners' error judgment in written English. Doctoral dissertation, University of Houston.

HAKUTA, K. and DIAZ, R.M. 1985, The relationship between degree of bilingualism and cognitive ability: A critical discussion and some new longitudinal data. In K.E. NELSON (ed.) *Children's Language,* vol. 5. Hillsdale, NJ: Erlbaum.

HOOVER, W., MATLUCK, B. and DOMINQUEZ, D. 1982, *Language and Literacy Learning in Bilingual Instruction: Cantonese Site Analytic Study.* Final report submitted to NIE.

KATSAITI, L.T. 1983, Interlingual transfer of a cognitive skill in bilinguals. MA thesis, Ontario Institute for Studies in Education.

KEMP, J. 1984, Native language knowledge as a predictor of success in learning a foreign language with special reference to a disadvantaged population. Thesis submitted for the MA Degree, Tel-Aviv University.

KRASHEN, S.D. 1981, Bilingual education and second language acquisition theory. In CALIFORNIA STATE DEPARTMENT OF EDUCATION (ed.) *Schooling and Language Minority Students: A Theoretical Framework.* Los Angeles: Evaluation, Dissemination and Assessment Center.

LAMBERT, W.E. 1975, Culture and language as factors in learning and education. In A. WOLFGANG (ed.) *Education of Immigrant Students.* Toronto: Ontario Institute for Studies in Educatin.

LONG, M.H. 1983, Native speaker/non-native speaker conversation in the second language classroom. In M.A. CLARKE and J. HANDSCOMBE (eds) *On TESOL '82: Pacific Perspectives on Language Learning and Teaching.* Washington, DC: TESOL.

MCLAUGHLIN, B. 1984, Early bilingualism: Methodological and theoretical issues. In M. PARADIS and Y. LEBRUN (eds) *Early Bilingualism and Child Development.* Lisse: Swets & Zeitlinger.

RAMIREZ, C.M. 1985, Bilingual education and language interdependence: Cummins and beyond. Doctoral dissertation, Yeshiva University.

SCHACHTER, J. 1983, Nutritional needs of language learners. In M.A. CLARKE and J. HANDSCOMBE (eds) *On TESOL '82: Pacific Perspectives on Language Learning and Teaching.* Washington, DC: TESOL.

SKUTNABB-KANGAS, T. and TOUKOMAA, P. 1976, *Teaching Migrant Children's Mother Tongue and Learning the Language of the Host Country in the Context of the Socio-cultural Situation of the Migrant Family.* Helsinki: The Finnish National Commission for UNESCO.

SWAIN, M. 1986, Communicative competence: Some roles of comprehensible input and comprehensible output in its development. In J. CUMMINS and

M. SWAIN, *Bilingualism in Education: Aspects of Theory, Research and Practice*. London: Longman.

SWAIN, M. and LAPKIN, S. 1982, *Evaluating Bilingual Education*. Clevedon, England: Multilingual Matters.

SWAIN, M. and WONG FILLMORE, L.W. 1984, Child second language development: Views for the field on theory and research. Paper presented at the 18th Annual TESOL Conference, Houston, Texas, March.

TREGER, B. and WONG, B.K. 1984, The relationship between native and second language reading comprehension and second language oral ability. In C. RIVERA (ed.) *Placement Procedures in Bilingual Education: Education and Policy Issues*. Clevedon, England: Multilingual Matters.

WELLS, G. 1982, Language, learning and the curriculum. In G. WELLS, *Language, Learning and Education*. Bristol: Centre for the Study of Language and Communication, University of Bristol.

WONG FILLMORE, L.W. 1983, The language learner as an individual: Implications of research on individual differences for the ESL teacher. In M.A. CLARKE and J. HANDSCOMBE (eds) *On TESOL '82: Pacific Perspectives on Language Learning and Teaching*. Washington, DC: TESOL.

11 Conceptual Framework to Design a Programme Intervention for Culturally and Linguistically Different Handicapped Students

LILLIAM M. MALAVÉ

Review of the Literature

The literature in both bilingual and special education demonstrates the emphasis placed on selected concerns related to the education of culturally and linguistically different students (CLDS). Among the special concerns reflected in the literature we can identify: the over- and under-representation of CLDS in special education programmes; the inappropriate assessment and placement processes of these students; the unique features of special programmes designed to meet their needs; and the socio-personal and academic characteristics of these students.

The literature establishes relationships among the above listed concerns, and frequently explains some of these concerns in terms of the influence that they have upon each other. For example, the disproportional referral and placement of CLDS in special education programmes (Rodriguez, Prieto & Rueda, 1984; Mercer, 1977; Cummins, 1984; Ysseldyke & Algozzine, 1981) has prompted efforts to study variables that influence the referral and placement process of these students. Variables cited to explain the over- and under-referral of CLD–LEP (Limited English Proficient) students to special education programmes include: acculturation level, inadequate assessment, language problems, poor school progress, academic-cognitive difficulties, and special learning problems. Collier (1988) documents a strong relationship between level of acculturation and degree of placement. She indicates that contrary to theoretical expectations, placed students, when compared with non-placed ones, appear to be highly acculturated. This notion is reinforced by the finding that referrals decrease when CLDS enrolment increases and bilingual programmes are available (Collier, 1988; Finn, 1982). The negative consequences of biased assessment have been explained in terms of inappropriate instruments (Baca & Bransford, 1981; Samuda, 1976; Bernal, 1979), and inadequate or non-existent programmes (Bernal & Reyna, 1975; Ramirez & Castaneda, 1974). Special alternative assessment instruments and procedures (De Avila & Pulos, 1978; Laosa, 1978; Mercer & Lewis, 1978, 1979; Bernal, 1984; Cummins, 1984; Guildford & Fruchter, 1973; Mercer & Lewis, 1979) as well as unique instructional programmes have been recommended by researchers in the fields of bilingual and special education (Cummins, 1984; Collier, 1988).

Unique language instructional programmes and approaches to teaching the CLD/special students are presently being discussed in the literature (Cummins, 1984; Bernal, 1984; Valencia, 1984) of both bilingual and special education. Programmes discussed focus on: developing higher order thinking processes; encouraging students to engage in independent activities; responding to performance with reduced second language references; and stressing creative tasks to allow performance and expression of ideas through the child's native culture, and L1 and L2 (Valencia, 1984; Cummins, 1991; Hartley, 1988). Mathematics and science are viewed as unique areas for educating LEP students (Valencia, 1985; Kaplan, 1982). The effective school literature also provides information regarding instructional practices for culturally and linguistically different students. Some unique features related to the education of LEP–CLD students cited in the literature are: the utilisation of L1 to mediate instruction, social contact with native-like L2 peers, teacher use of L1 to transmit cultural information, initial level of L2 of the student, and the quality of instructional variables (Malavé, 1988).

This chapter discusses a conceptual framework that proposes the enrichment of curriculum and instructional approaches based on the strengths of the individual LEP child, not on his/her deficits. It recommends the development of specially designed programming that can be adapted to subject matter instruction, such as science and mathematics, to meet the needs of CLDS who are LEP. The paradigm includes variables relevant to the education of LEP students which have been identified in the fields of bilingual and special education as well as the effective school research literature.

A Conceptual Framework for Content and Procedural Knowledge

The basic premise of the conceptualisation developed by Cawley & Miller (1986) establishes that there are differential effects of curriculum or knowledge structures, and instructional or task structures, on the student's performance. This premise denotes that children need to possess both prior content knowledge and task capability to meet the demands of the school; students who possess both attributes represent the population for whom the schools are designed. Cawley & Miller (1986) claim that the differences among the students in this first category do not require the schools to make substantial modifications. Three additional categories are described: children who possess task capabilities but lack the knowledge sufficient to meet the demands of the school; children with knowledge levels consistent with their non-handicapped peers but who manifest specific task limitations (for example, learning disabled); and children who show substantial discrepancies in both level of knowledge and task performance. The authors suggest the need to effect curricular modifications to meet the needs of students in the second category; they also suggest instructional modifications for the third category of students. Nevertheless, the authors recognise that empirical evidence implies that curricular modifications may be necessary for this group of students. The fourth category of students require both instructional and curricular adjustments.

Cawley & Miller's (1986) conceptualisation sets the stage for developing a paradigm to illustrate the attributes and needs of LEP students who are handicapped according to task or content targets; the proposed adaptation is couched in terms of variables relevant to the attributes and needs of handicapped students who are LEP. To ignore the unique characteristics of these students is to run the risk of making claims and judgements about these students with a set of inappropriate assumptions.

A Paradigm for LEP Handicapped Students

The basic premise of the proposed paradigm establishes that children need to possess prior content knowledge, task capability and appropriate cognitive-academic linguistic skills to meet the demands of the school. It also proposes that there are differential effects of curriculum, instructional and cognitive-academic linguistic skills on the student's performance.

Lack of content knowledge, task capability and linguistic skill constitute obstacles for learning. The paradigm considers both content and procedural knowledge to suggest specially designed programming for handicapped students who are limited English proficient. It also incorporates unique instructional features to reduce obstacles for learning related to the cognitive-academic linguistic limitations of the student. The unique variables considered are: language(s) of instruction, cultural sensitivity of the curriculum and materials, and socio-personal characteristics of the students. The model suggests that programmes which consider the unique bilingual features allow access to target variables independent of the influence of obstacles created by the child's limited English language proficiency and her/his lack of familiarity with the cultural meaning of the curriculum and materials. In addition, the use of these variables reduces the disparity between the instructional approach and the learning characteristics of the CLD–LEP student. The reduction of obstacle variables is the focus of the specially designed programme.

The proposed paradigm adapts Cawley & Miller's (1986) conceptual framework of content and procedural knowledge to suggest curriculum and instructional changes that reflect the characteristics and needs of the target population. It recommends the use of culturally relevant curriculum that contains a set of tasks and different content across the tasks to convert it so that only one or the other varies at any given time. The same content that emerges from culturally relevant curriculum and materials can be used in a language that the child understands across a number of different behaviours. Familiar content can be used to enhance the students' acquisition of procedural knowledge through the proficient language. One can take a set of tasks in which the learner is capable and construct items from different culturally relevant topics in a language which the child understands, to increase content knowledge. Furthermore, familiar content knowledge across tasks can enhance the acquisition of procedural knowledge. To effect instructional modifications the paradigm considers socio-personal and learning characteristics of the students. For example, the literature documents that CLD students respond effectively to instructional approaches that include teacher instructional initiation but permits student-to-student interaction, foster activities which promote social contact with native or near-native L2 peers and teachers, encourage the use of L2 in meaningful social settings, include activities at an appropriate L2 level, and encourage topic building (Garcia, 1983; Wong Fillmore, 1976, 1981; Tikunoff, 1981, 1985; Wong Fillmore et al., 1985). Figure 11.1 illustrates the proposed paradigm.

CONTENT KNOWLEDGE

	Has	*Does Not Have*
	I	II

— Has knowledge L1 C1 (not in L2)
— Has task in L1 C1 (not in L2)

— Needs:
A. Instruction in L1
B. L2 appropriate instruction (according to ability)
C. To develop L2 to integrate knowledge and task in L1 C1 to L2 and perform appropriately
D. L2 and L1 C1 culturally relevant material and instruction

— Has task in L1 C1 (not L2)
— Does not have knowledge L1 C2 (nor L2)

— Needs:
A. Instruction in L1
B. L2 appropriate instruction (according to ability)
C. Needs to develop L2 appropriately to integrate CK and T in L2
D. L2 and L1 C1 culturally relevant curricula
E. Curriculum that focuses on task in L1 C1 to develop content

Examples of Obstacles:
Lack of L1 and L2 appropriate instruction

Lack of L1 C1 relevant curriculum and materials
Incongruent instructional approaches

Examples of Obstacles:
Lack of L2 and CK in L1 C1 or L2 C2
Lack of L2 appropriate instruction
Lack of L1 C1 relevant curriculum and materials
Incongruent instructional approaches

TASK PERFORMANCE HAS

FIGURE 11.1 *A conceptual framework to design a programme intervention for culturally and linguistically different handicapped students*

	III	IV
TASK PERFORMANCE DOES NOT HAVE	— Has content knowledge in L1 C1 (not L2)	— Does not have CK in L1 C1 or L2 C2
		— Does not have T in L1 C1 or L2 C2
	— Does not have task in L1 C1 or L2	— Does not have L2 in L1 C1 or L2 C2
	— Needs: A, B, C, D, in I, II and	— Needs: A, B, C, D, in I, II and
	E. to develop instruction that focuses on content to develop task	F. to develop CK and T in dominant language

Examples of Obstacles:
Lack of L2 and L2 appropriate
  instruction
Lack of L1 C1 relevant
  curriculum and materials
Lack of T in L1 C1 or L2
Lack of congruent instructional
  approach

Examples of Obstacles:
Lack of L2
Lack of CK in L1 C1 or L2 C2
Lack of C1 relevant
  curriculum and materials
Lack of T in L1 C1 or L2 C2
Lack of congruent instructional
  approach
Lack of L2 appropriate level
  instruction

FIGURE 11.1 *Continued*

As illustrated in Figure 11.1, this model incorporates instruction in the student native (L1) or dominant language (L1 or L2). It assumes that language dominance is determined by the student's ability to demonstrate cognitive-academic linguistic proficiency. (A student who demonstrates a higher level of cognitive-academic linguistic proficiency in L1 than in L2 is considered L1 dominant, and vice versa.) Additional elements include the use of L1 as a carrier of cultural information, and the incorporation of culturally relevant curriculum and materials to mediate instruction. It proposes that the use of L1 and culturally relevant curriculum and materials can reduce obstacle variables. L1 and culturally relevant curricula facilitate understanding and meaningful interpretations. Instruction can then be targeted to further the acquisition of content knowledge, and/or task accomplishment without the interference of obstacle variables resulting from the LEP status. It is expected that the isolation of linguistic obstacles promotes the integration of L2 development with the acquisition of content knowledge and task performance. The student's level of L2 proficiency becomes a determinant of the language complexity reflected in the academic activities. All L2 activities, including those designed to promote L2 proficiency, must guarantee that the student has adequate L2 skills to comprehend the content and understand the procedures even though they may contain new language, content and/or procedural knowledge. The paradigm is based on the notion that an enrichment programme is designed to take into consideration the linguistic strengths of the student and not his/her deficits.

The first quadrant of Figure 11.1 illustrates the attributes of a student who has acquired content knowledge and masters the task required but lacks the necessary cognitive-academic English (L2) language proficiency. A student who falls in this quadrant is often referred to special education because of poor academic performance, discipline problems, inadequate assessment, language problems, or non-existence of alternative programmes. However, it is possible that this student is encountering learning obstacles related to his/her language limitations (LEP status). The literature fully documents the under- and over-referral and representation of LEP students in special education classes as a result of language and culturally related issues. The obstacle variables identified in Quadrant I include: incongruent instructional approaches, lack of L2 proficiency, need for L1 C1 relevant curriculum and materials, and inappropriate L2 level related instruction. Substantial curricular and instructional modifications are required to enhance the instructional process and make learning a meaningful experience for the students in this quadrant. Modifications require the incorporation of significant language and culturally related instructional mediators, and the adoption of culturally relevant curriculum and materials.

Quadrant I suggests curricular and instructional changes that reflect the needs of a student who has acquired sufficient content knowledge and can master the task in his/her first language but lacks proficiency in the second language to demonstrate successful performance. Contrary to the assumptions included in the model designed for English proficient students (Cawley & Miller, 1986), the proposed paradigm recognises that instruction for Quadrant I LEP students requires substantial instructional and curricular modifications. Schools do not promote acceptable curriculum and instructional practices to meet the needs of these LEP students. The academic tasks and content knowledge necessary to perform successfully reflect dependence on prior knowledge and task capability at a cognitive-academic language level which LEP students do not possess. Grade level expectations reflect an academic-linguistic proficiency which is generally determined by the years of English language schooling.

An LEP student in Quadrant I will probably not perform successfully in a traditional classroom. However, this student's performance can be enhanced when instructed with culturally relevant curriculum and materials and through a language that he/she understands. A teacher who uses L1 during instruction and makes use of C1-related content and materials enhances the students' opportunity to identify with the teacher and the instructional process. This identification reduces discontinuities between the school and the CLD student who is LEP. The use of L1 lessens the possible status difference between the home and school languages, resulting in an increased motivation towards learning. Another example of the importance of language as an instructional mediator is the use of L1 or L2 appropriate levels of instruction to reduce the amount of extraneous vocabulary encountered when learning in a non-cognitive-academic proficient language. Instruction in L1 and appropriate L2 instructional level promote meaningful interpretations and decrease misunderstanding resulting from the inability to distinguish subtle variations in the language. The removal of an unfamiliar language as an acquisition requirement facilitates learning the content and mastering the tasks. The use of L1 for instructional purposes also provides an avenue to transmit culturally relevant information; such information and materials allow students to work with concepts in which they have had first-hand experience. Substantial amounts of native (L1) language have also been associated with positive learning behaviours for LEP students.

In addition, it is necessary to provide a learning–teaching environment congruent with his/her socio-personal and learning characteristics. An appropriate learning–teaching environment for these students must consider their unique socio-personal characteristics. The literature documents that students who come from non-English cultural and linguistic backgrounds respond positively to instruction that permits student interaction even though it may be teacher-initiated; encourages social contact with native or near-native L2 peers and teachers; stimulates the use of L2 in meaningful settings; encourages topic building; and implements activities at appropriate L1 and L2 levels. It is also suggested that specially designed programme activities for Quadrant I students should focus on developing higher thinking skills; encourage students to engage in creative activities; stress creative tasks to allow performance and expression of ideas through the child's dominant or preferred language and native culture; and emphasise comprehension, problem solving and socio-personal understanding.

Students in Quadrant II possess task capability in their native language but do not have the knowledge sufficient to meet the academic demands of the school in either L1 or L2. For example, a child may be able to read well, but lacks prior knowledge in both L1 and L2 to understand the present content. This student can also be one who could understand the procedural knowledge presented through L1 C1 relevant material but lacks familiarity with the L2 culturally related information necessary to perform well using L2. Students in Quadrant II have procedural knowledge in L1 C1 but not necessarily in L2 C2; do not have content knowledge in L1 C1, nor in L2 C2; need appropriate L2 level of instruction; can benefit from instruction through L1; can benefit from L2 and L1 C1 culturally relevant curriculum and materials; need instruction that focuses on task in L1 C1 to acquire content; and need to develop L2 appropriately to integrate content knowledge and task in L2. The obstacles identified include: lack of L2 proficiency, insufficient content knowledge in both L1 C1 and L2, need for L2 appropriate level of instruction, absence of L1 C1 relevant curriculum and materials, and need for congruent instructional approaches. These students require both curriculum and instructional modifications that address their unique language, cultural and socio-personal needs; and curricular modifications which focus on curricula that consider the level of prior knowledge which the child brings to the classroom.

Students in Quadrant III demonstrate in their dominant language a knowledge level consistent with their non-handicapped peers; however, they do not reveal the same level of task capability that their peers manifest. These students appear to possess average to near average ability but their level of task capability can be indicative of a learning disability (Cawley, 1988). The instructional modifications offered for Quadrant I students are consistent with Cawley and Miller's conceptualisation. There is a need for instructional modifications to foster task acquisition. The curriculum level appears to be appropriate but the instructional approaches need to vary to reduce procedural obstacles. In addition, the authors suggest the need for curricular modifications to address contradictory empirical evidence. Similarly, the model formulated to meet the needs of CLD–LEP handicapped students proposes both curricular and instructional modifications. These modifications correspond to the model's definition of this quadrant's target students: children who are limited English proficient (LEP) and do not reveal the same level of task capability in L1 C1 that their peers manifest, even though they demonstrate a similar knowledge level in L1 C1. The proposed paradigm suggests instructional and curricular modifications in the areas of language of instruction, L2 level of instruction, cultural relevance of the curriculum, integration of L2 with knowledge and task required, and instruction to focus on content knowledge and to foster task performance. Obstacle variables identified are: lack of L2, need for appropriate L2 level of instruction, insufficient L1 C1 relevant curricula, absence of congruent instructional approaches, and inability to perform the task successfully.

The students in the fourth quadrant differ in that they manifest low levels of both content knowledge and task performance: these students require both instructional and curricular modifications. The curriculum needs to be modified to consider the level of prior knowledge the child brings to the school, and the instructional approaches need to reduce the interference resulting from procedural obstacles. Furthermore, in order to address the needs of CLD–LEP handicapped students specially designed programming must provide instruction in the dominant language of the child, facilitate appropriate L2 level of instruction, include L2 and L1 C1 culturally relevant curricula, and foster the development of L2 to integrate knowledge and task in L1 C1 to L2. The variable obstacles identified include: need for L2 proficiency; need for prior content knowledge; insufficient L1 C1 relevant curricula; lack of task capability; and absence of congruent instructional approaches.

The proposed model establishes that in all the four quadrants handicapped CLD, who are LEP, benefit from instructional and curricular modifications to incorporate the unique instructional features. The modifications require these curricular and instructional changes in order to: provide instruction in L1; include L1 C1 culturally relevant material; provide appropriate L2 level of instruction; and consider target students' socio-personal characteristics. Among the socio-personal characteristics that seem to influence the teaching–learning process of CLD students and which are cited frequently in the literature we find: social contact with near or native-like L2 peers and teachers; initial level of L2 of the student; student-to-student interaction in teacher-initiated instruction; student participation in topic building activities; meaningful use of L2 in social settings; and participation in appropriate L2 level instructional activities.

To summarise, the paradigm for CLD–LEP handicapped students establishes that curricular and instructional modifications are necessary to meet the students' deficiencies in content knowledge and/or task capability and language proficiency. Quadrant I emphasises the unique bilingual curricular and instructional modifications, because the students in this quadrant do not demonstrate any content or task deficiency when they perform in their native language. Therefore, the recommendations are limited to modifications that reflect the unique bilingual instructional features. While greater emphasis is given to this notion during the discussion of the implications of Quadrant I, this premise needs to be incorporated throughout the complete paradigm. The additional three quadrants reflect the need for curricular and instructional modifications to address both content and task deficiencies and the unique needs of the target population.

Quadrant II illustrates the need for curricular and instructional modifications to address the students' unique bilingual needs and attributes, but in addition, it also shows the modifications necessitated by their inability to manifest prior content knowledge in either language (L1 or L2). Quadrant III also considers the unique bilingual needs and attributes of the students but suggests modifications for students who need to improve their task performance. The last quadrant stresses the need to design programmes considering the students' inability to demonstrate required prior content and task knowledge, and their limited cognitive-academic English language skills. The instructional programme suggested for these students requires instructional and curricular modifications to address their task, content and cognitive-academic linguistic deficiencies.

Conclusions

The proposed paradigm provides a framework to address the unique needs of culturally and linguistically different handicapped students who are limited English proficient. It establishes the differential effects of content knowledge and task structures on the students' performance. It suggests curricular changes when content deficiencies are identified, and instructional modifications when insufficient task capability is demonstrated. It implies that, by definition, handicapped students who are linguistically different or LEP and culturally diverse necessitate the development of specially designed programming to address their unique needs and attributes. The proposed paradigm for CLD–LEP handicapped students incorporates features to reduce the effect of selected obstacle variables. This framework illustrates the need for instructional modifications to consider the linguistic and socio-personal characteristics of these students, and curricular adjustments to address the need to provide culturally relevant curricula and instruction in the dominant or native

(L1) language of the student. It also suggests the need to effect both instructional and curricular changes to develop curricula and provide instruction which takes into consideration the second language (L2) ability of the student. This framework implies that the implementation of a specially designed programme, which considers the influence that the identified obstacle variables have on the teaching–learning process, increases opportunities for students to participate and succeed in meaningful academic activities. It establishes that successful instructional programmes for LEP–CLD handicapped students focus on the following: higher order thinking skills; performance on responses with reduced non-dominant language interference; creative tasks that allow the expression of ideas through the native culture and language; student-to-student interaction and meaningful social contact; comprehensible L2 level of instruction; and social contact with native or near native-like speakers of L2.

References

BACA, L. and BRANSFORD, J. 1981, Meeting the needs of bilingual handicapped children. *Momentum* 26–51. Boulder, CO: The University of Colorado.

BERNAL, E.M., JR 1979, The education of culturally different gifted students. Paper presented for the National Society for the Study of Education, Chicago.

— 1984, Gifted migrant students: An empirical system for their identification and selection. In A.A. VALENCIA (ed.) *Viable Strategies for Advancing the Education of Gifted/Talented Migrants*. Fresno, CA: California State University.

BERNAL, E.M. and REYNA, J. 1975, Analysis and identification of giftedness in Mexican American children: A pilot study. In B.O. BOSTON (ed.) *A Resource Manual of Information in Educating the Gifted and Talented* (pp. 53–60). Reston, VA: The Council for Exceptional Children.

CAWLEY, J.F. 1988, *Practical Mathematics, Appraisal of the Learning Disabled*. Rockwell, MD: Aspen Publishers.

CAWLEY, J.F. and MILLER, J.H. 1986, Appraisal therapy in mathematics. *The Educational Therapist* 7, 2–5.

COLLIER, C. 1988, Comparisons of acculturation and education characteristics of referred and non-referred culturally and linguistically different children. In L. MALAVÉ (ed.) *NABE '87: Theory, Research, and Applications: Selected Papers*. Falls River, MA: National Dissemination Center.

CUMMINS, J. 1984, *Bilingualism and Special Education: Issues in Assessment and Pedagogy*. San Diego: College Hill Press.

DE AVILA, E.A. and PULOS, S.M. 1978, Developmental assessment by pictorially presented Piagetian material: The cartoon conversion scales (CCS). In G.I. LUBIN, M.K. POULSON, J.F. MAGARY and M. SOTO-MACALISTER (eds) *Piagetian Theory and its Implications for Helping Professions*. Los Angeles: University of Southern California Press.

FINN, J.D. 1982, Patterns in special education placement as revealed by the OCR surveys. In K.A. HELLER, W.H. HOLTZMAN and S. MESSICK (eds) *Placing Children in Special Education: A Strategy for Equity*. Washington, DC: National Academy Press.

GARCIA, E. 1983, Instructional discourse in a kindergarten classroom. In L. MALAVÉ (ed.) *NABE '87: Theory, Research and Application: Selected Papers*. Falls River, MA: National Dissemination Center.

GUILDFORD, J.P. and FRUCHTER, B. 1973, *Fundamental Statistics in Psychology and Education* (5th edn). New York: McGraw-Hill.

HARTLEY, E.A. 1988, How can we meet all their needs? Incorporating education for the gifted and talented in the multicultural classroom. In L. MALAVÉ (ed.) *NABE '87: Theory, Research, and Application: Selected Papers*. Falls River, MA: National Dissemination Center.

KAPLAN, S.N. 1982, Curriculum development for the culturally different gifted/talented. In *Curriculum for the Gifted*. The National State Leadership Institute for the Gifted and Talented. Ventura, CA: Office of Ventura County Superintendent of Schools.

LAOSA, L. 1978, Maternal teaching strategies in Chicano families of varied educational and socioeconomic levels. *Child Development* 49, 1129–35.

MALAVÉ, L. (ed.) 1988, *NABE '87: Theory, Research, and Application*. Falls River, MA: National Dissemination Center.

MERCER, J.R. 1977, Identifying the gifted Chicano child. In J. MARTINE (ed.) *Chicano Psychology* (pp. 329–52). New York: Academic Press.

MERCER, J.R. and LEWIS, J.F. 1978, Using the system of multicultural pluralistic assessment (SOMPA) to identify the gifted minority child. In A.V. BALDWIN. G.H. GEAR and L.J. LUCITO (eds) *Educational Planning for the Gifted: Overcoming Cultural, Geographic, and Socioeconomic Barriers*. Reston, VA: The Council for Exceptional Children.

— 1979, *System of Multicultural Pluralistic Assessment: Conceptual and Technical Manual*. Riverside, CA: Institute for Pluralistic Assessment and Training.

RAMIREZ, M. and CASTANEDA, A. 1974, *Cultural Democracy, Bicognitive Development and Education*. New York: Academic Press.

RODRIGUEZ, R.F., PRIETO, A.G. and RUEDA, R.S. 1984, Issues in bilingual/multicultural special education. *Journal of the National Association for Bilingual Education* 8(3), 55–65.

SAMUDA, R.J. 1976, Problems and issues in assessment of minority group children. In R.L. JONES (ed.) *Mainstreaming and the Minority Child*. Reston, VA: The Council for Exceptional Children.

TIKUNOFF, W.J. 1981, *Second Quarter Report for Significant Bilingual Instructional Features Study*. San Francisco: Far West Laboratory for Educational Research and Development.

— 1985, *Applying Significant Bilingual Instructional Features in the Classroom*. Rosslyn, VA: National Clearinghouse for Bilingual Education.

VALENCIA, A.A. 1984, Cognitive and interactive learning approaches for gifted/talented migrant students. In A.A. VALENCIA (ed.) *Variable Strategies for Advancing the Education of Gifted/Talented Migrants*. Fresno, CA: California State University.

— 1985, Curricular perspectives for gifted limited English proficient students. *Journal of the National Association for Bilingual Education* 10(1), 65–77.

WONG-FILLMORE, L. 1976, *The Second Time Around: Cognitive and Social*

Strategies in Second Language Acquisition. Parts I, II. Ann Arbor, MI: UMI Dissertation Information Services.

— 1981, Second quarterly report 1980–81 for learning English through bilingual education. Unpublished document.

WONG-FILLMORE, L., AMMON, R., MCLAUGHLIN, B. and AMMON, M.S. 1985, *Final Report for Learning English Through Bilingual Instruction.* NTE Report prepared for the Office of Bilingual Education and Minority Language Affairs, and the Department of Education; NIE-400-80-0030, National Clearinghouse for Bilingual Education, Arlington, VA.

YSSELDYKE, J.E. and ALGOZZINE, B. 1981, Diagnostic classification decisions as a function of referral information. *Journal of Special Education* 15(4), 429–35.

12 Communication Perceptions Between Hispanic Parents of Learning Handicapped Children and Special Education Teachers

JANICE A. CHAVEZ, DAVID P. LOPEZ
and LOUISE F. BURTON

The purpose of this study was to determine the nature and level of communication between Spanish-speaking parents of learning handicapped children and the special education teachers who serve these children. Presently, there exists little research examining the home–school communication process and the importance parents have in this process.

It is well recognised that parents provide valuable input into the educational programme of their child. For parents of handicapped children, involvement has been mandated by special education legislation. The intent of PL 94–142, the Education for All Handicapped Children Act, is to provide the most appropriate individual educational plan to meet the needs of the handicapped child.

Educators are aware of the importance of including parents in all aspects of the programme for handicapped students and recognise the potential benefits and barriers to achieving optimal parental involvement (Yoshida, Fenton, Kaufman & Maxwell, 1978). Parent input is particularly critical when the special needs child is culturally and linguistically different. Positive parent involvement requires ongoing communication with school personnel; frequently the teacher is the major source of school contact with the parent.

According to Witt, Miller, McIntyre & Smith (1984), special education has not approached the degree of participatory partnerships needed for a sharing relationship between parents and schools. Satir (1972) concluded that communication is the most important factor influencing relationships among individuals. In a review of the literature on school–parent interactions, Beals & Beers (1982) described three communication approaches between these parties: (1) tell parents what they need to know; (2) bring parents in and put them to work; (3) I talk, you talk, we talk. The first approach focuses on parent education, the second emphasises parents as active participants in school activities, and the third implies honest and open communication as the basis for parent–teacher interactions. The latter approach, which involves shared communication, is recommended. Yet, parents and teachers may enter this communication process with reluctance. Parents bring to the relationship their past experiences with school which may have been negative or unproductive; on the other hand, teachers frequently hold anxieties or feelings of inadequacy regarding the conference (Price & Marsh, 1985).

Developing open communication can become even more difficult when the child's parents are culturally and linguistically different. The greatest challenge occurs in overcoming the communication barriers that exist when the teacher does not speak the language of the home, when parents are unfamiliar with educational terminology, and when teachers have limited knowledge of the parent's culture (Burton & Chavez, 1984). When these barriers exist, interactions between parents and teachers can be threatening and nonproductive.

Baca & Cervantes (1984) emphasise the importance of schools establishing a bond with bilingual parents of exceptional children. A bonding relationship requires a respect for the parent's culture and a sharing atmosphere which supports mutual goals for the child. However, little is known about the communication relationships which occur between bilingual/bicultural parents and the teachers of their handicapped children. In response to this void, the purpose of this study was to examine the communication between Hispanic parents of learning handicapped children and the teachers who serve these children.

Method

Two questionnaires were developed to determine the communication perceptions of Hispanic parents with learning handicapped children and of special education teachers. In order to allow comparisons between parents and teachers, parallel questionnaires were constructed; however, administration procedures differed between the two groups. Teachers were requested to respond to the questionnaire in writing, while parents were individually interviewed in their dominant language, English or Spanish, by trained bilingual graduate students. A small rural school district in central California was selected as the research site. The teacher questionnaire was distributed to 14 special education teachers, with a 100% return rate. Fourteen parents from a pool of approximately 45 Hispanic parents agreed to participate in this study. The Spanish-speaking parents were administered the parallel questionnaire during a 20–30 minute scheduled interview at a school site.

Results

The results from parents and teachers regarding the home–school communication are shown in Table 12.1. Results from data tabulation of the parent responses indicated that, of the 14 parents, two spoke only English in the home, three spoke only Spanish and nine spoke both English and Spanish (Spanish being the dominant language). The number of children in the family ranged from one to 10 with the mean being 4.4 children. Of the 11 fathers living in the home, six were farm labourers and the others were employed as painter, truck driver, construction worker or automobile salesperson. Of the mothers listing an occupation, six were farm labourers, five held positions in the school district or a small business, and three indicated they were homemakers.

Parent responses to questions regarding their handicapped children were also analysed. It was found that the children ranged from 8 to 19 years of age, with a mean age of 13.4 years. All children in the study were identified as learning handicapped. In response to the parents' perceptions of their child's exceptionality category, seven parents stated that their child was 'learning handicapped', three reported a specific disability (dyslexia, fine-motor problems, or reading problems), and four reported they were unaware of their child's label.

Twelve children attended a resource specialist programme and two attended a special day class. The majority of parent respondents were unclear as to the specific type of classroom (special day class or resource specialist programme) in which their child was enrolled. When the placement was a resource programme, six parents whose children attended this programme held misconceptions regarding the service delivery and six had no idea of their children's specific special education placement.

TABLE 12.1 *A comparison between parent and teacher perceptions on school–home communication*

Related question	Selections	Responses Parent	Teacher
Home language(s)	English	2	11
	Spanish	3	3
	Eng/Sp	9	
Special education programme	Resource Room	0	12
	Special Day Class	2	2
	Teacher's help, maths class, reading class	6	
	Unaware	6	
Exceptionality category	Learning handicapped	7	12
	Specific disability	3	
	Unaware	4	
Type of communication	Letters	13	12
	Telephone calls	11	10
	Home visits	1	2
Interpreter provided	Yes	14	14
	No	0	0
Frequency of communication	0 times/month	2	2
	1 to 2 times/month	10	11
	3 to 4 times/month	1	1
	5 or more times/ month	1	0
Topics of discussion	attendance	10	13
	medication	9	3
	illness	12	9
	health issues	14	8
	clothing/materials	9	3
	transportation		
	discipline	13	9
Information of educational needs	Yes	11	14
	No	3	0
Home teaching activities	Yes	8	14
	No	6	0
Comfort in asking questions	Yes	4	14
	No	10	0

However, the two parents with children attending the special day class were aware of their child's special placement.

Teachers and parents were asked to respond to similar questions related to the method, language, frequency and topic of communication. With reference to the method, both groups agreed that 'letters' and 'telephone calls' were the usual means of communication. Few teachers and parents indicated that 'home visits' were used for this purpose.

When asked to identify the language used for home–school communication, teachers stated that they used English most of the time and Spanish with the assistance of an interpreter. It should be noted that two parents reported speaking English in the home and 12 indicated they spoke both Spanish and English (Spanish being the dominant language). Both groups agreed that a Spanish interpreter, usually a teacher's aide, was provided when necessary. The majority of parents and teachers indicated that contacts occurred one to two times per month.

Teachers and parents were asked if they discussed attendance, medication, illness, health issues, clothing/materials, transportation or discipline topics during school conferences. The topics most frequently identified by over half of the parents and teachers were health, discipline, illness and attendance issues. Transportation and medication were identified by over half of the parents, although few teachers identified these topics as frequent discussion topics.

In reference to the question, 'Has the school provided information about your child's educational needs?', all 14 teachers reported that parents were well informed. Eleven parents felt teachers made attempts to provide general information on their child's educational needs, while three parents indicated they did not receive this type of information. Moreover, eight parents reported that the teacher provided them with specific activities to help their child at home, while six parents reported that teachers did not provide them with home-related activities. The responses from parents regarding their feelings on asking questions of their child's teacher showed that ten of the parents were uncomfortable asking questions. On the other hand, all 14 teachers indicated that they felt quite comfortable about asking questions of parents.

Teachers and parents were asked to list additional areas that they felt were important to include in the school conference. Teachers desired more information from parents on home monitoring of the child's progress, discipline measures used in the home and ways to increase the child's self-concept. Parents were more interested in acquiring information on how to help their child at home and possible causes for their child's learning difficulties.

Conclusions and Recommendations

This study was conducted to determine the nature and level of communication between Hispanic parents of learning handicapped children and the special education teachers who service these students. Due to the small parent and teacher sample size from one school district and the lack of a control group, caution should be exercised in making generalisations to the larger population. Although this study has its limitations, the findings have important implications for similar school districts who serve rural, Spanish-speaking, learning handicapped children and their parents. The following results, interpretations and recommendations also indicate a need for further research in the area of school–home communication.

In this study it was found that both parents and teachers agreed that letters served as the most common communication method, followed by telephone calls and home visits. Telephone and letter correspondence was made approximately one to two times per month. Although these forms of communication, which were made in English, were the most efficient method used, they were not the most effective since many parents spoke primarily Spanish. For example, a majority of parents in this study held misconceptions regarding their child's exceptionality and classroom placement. These misconceptions seemed to be the result of misinterpretation of written materials or telephone calls made to parents. Culturally and linguistically different parents with limited educational experience, minimal literacy skills, and an unfamiliarity with English language may easily misunderstand the information on the educational status of their children; therefore, it is imperative that teachers working with such parents consider less usage of written materials and/or telephone messages containing educational jargon. School personnel should not assume that, when parents speak limited English, effective communication is taking place, particularly when communicating on important and such technical matters as a child's placement and progress in special education. By increasing the amount of home visits made in English and Spanish, the interactions will not only become more personalised but also enhance the dissemination of more accurate information.

It is understandable why parents feel uncomfortable asking questions of teachers, as found in this study. First, Hispanic parents, as well as other parents, often feel intimidated by institutions such as the school. The feelings of apprehension may be compounded by the parent's past experiences in dealing with institutions and schools, particularly when those experiences have been negative. Secondly, Hispanic parents tend to hold a deep respect for the school and its mission. Because of this respect, parents may feel that the information the teacher provides regarding their child is accurate and should not be questioned or challenged. Hispanic parents, because of respect and/or intimidation, perceive teachers as educational experts: school personnel should never confuse or misinterpret these feelings by Hispanic parents as a lack of interest in their child's education. Educators must become familiar with the cultural background of parents in their service area.

Local school districts and university teacher training programmes should make every attempt to increase the number of bilingual special education teachers who are able to communicate readily with Spanish-speaking parents. A bilingual teacher with special education training would be capable of explaining technical diagnostic and prescriptive information to Spanish-speaking parents who would not otherwise understand the same information given in English. Parents in an interactional situation usually feel more comfortable asking questions of a person who speaks and understands their language, is knowledgeable of their culture and is informed on special education procedures.

Trained teachers, or at least trained interpreters, are desperately needed in order to properly translate the complex terms on the individual education plan (IEP), diagnostic reports, and during school conferences and meetings. Translating technical information from one language to another requires specialised training and extensive experience. It should not be assumed that any bilingual education teacher, teacher's aide, or school secretary who is bilingual is capable of conveying the appropriate message when translating from English to Spanish.

Educators must continue to probe further into the communication efforts between school and home. Suggestions for further research should include the following modifications and extensions of the present study:

(1) A comparison of communication perceptions between Hispanic parents and teachers of special education children
(2) The effect of parent involvement programmes on bilingual, learning handicapped student achievement
(3) A comparison of communication perceptions between bilingual parents and regular education teachers
(4) The identification of sociocultural/psychological barriers which impede

communication between Hispanic parents and special education teachers.

The findings and implications of the present study and the recommendations for future research will hopefully assist parents and teachers in communicating more effectively with one another. In improving communication between parents and teachers, the Hispanic learning handicapped child will ultimately benefit.

References

BACA, L.M. and CERVANTES, H.T. 1984, *The Bilingual Special Education Interface*. St Louis: Times Mirror/Mosby College Publishing.

BEALS, A. and BEERS, C.S. 1982, What do you say to parents after you say hello? *Teaching Exceptional Children* 15(1), 34–8.

BURTON, L.F. and CHAVEZ, J.A. 1984, Serving exceptional children in rural America: The one room school house revisited. Paper presented at the 62nd Annual Convention of the Council for Exceptional Children, Washington, DC. (ERIC Document Reproduction Service No. ED 249 711.)

PRICE, B. and MARSH, G. 1985, Practical suggestions for planning and conducting parent conferences. *Teaching Exceptional Children* 17(4), 274–8.

SATIR, V. 1972, *Peoplemaking*. Palo Alto, CA: Science and Behavior Books.

WITT, J.C., MILLER, C.D., MCINTYRE, R.M. and SMITH, D. 1984, Effects of variables on parental perceptions of staffing. *Exceptional Children* 51(1), 27–32.

YOSHIDA, R.K., FENTON, K.S., KAUFMAN, M.J. and MAXWELL, J.P. 1978, Parental involvement in the special education pupil planning process: The school's perspective. *Exceptional Children* 44(7), 531–4.

13   Can Schools Promote Additive Bilingualism in Minority Group Children?[1]

RODRIGUE LANDRY and RÉAL ALLARD

In this chapter, we discuss the relative contribution of the school to the development of an additive type of bilingualism. This discussion is based on both a theoretical framework and some empirical data. Following a general introduction, we present a model of bilingual development in which social and psychological factors which contribute to additive and subtractive bilingualism are defined. Within that framework, a global definition of additive bilingualism is proposed. We then present data which address the question of the contribution of schooling to the bilingual development of minority francophone students in Eastern Canada. Results are discussed in terms of the contribution of schooling to the development of additive bilingualism when the effects of other social factors are taken into consideration.

Introduction

Lambert (1975) made an important distinction between two types of bilingualism. In trying to account for important contradictions in research results on the cognitive and affective consequences of bilingualism, Lambert noted that in certain conditions the learning of a second language (L2) had no negative impact on the maintenance of the mother tongue (L1) and that this type of bilingualism could lead to positive cognitive consequences. This was referred to as *additive bilingualism*. Lambert also noted that in other conditions, the learning of L2 led to less efficient L1 acquisition, a *subtractive* type of bilingualism which could be related to negative cognitive consequences. According to this framework, when bilingualism is additive, the learning of L1 and L2 are complementary processes. When bilingualism is subtractive, this process becomes competitive and one language is learned to the detriment of the other (Hamers & Blanc, 1983).

The effects of schooling on the acquisition of bilingualism may differ depending on the type of bilingual programme and on whether the children are from minority or majority linguistic groups. In majority groups, most forms of bilingual education lead to an additive type of bilingualism. For example, majority anglophone children in Canada educated within a total immersion programme in which French is the dominant language of instruction acquire a functional proficiency in the second language with no negative impact on the development or maintenance of their first language (Lambert & Tucker, 1972; Swain & Lapkin, 1982; Genesee, 1983, 1987; Cummins & Swain, 1986). In minority groups, many forms of bilingual education lead to a subtractive type of bilingualism (Skutnabb-Kangas, 1983, 1984; Cummins, 1984; Hamers & Blanc, 1983). Some have even argued that most forms of bilingual education for minority groups may lead to the 'soft assimilation of these groups' (Paulston, 1980; Bibeau, 1982). Cummins (1986) theorised that additive bilingualism for minority group children is possible, but only when the value of L1 as a minority language is officially recognised and the minority group becomes 'empowered' to offer strong pedagogical programmes in its first language. Skutnabb-Kangas (1983) has neatly summarised this issue into one pedagogical principle, namely, that it is essential to provide 'support via instruction in the language which is otherwise less likely to develop' (p. 130). This principle applies to both minority and majority groups. For majority groups, stronger bilingualism is obtained when children are instructed via their second language as in total immersion programmes; for minority groups, however, schooling should be predominantly in the first language, since it is less likely to develop through general societal support. Research has shown that minority group children educated mainly via their first language not only better maintain their mother tongue, but also that they may be better prepared to learn their second language (Cummins & Mulcahy, 1978; Cummins, 1986; Hamers & Blanc, 1983; Hébert et al., 1976; Landry & Allard, 1985; Landry, 1979; Skutnabb-Kangas & Toukomaa, 1976; Toukomaa & Skutnabb-Kangas, 1977; Skutnabb-Kangas, 1983, 1984; Willig, 1985).

The school is not the only factor that favours language maintenance for minority group children. It has been argued that societal pressures are so strong that linguistic assimilation may occur, at least to some extent, even when minority education programmes are implemented (Mougeon & Canale, 1980; Mougeon & Heller, 1986). Edwards (1985) has suggested that schooling, when compared to other social factors, plays a negligible role in language maintenance and loss for minority groups. In the model described below, schooling is shown to be essential, yet only one of several social factors which may contribute to an additive type of bilingualism for minority group children.

A Macroscopic Model of Bilingual Development

In this section we give a brief overview of a general model of the determinants of additive and subtractive bilingualism (Landry, 1982, 1984; Landry & Allard, 1984, 1987a, 1987b). Before describing the model, it is important that the terms 'additive' and 'subtractive' bilingualism be clearly defined. These terms have been mainly associated with the cognitive consequences of bilingualism (Lambert, 1975; Cummins, 1978, 1979; Hamers & Blanc, 1983). Cummins (1976, 1978, 1979, 1981) presented a theoretical framework in which he argued that, to avoid negative cognitive consequences, the bilingual experience must allow the child to reach a critical threshold of 'native-like' proficiency in at least one language. Furthermore, Cummins' linguistic interdependence hypothesis states that the acquisition of L2 is dependent on the development of L1. It is our contention, however, that the emphasis on cognitive consequences as the defining criteria of additive and subtractive bilingualism makes this theoretical construct of little relevance in the distinction between minority and majority group bilingualism. Additive bilingualism has been associated with positive cognitive consequences such as mental flexibility, creativity and metalinguistic awareness. Although such effects may be possible, those found tend to be of low magnitude and they do not seem to be related to a significant increase in global intellectual functioning (Landry, 1984; McLaughlin, 1984). The defining characteristic should not be whether bilingual experience leads to positive cognitive consequences (although these could be considered an extra bonus to additive bilingualism) but whether the bilingual experience provides the advantages of a second language without any negative impact on the development of one's first language. Even without gains in cognitive functioning or ability, the learning of a second language can still be additive. And even without the loss of cognitive abilities, bilingualism can be subtractive. A global definition of these two types of bilingualism should incorporate cognitive, affective and behavioural aspects of linguistic development. Complete additive bilingualism should encompass (a) a high level of proficiency in both communicative and cognitive-academic aspects of L1 and L2; (b) maintenance of a strong ethnolinguistic identity and positive beliefs towards one's own language and culture while also holding positive attitudes towards the second language and culture; and (c) the opportunity to use one's first language without diglossia, that is without one's language being used exclusively for less valued social roles or domains of activity (Landry, 1984; Landry & Allard, 1987a, 1987b). The latter definition encompasses not only the psychological effects of bilingualism but also the social consequences of bilingual experiences (Landry, 1987). When a person ceases to use or value his or her language, it is not only the linguistic proficiency and the psychological disposition of the individual which are affected but also the ethnolinguistic vitality of the community (see Figure 13.1).

Although we often refer to additive and subtractive bilingualism in dichotomic terms, the model views these two types of bilingualism in relative terms and as being on a continuum. The same can be said of the concepts of minority and majority when referring to different linguistic groups. The model is referred to as a macroscopic model in the sense given by DeRosnay (1975). The macroscope, according to DeRosnay, is a cognitive tool needed when dealing with the complexities of social and living systems. In order to understand a complex system, a global-analytic approach is needed; that is, we should conceptualise the whole and the parts of the system simultaneously. The model presented (see Figure 13.1) integrates within a single framework the sociological and the psychological aspects of bilingualism. These have generally been analysed as isolated facets of the bilingual phenomenon. The process of studying a phenomenon as complex as that of bilingualism from a single perspective is a form of analytic reductionism (Landry, 1985) which leads to an incomplete picture of the analysed phenomenon. It is only recently that research has aimed at integrating both the individual and society as complementary factors in bilingual development (Prujiner *et al.*, 1984; Blanc & Hamers, 1987).

The challenge of this macro–micro dichotomy has been well stated by Blanc (1987: 4):

> While one accepts that this analysis of the objective social conditions should come first, human social behaviour cannot be properly understood unless we can discover the subjective representations of social reality that mediate between social conditions and the effects of thesc on individual and collective behaviour . . . The difficulty lies in how to relate them without reducing one level to the other, as has too often been the case.

The model presented in this chapter attempts to link three levels of

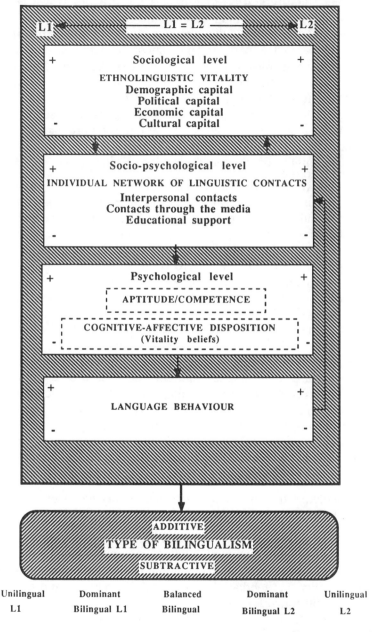

FIGURE 13.1 *Macroscopic model of the determinants of additive and subtractive bilingualism*

analysis which, considered together, provide a global overview of the variables involved in bilingual development. It is understood that each of these variables can be further analysed. Only multidisciplinary research could lead to a full account of bilingualism. The model presented is not considered complete; it is a preliminary attempt at this integrative process. The model, which originated from a multidisciplinary approach to bilingualism (Prujiner et al., 1984), adapts and integrates variables drawn from several sources (e.g. the notion of ethnolinguistic vitality from Giles, Bourhis & Taylor, 1977; the notion of communication networks from Milroy, 1980 and others; the notions of cognitive-academic linguistic proficiency and interpersonal communicative skills from Cummins, 1979, 1981). Despite the eclectic nature of the model, it attempts to make a coherent link between complementary dimensions of bilingualism and encompasses notions such as the family, the school and the social milieu which have not been clearly integrated in other models. It also introduces the concept of belief to account for some cognitive-affective aspects of bilingualism (Allard & Landry, 1986, 1987a). The goal of the model is more the prediction of the degree and type of bilingualism than the explanation of the underlying processes involved.

The sociological level

As depicted in Figure 13.1, the individual residing in a social environment in which two languages are in contact belongs to a linguistic community which has a relative degree of ethnolinguistic vitality (Giles, Bourhis & Taylor, 1977). This vitality could be measured by looking at certain sociological indices indicative of a community's resources or 'capital' (Bourdieu, 1980) in demographic, economic, political and cultural terms (Prujiner et al., 1984). The more a linguistic community controls its social institutions (Allardt, 1984; de Vries, 1984) or shows institutional completeness (Breton, 1964), the more it will develop as a distinct and active entity. The study of the power struggle between two linguistic communities at the macro-social level constitutes in itself a complex field of analysis (Prujiner, 1987). The present model is less concerned with the dynamics of this power struggle than with the link between the vitality of the community at the sociological level and the linguistic contacts of the members of the community. Ethnolinguistic vitality is theorised as the major determinant of the probability of linguistic contacts at the individual level. A major advantage of incorporating the concept of ethnolinguistic vitality within the model is that it makes it possible to study minority and majority linguistic groups in relativistic terms; that is, ethnolinguistic vitality is viewed as a continuous variable whereas the majority and minority status of groups are typically viewed in terms of a dichotomous variable.

The social–psychological link

The individual experiences the relative vitality of the linguistic communities within the meta-social system through a social network. The individual is the centre of a complex network which favours various forms of linguistic contacts. By measuring the strength of these networks, one can evaluate the individual's opportunities for bilingual experience. The network of the individual is what links the social structural variables and the representations of the individual at the psychological level (Hamers, 1987). Previous work on social communication networks (Milroy & Margrain, 1980; Milroy, 1980; Prujiner et al., 1984; Rogers & Kincaid, 1981; Blanc, Clément, Deshaies & Hamers, 1984; Hamers, 1987) has dealt mainly with interpersonal contacts. In our research, we have used the term 'individual network of linguistic contacts' (INLC) to refer to contexts in which multiple forms of linguistic contacts can be experienced. Networks provide the opportunities for linguistic contacts which can be oral or written, input or output, formal or informal, interactive and non-interactive. The context within which contacts take place may also require more or less cognitive involvement. Languages cannot be acquired unless there are enough opportunities to use them: not only is comprehensible input necessary (Krashen, 1981) but also a sufficient amount of comprehensible output by the language learner is required (Swain, 1985). All of these forms of linguistic contacts are experienced via the individual's INLC. In the model, language behaviour is seen as separate from the INLC; in reality, this behaviour occurs within the network. The network, as measured in our research, refers to the opportunities provided to the individual to use the language, whereas language behaviour is the actual use of the language within the network.

The model identifies three types of opportunities for linguistic contacts: *interpersonal contacts, contacts through the media* and *educational support*. It is hypothesised that the interactive nature and the low to medium cognitive involvement typically favoured by interpersonal contacts contribute mostly to the development of 'basic interpersonal communication skills' (as defined by Cummins, 1979). Educational support provides linguistic contexts which are typically formal, context-reduced and non-interactive (Resnick, 1987); this type of contact is, therefore, expected to contribute most to cognitive-academic linguistic proficiency or the ability to use the language as a tool for abstract reasoning (Cummins, 1979). Contacts through the media can involve much or little cognitive involvement and may, therefore, relate equally to communicative and cognitive-academic aspects of proficiency. Each type of linguistic contact in the individual's INLC can also be analysed into sub-networks. We can measure the relative strengths of the L1 network, of the L2 network and of a mixed network (L1/L2) in which both languages are used more or less simultaneously.

Finally, another way of analysing the INLC construct is to look at the relative strengths of the L1 and L2 networks in different 'milieux de vie' of school-aged children. Landry & Allard (1987a, 1987b) have identified three milieux which are part of the 'counterbalance model of bilingual experience' (see Figure 13.2). These are the *family* milieu, the *school* milieu and the *socio-institutional* milieu.

According to this model, additive bilingualism for a minority group's members is only possible when the frequency of opportunities for linguistic contacts in L1 can compensate for the dominance of L2. This counterbalancing effect may occur when the group controls enough social

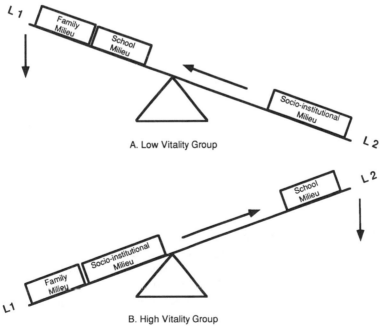

FIGURE 13.2 *The counterbalance model of linguistic contacts in bilingual experience*

institutions so that contacts are relatively frequent in L1 in the socio-institutional milieu. In most cases, to counterbalance the predominance of L2, it becomes necessary for the ambient atmosphere of both the family milieu and the school milieu to be almost completely unilingual in L1. The efforts of many minority francophone communities in Canada to gain administrative control of their own schools is an attempt to create this linguistic ambience which educational leaders see as a necessity for the survival of French in their community. The minority child must have opportunities for L1 linguistic contacts not only in the school but also in other social institutions. Opportunities for language maintenance in the home would also act as an important counterbalance to the dominance of L2 in the society at large.

As shown in Figure 13.2, the situation is different for the majority group. The family and the socio-institutional milieu typically contribute only to L1 unilingualism for majority group members. Only the school can act as a counterbalancing force to increase the relative strength of the L2 network. Intensive second language programmes such as total immersion have contributed largely to additive bilingualism among majority group individuals, but several researchers are warning that unless opportunities for L2 contacts are extended in the larger community, the level of bilingualism attained via schooling is compromised (Pellerin & Hammerly, 1986; Harley, 1984; Genesee, 1983; Cummins & Swain, 1986) and, we would add, probably short-lived.

The psychological dimension and linguistic behaviour

Linguistic experiences cumulated within the INLC will enhance one's psychological disposition to use a language. The *aptitude/competence* component refers to the ability to learn and use the language, and the belief or *cognitive-affective disposition* component refers to the willingness to use and learn the language. Intellectual aptitude is hypothesised to be more strongly related to cognitive-academic linguistic proficiency than to the communicative aspects of competence (Cummins, 1984, 1983; Cummins & Swain, 1986; Genesee, 1976, 1978). Proficiency in language may also be related to specific linguistic aptitudes (Carroll, 1973). Notwithstanding the role of aptitude, it is the overall linguistic experience within the INLC which will lead to competence in the language. Competence then becomes the foundation for further language experiences and, therefore, promotes the maintenance of the INLC.

Competence is necessary but not sufficient to maintain language usage within a bilingual individual's network. The individual must also want to learn and use a language. This willingness to learn and use a language is dependent on the individual's beliefs pertaining to that ethnolinguistic group's vitality (Allard & Landry, 1986, 1987a, 1987b). Beliefs have been found to be very good predictors of L1 and L2 use (Allard & Landry, 1986, 1987b; Landry & Allard, 1984, 1985). A person's general and personal beliefs contribute to the formation of behavioural intentions (Kreitler & Kreitler, 1972, 1976, 1982); when behavioural intentions conducive to using a language are paired with the necessary competencies, an individual will continue using it and, therefore, maintain his INLC in that language. For bilingual individuals, beliefs and competence are complementary and mutually reinforcing factors which influence the use of each language.

Types and degree of bilingualism

As shown in Figure 13.1, bilingualism is the end result of a complex interactive process involving variables at the individual and at the societal level. Different configurations of interaction among these variables will lead to different profiles of bilingualism. When ethnolinguistic vitality and the resulting INLC patterns favour only or mainly L1, the individual will maintain L1 unilingualism or become a bilingual dominant in L1. Dominant L1 bilingualism will typically be additive in nature but may also be subtractive; subtractive bilingualism would be minimal in this case but would occur when the learning of L2, while not strong enough to overwhelm the development of L1, could still hamper its development. Such subtractive effects have been found in francophone minority students schooled in French who have strong L2 networks (Landry, 1979).

When INLC patterns favour L2 more strongly than L1, bilingualism becomes a subtractive process. As was discussed above, it is the overall pattern which must be considered here and not only a part of the INLC. Majority group children may be schooled exclusively in L2 with very few adverse effects mainly because of extensive support for L1 in the family and socio-institutional milieux. For minority group children, schooling via L2 is a subtractive process since the remaining networks are not strong enough to ensure the maintenance of L1.

In theory, balanced bilingualism is possible but it is probably rare in reality. This type of bilingualism would occur when INLC patterns favour both languages equally. Balanced bilingualism can be additive or subtractive. When L2 experience builds on a strong L1 foundation, the child may become highly competent in both languages; however, when linguistic experiences are such that the child has inadequate models in both L1 and L2, the end result may be weak development of both languages. Subtractive bilingualism would also occur if the individual's ethnolinguistic identity is weakened or if the person's beliefs favour L2 at the expense of L1, thereby indicating relinquishment or abandonment of one's language. As specified earlier in the proposed definition, additive bilingualism involves not only linguistic competence but also language behaviour and one's cognitive-affective disposition towards the language. Positive cognitive consequences related to additive bilingualism could also be considered, as discussed above, a possible bonus of the bilingual experience.

An Empirical Study

Following the theoretical model, it is hypothesised in the present study that for minority group children, schooling exercises a counterbalancing effect by increasing INLC patterns in favour of L1. The school alone, however, cannot fully compensate for the lack of L1 contacts in the family and in the social milieu. The lower the vitality of a minority linguistic group, the more the school is needed to counterbalance L2 dominance in the social milieu. In the study, we analyse as dependent variables the following ingredients of additive bilingualism: communicative and cognitive-academic linguistic proficiency, beliefs and identity, the frequency of language behaviour and the type of linguistic variety favoured. In other words, it is hypothesised that when group vitality and individual INLC in L1 are low, being schooled in L1 will enhance L1 development but will not hamper L2 development. Inversely, when L1 vitality is high, being schooled in L2 will lead to better L2 development but not necessarily to less L1 development.

Methodology

The results presented in this chapter involve only francophone minority students. The results of anglophone and francophone majority group students who also participated in the study are being analysed elsewhere (Allard & Landry, in press; Landry & Allard, in press).[2]

Population

Eight high schools in the Maritime provinces of Canada (five in New Brunswick, two in Nova Scotia and one in Prince Edward Island) housed the francophone minority students involved in the present analyses. These were chosen so as to represent a continuum of ethnolinguistic vitality. A total of 725 subjects were tested in these eight high schools. In large high schools, a representative sample of approximately 20% of the total population of grade 12 students was selected; in small high schools, the total population of grade 12 francophone students was tested.

In New Brunswick, francophones represent about one-third of the population but some areas are more francophone than others. Most students from all five high schools chosen have received instruction in French from grade 1 to grade 12 except for regular courses in English as a second language. Because of variations in the ethnolinguistic vitality of the communities involved, the degree of francophone ambience in each school varies even if the language of instruction is always French. The regions of Caraquet and Edmundston represent areas which are almost totally francophone; the Bouctouche region is highly francophone but it is close to the neighbouring city of Moncton which has an anglophone majority. Bathurst is a city which has approximately an equal number of francophones and anglophones; however, many students attending the francophone high school in Bathurst come from neighbouring villages which are predominantly French. The town of Dieppe which is predominantly francophone shares its limits with the city of Moncton which is only about one-third francophone. Many students attending the francophone high school of Dieppe are from Moncton, but many also come from areas outside the city, some of which are predominantly French.

In Prince Edward Island, francophones represent only 5% of the population. In the area of Abraam Village, however, where Evangeline School is situated, francophones constitute about two-thirds of the mostly rural population. The instruction received by the francophone students of this high school has been predominantly French, but the educational support has not been as strong as in New Brunswick.

In Nova Scotia, francophones represent about 4% of the province's population. In the areas where the two schools participating in the study are situated, francophones outnumber anglophones in a ratio of approximately 2 to 1. When considering all the schools participating in the study, French educational support has been lowest in Nova Scotia.

Instruments

The questionnaires and tests related to the variables analysed in this report are listed below.

(1) *Oral communicative competence in French.* This variable was tested through a self-evaluation questionnaire in which the subjects rated their ability to communicate in a variety of situations ranging in levels of difficulty (e.g. asking a phone number, describing family members, discussing politics, discussing the capital punishment issue). The subjects rated their ability to communicate in standard French and in their vernacular language. Scores reported could range from 1 to 9, the latter referring to 'native-like' ability. The self-evaluations of the ability to communicate in standard French are the ones reported in the present analyses.

(2) *Oral communicative competence in English.* This questionnaire involved the same language tasks used to evaluate oral communicative competence in French, but the subjects rated their ability to communicate in English.

(3) *French cognitive-academic linguistic proficiency.* A cloze test of approximately 325 words and requiring 65 answers was used. Testing time was 20 minutes. Both the 'exact' and 'acceptable word' scoring procedures were used, the latter being reported here. Scores could range from 0 to 65.

(4) *English cognitive-academic linguistic proficiency.* A cloze test of approximately 330 words and requiring 66 answers was used. Testing time was 20 minutes. Using the 'acceptable word' scoring procedure, scores could range from 0 to 66.

(5) *Beliefs in ethnolinguistic vitality.* This questionnaire related eight different categories of beliefs to twelve different indices of ethnolinguistic vitality (Allard & Landry, 1987a). A factor analytic study of the eight beliefs concerning French vitality and of the eight beliefs concerning English vitality has been undertaken (Allard & Landry, 1987b). These analyses have yielded the following factor scores: (1) general beliefs towards French ethnolinguistic vitality, (2) personal beliefs towards French ethnolinguistic vitality, (3) general beliefs towards English ethnolinguistic vitality, (4) personal beliefs towards English ethnolinguistic vitality. General beliefs refer to the perception of the objective situation by the individual, and personal beliefs are more closely related to feelings of belonging, personal values, expectancy of fulfilling one's needs in the language and the personal goals of the individual. These factor scores have a mean of 0.0 and a standard deviation of 1.00.

(6) *Language behaviour in French.* Subjects rated the frequency of use of French (1 = never, 9 = always) in 15 different contact situations. The mean score is reported.

(7) *Language behaviour in English.* Subjects rated the frequency of use of English in the same contact situations as in the questionnaire on French language behaviour. The mean score is reported.

(8) *Variety of language spoken.* Subjects rated the linguistic variety (vernacular) in which they generally felt more at ease. The scale ranged from 1 (standard English) to 7 (standard French), the midpoint of 4 referring to 'franglais' or 'Frenglish', a strong mixture of French and English in spoken language.

(9) *Francophone identity.* Subjects rated their francophone identity on a 1 to 9 scale from a variety of perspectives (culture, language, ancestors, ethnic origins, etc.). The mean score is reported. A score of 1 equals a non-francophone identity and a score of 9 equals a completely francophone identity.

(10) *Anglophone identity.* Subjects rated their anglophone identity on the same scales as for francophone identity. Scores could range from 1 to 9, the latter indicating a completely anglophone identity.

(11) *Non-verbal intellectual aptitude (IQ).* The abstract reasoning scale of the Differential Aptitude Tests (Bennett, Seashore & Wesman, 1974) was administered. Testing time was 25 minutes. The maximum score on this scale is 50.

(12) *Socio-economic status (SES).* Data on the father's and mother's occupation and level of education were collected. Occupation was categorised on a 1 to 7 scale using the indices developed by Blishen & McRoberts (1976). Subjects reported their parents' level of education on a 1 to 7 scale. The mean of these four 1 to 7 scales is used as an SES index for the present analyses.

(13) *Demographic vitality.* Using the census data of 1981, the percentage of persons reporting French as mother tongue (first language spoken and still understood) is used as an index of demographic vitality. Subjects' scores are the percentages reported by Statistics Canada for their town or village. This procedure offers more variability and accuracy than provincial or regional rates.

(14) *Individual network of linguistic contacts (INLC).* As discussed in the theory section of this chapter, the INLC consists of three types of contact. *Interpersonal contacts* were measured by a 38-page questionnaire which analysed different structural dimensions of interpersonal contacts with francophones and anglophones. For the present analyses only contacts with francophones are considered. Contacts with the *French and English media* were measured by a

separate questionnaire in which subjects rated their overall access
to twelve different media sources since early childhood. Only contacts
with the French media are considered in the present analyses.
Responses were given on a 1 to 9 scale. *Educational support* was
measured by seven questions, each one being answered for each
school year from kindergarten to grade 12. Subjects responded to
all questions on a 1 to 5 scale. Requested were information
concerning the proportion of French instruction, the proportion of
French educational materials, the language used by teachers, the
language used by students, the language used during extracurricular
activities, the language used by the school administration and the
proportion of francophones and anglophones in the school. The
mean total score may be seen as a measure of the school's overall
French ambience: a score of 1 indicates an English ambience and a
score of 5 a completely French ambience.

Procedure

Testing was done over two days and required a total of five 50-
minute class periods (three periods on day 1 and two periods on day 2
or vice versa). All the testing in the eight schools involved was done
between mid-November 1985 and mid-January 1986. The two testing days
were never consecutive but were usually within the same week for a
particular school. Except for the French and English cloze tests (20
minutes each) and the non-verbal aptitude test (25 minutes), which were
timed, subjects responded to the questionnaires at their own pace.
Subjects were tested in groups, either in their respective classrooms or
in larger groups when this was possible.

Design for statistical analyses

Data were entered on the computer via terminals and the statistical
analyses were made using programs from the Statistical Package for Social
Sciences (SPSS Inc., 1986). For the present analyses, the minority
francophone grade 12 students were categorised as high or low using the
median as a cut-off point on the following independent variables:
demographic vitality, INLC and educational support. Since many students
reside in towns and villages which are predominantly French, the median
cut-off score for local demographic vitality is relatively high (79.5%).
Since educational support was isolated for analysis, the INLC score is
composed of only interpersonal contacts with francophones and contacts
with the French media. To make a composite INLC scale, the total mean
score for francophone interpersonal contacts with francophones and the

total score for French media were both transformed to the same 100-point scale and then multiplied by each other. This product was again transformed to a 100-point scale. After these procedures, the median cut-off score on this composite INLC scale is 36.87. Finally, the median cut-off score for educational support is 4.655 on a 1 to 5 scale. It is reminded that this score is intended as an overall estimate of the French ambience of the school.

Having categorised the students as high or low on three independent variables, 3 × 2 analyses of covariance were undertaken for each of the following dependent variables: communicative competence in L1 and L2, cognitive-academic competence in L1 and L2, language behaviour in L1 and L2, variety of spoken French, personal and general beliefs in L1 and L2, and francophone and anglophone identity. Non-verbal IQ and SES were used as covariates.

Results

In this section, the results of the analyses of covariance are presented for the following groups of variables: linguistic competence, beliefs, identity, language variety and language behaviour. Descriptive statistics for all variables are presented in Table 13.1. For each dependent variable, mean scores are presented for the subjects who were below and for those who were above the cut-off scores on the three independent variables involved: demographic vitality, INLC and educational support. Levels of significance for the differences in means are drawn from one-way analyses of variance. In order to highlight the possible influences of the educational support variable, the data reported below are presented in a format different from that used in Table 13.1. These data are presented in graphic form in Figure 13.3. The subjects who were high and those who were low on demographic vitality (DV) and INLC are further split up as high or low in L1 educational support. Three-way analyses of covariance were used to analyse these data.

Linguistic competence

The results are presented separately for communicative competence and cognitive-academic competence in both French and English. Graphic results for each measure of linguistic competence are presented in Figure 13.3.

Reporting first for communicative competence in French (L1), the two main effects of demographic vitality and INLC were statistically

TABLE 13.1 Descriptive statistics and level of significance of simple main effects for the dependent variables of the study by low and high levels of L1 demographic vitality, INLC, and educational support[a]

Dependent variables	Demographic vitality Low		Demographic vitality High		INLC Low		INLC High		Educational support Low		Educational support High	
	N	Mean (SD)	N	Mean (SD)	N	Mean (SD)	N	Mean (SD)	N	Mean (SD)	N	Mean (SD)
Communicative competence L1	300	5.73 (1.72)	262	6.56 (1.55)	306	5.73 (1.68)	266	6.59 (1.52)	326	5.80 (1.75)	298	6.48 (1.55)
Communicative competence L2	296	6.57 (1.98)	288	5.49 (1.96)	294	6.54 (1.94)	306	5.48 (2.01)	319	6.56 (1.95)	333	5.45 (1.99)
Cognitive-academic competence L1	298	27.35 (9.61)	288	32.49 (8.17)	295	27.66 (9.63)	302	32.36 (8.28)	314	27.32 (9.94)	321	32.02 (8.09)
Cognitive-academic competence L2	297	32.15 (10.45)	287	23.67 (11.71)	294	32.53 (10.16)	299	23.68 (11.46)	315	32.08 (10.65)	318	23.86 (11.31)

	N	Mean (SD)	N	Mean (SD)	N	Mean (SD)	N	Mean (SD)	N	Mean (SD)	N	Mean (SD)
Personal beliefs L1	300	-0.34 (1.08)	287	0.36 (0.82)	297	-0.39 (0.95)	302	0.47 (0.82)	317	-0.45 (1.00)	333	0.46 (0.79)
Personal beliefs L2	300	0.28 (0.90)	287	-0.26 (1.08)	297	0.33 (0.85)	302	-0.34 (1.08)	317	0.45 (0.87)	333	-0.45 (0.97)
General beliefs L1	300	-0.36 (0.99)	287	0.43 (0.90)	297	-0.24 (0.97)	302	0.24 (1.07)	317	-0.10 (0.97)	333	0.09** (1.09)
General beliefs L2	300	0.23 (0.94)	287	-0.29 (1.06)	297	0.16 (0.95)	302	-0.15 (1.09)	317	0.01 (0.89)	333	-0.02* (1.15)
Francophone identity	314	7.34 (1.69)	293	8.22 (1.06)	309	7.32 (1.63)	310	8.33 (0.94)	337	7.25 (1.70)	337	8.29 (1.00)
Anglophone identity	310	4.77 (2.29)	293	3.85 (2.18)	308	4.81 (2.22)	307	3.71 (2.20)	336	4.93 (2.30)	332	3.60 (2.04)
Language variety	266	4.64 (1.61)	268	5.47 (1.33)	276	4.55 (1.62)	276	5.61 (1.18)	301	4.57 (1.63)	296	5.57 (1.17)
Language behaviour L1	314	5.75 (1.73)	298	7.30 (1.07)	314	5.60 (1.54)	313	7.41 (1.08)	340	5.82 (1.67)	340	7.24 (1.18)
Language behaviour L2	312	5.59 (1.71)	298	3.98 (1.50)	312	5.49 (1.51)	311	4.01 (1.63)	338	5.65 (1.59)	340	3.91 (1.50)

[a] Excepting those indicated by asterisks, all simple main effects are significant at $p < 0.001$

* ns

** $p < 0.05$

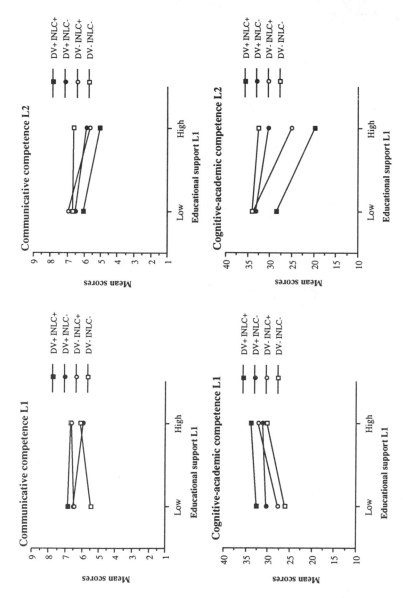

FIGURE 13.3 *Communicative and cognitive-academic competence in L1 and L2 for low and high levels of L1 demographic vitality (DV), INLC and educational support*

significant, $F(1, 488) = 8.412, p < 0.01$ and $F(1, 488) = 18.577, p < 0.001$, respectively. As a main effect, educational support in L1 was not significantly related to communicative competence in L1 but there was a significant demographic vitality by educational support interaction, $F(1, 488) = 5.172, p < 0.05$. (The means needed to interpret this interaction and others reported below are presented in Table 13.2). The present interaction seems to indicate that high educational support in L1 is related to an increase in L1 communicative competence when demographic vitality is low but not when demographic vitality is high (see Table 13.2, A). Only one covariate, SES, had a statistically significant effect, $F(1, 488) = 22.217, p < 0.01$.

TABLE 13.2 *Means needed for the interpretation of the two-way interactions between educational support and demographic vitality or INLC*

Dependent variables		Variables interacting with educational support			Means	
					Educational support	
					Low	High
A. L1 communicative competence	DV	($p < 0.05$)	High		6.70	6.52
			Low		5.60	6.33
B. L2 communicative competence	INLC	($p < 0.05$)	High		6.40	5.19
			Low		6.64	6.27
C. L1 cognitive-academic competence	DV	($p < 0.05$)	High		31.65	33.26
			Low		26.28	31.08
D. L2 cognitive-academic competence	INLC	($p < 0.01$)	High		30.57	20.91
			Low		33.87	31.46
E. L1 personal beliefs	DV	($p = 0.064$)	High		−0.08	0.52
			Low		−0.56	0.37
F. L2 general beliefs	DV	($p < 0.05$)	High		−0.21	−0.34
			Low		0.08	0.61
	INLC	($p = 0.071$)	High		−0.09	−0.21
			Low		0.03	0.40
G. Language variety	INLC	($p < 0.05$)	High		5.47	5.71
			Low		4.28	5.22
H. Language behaviour in L2	INLC	($p < 0.05$)	High		5.10	3.54
			Low		5.79	4.84

For communicative competence in English (L2), the main effects of INLC and educational support were both statistically significant, F (1, 511) = 7.240, $p < 0.01$ and F (1, 511) = 15.449, $p < 0.001$, respectively. The effect of demographic vitality was close to statistical significance, $F(1, 511) = 3.658$, $p = 0.056$. Low educational support in French, a weak French INLC and low L1 demographic vitality all contributed to L2 communicative competence. However, there was a significant educational support by INLC interaction, $F(1, 511) = 4.041$, $p < 0.05$ (see means in Table 13.2, B). When the French INLC was low, being schooled predominantly in French did not hamper the development of English communicative proficiency as much as when the French INLC was high. Only SES had a significant effect as a covariate, $F(1, 511) = 13.731$, $p < 0.001$.

Turning to cognitive-academic competence in French, both covariates were statistically significant, $F(1, 533) = 52.407$, $p < 0.001$ and $F(1, 533) = 6.602$, $p < 0.05$ for non-verbal IQ and SES respectively, and all three main effects were also statistically significant, $F(1, 533) = 20.746$, $p < 0.001$ for demographic vitality, $F(1, 533) = 9.386$, $p < 0.01$ for INLC, and $F(1, 533) = 6.634$, $p < 0.05$ for educational support. There was also a significant demographic vitality by educational support interaction, $F(1, 533) = 5.901$, $p < 0.05$, which indicates that the effect of low French educational support was less detrimental to L1 cognitive-academic competence when L1 demographic vitality was high than when L1 demographic vitality was low (see Table 13.2, C).

The analysis concerning cognitive-academic proficiency in English showed both covariates to be statistically significant, $F(1, 529) = 100.552$, $p < 0.001$ and $F(1, 529) = 15.424$, $p < 0.001$ for non-verbal IQ and SES respectively. All three main effects were statistically significant, $F(1, 529) = 4.353$, $p < 0.05$; $F(1, 529) = 33.446$, $p < 0.001$; and $F(1, 529) = 47.333$, $p < 0.001$, for demographic vitality, INLC and educational support respectively. There was also a significant INLC by educational support interaction, $F(1, 529) = 9.685$, $p < 0.01$. As can be observed in Figure 13.3 and Table 13.2 D, high educational support in French when INLC in French was low did not seem to hamper English cognitive-academic proficiency significantly. However, when INLC in French was high, less educational support in French was related to better English cognitive-academic skills.

Beliefs

The graphic results for personal and general beliefs in L1 and L2 are presented in Figure 13.4. As can be observed, personal beliefs are especially affected by the degree of educational support. The effects of language of instruction and school ambience seem decisive on whether the student will have stronger personal beliefs towards French or towards English. For L1 personal beliefs, covariates did not reach statistical significance, nor did the effect of demographic vitality. Both INLC and educational support, however, were highly significant, $F(1, 536) = 39.170$, $p < 0.001$ and $F(1, 536) = 51.487$, $p < 0.001$, respectively. The demographic vitality by educational support interaction is very close to statistical significance, $F(1, 536) = 3.451$, $p = 0.064$. There was a tendency for educational support to compensate for low demographic vitality in the promotion of L1 personal beliefs (see Table 13.2, E).

For L2 personal beliefs, the covariates and the main effect of demographic vitality were again non-significant. However, a low L1 INLC, $F(1, 536) = 11.804$, $p < 0.01$, and especially a low L1 educational support, $F(1, 536) = 66.433$, $p < 0.001$, were related to strong L2 personal beliefs. None of the interactions reached statistical significance.

The patterns of effects for general beliefs and personal beliefs were different. For L1 general beliefs, the stronger effect came from demographic vitality: high L1 demographic vitality was related to stronger L1 general beliefs, $F(1, 536) = 78.168$, $p < 0.001$. The main effects of INLC and educational support were also significant. A stronger INLC in L1 was related to stronger L1 general beliefs, $F(1, 536) = 5.479$, $p < 0.05$, but high educational support in L1 was related to lower L1 general beliefs, $F(1, 536) = 12.223$, $p < 0.01$. This effect occurs when results are adjusted for covariates and other independent variables. There were no significant interactions and the covariates were also not statistically significant.

A similar pattern is observed in the L2 general beliefs results. The main effect of demographic vitality was highly significant, $F(1, 536) = 31.878$, $p < 0.001$. The lower the L1 demographic vitality, the stronger were the L2 general beliefs, the higher the L2 group vitality was perceived to be. A weak INLC in L1 also tended to be related to strong L2 general beliefs, but this trend was not statistically significant, $F(1, 536) = 2.892$, $p = 0.09$. The main effect of educational support was statistically significant, $F(1, 536) = 7.069$, $p < 0.01$, but similarly to L1 general beliefs, the language of instruction was related to general beliefs in the other language: high educational support in L1 seemed to favour stronger L2 general beliefs. There was also a significant educational support by demographic vitality interaction, $F(1, 536) = 6.747$, $p < 0.05$. The lower the demographic vitality, the more educational support in L1 favoured

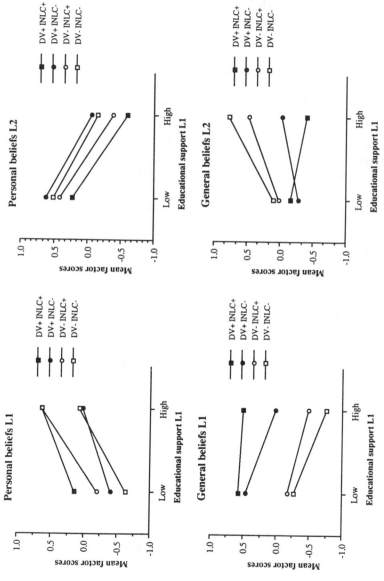

FIGURE 13.4 *Personal and general beliefs in L1 and L2 for low and high levels of L1 demographic vitality (DV), INLC and educational support*

L2 general beliefs (see Table 13.2, F). The INLC by educational support interaction also showed a similar pattern of effect but it did not quite reach the 0.05 level of significance, $F(1, 536) = 3.265$, $p = 0.071$ (see Table 13.2, F). The effect of non-verbal IQ as a covariate was not statistically significant but the effect of SES was very close to statistical significance, $F(1, 536) = 3.636$, $p = 0.057$.

Ethnolinguistic identity

Graphic results for francophone and anglophone identity are presented in Figure 13.5. As can be seen, francophone identity was stronger than anglophone identity for most subjects. For francophone identity, all three main effects were statistically significant: high L1 demographic vitality, a strong INLC in L1 and high educational support in L1 were positively related to a stronger francophone identity, $F(1,530) = 4.609$, $p < 0.05$; $F(1, 530) = 20.679$, $p < 0.001$; $F(1, 530) = 21.568$, $p < 0.001$, respectively. Covariates and interactions did not reach statistical significance.

For the anglophone identity scores, only two of the main effects were statistically significant. When adjusted for main effects and covariates, the effect of demographic vitality was not statistically significant. However, both a weak INLC in L1 and low educational support in L1 were related to a stronger anglophone identity, $F(1, 527) = 11.121$, $p < 0.01$ and $F(1, 527) = 14.120$, $P < 0.001$, respectively. None of the interactions and none of the covariates were statistically significant.

Language variety

Subjects were asked to rate their vernacular mother tongue on a linguistic continuum ranging from 1 to 7, a high score indicating that the language variety spoken was rated as close to the linguistic norms of standard French. It was hypothesised that high L1 demographic vitality, a strong INLC in L1 and high educational support in L1 would contribute to less interference from L2 (i.e. a lesser degree of language mixing). These hypotheses seem to be supported by the data (see Figure 13.6). Higher language variety scores were found when demographic vitality, INLC and educational support in L1 were high. The effects of INLC and educational support were highly significant, $F(1, 466) = 24.245$, $p < 0.001$ and $F(1, 466) = 12.582$, $p < 0.001$, respectively, but the effect of demographic vitality was only close to statistical significance, $F(1, 466) = 3.305$, $p = 0.070$). There was, however, a statistically significant INLC by educational support interaction, $F(1, 466) = 5.328$, $p < 0.05$. The effect of educational support in L1 was not as strong when INLC scores

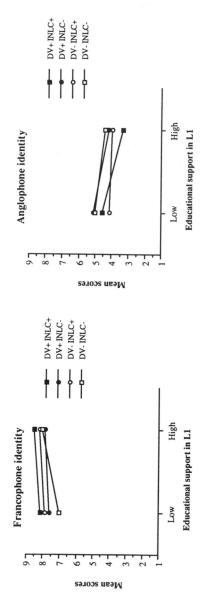

FIGURE 13.5 *Francophone and anglophone identity for low and high levels of L1 demographic vitality (DV), INLC and educational support*

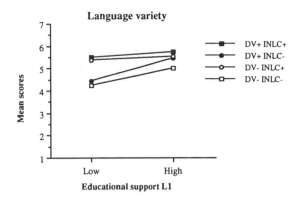

FIGURE 13.6 *Language variety for low and high levels of L1 demographic vitality (DV), INLC and educational support*

in L1 were high; in other words, when subjects already had a strong L1 language network, the degree of educational support in French was less related to language variety than when the INLC in L1 was weak. Under the condition of low educational support in French, the variety of French spoken was more heavily influenced by the English language when the INLC in French was weaker (see Table 13.2 G).

Language behaviour

The language behaviour profiles for both L1 and L2 are presented in Figure 13.7. Generally, the francophone minority students spoke French more frequently than English but again, all three independent variables were positively related to both L1 and L2 behaviours. Language behaviour in L1 was significantly related to high L1 demographic vitality, $F(1, 536) = 31.452$, $p < 0.001$, to a strong INLC in L1, $F(1, 536) = 82.866$, $p < 0.001$, and to strong educational support in L1, $F(1, 536) = 31.850$, $p < 0.001$. There were no significant interactions but there was a significant effect of non-verbal IQ as a covariate, $F(1, 536) = 7.200$, $p < 0.01$. Language behaviour in L2 was negatively related to L1 demographic vitality, $F(1, 533) = 21.150$, $p < 0.001$, to the strength of the INLC in L1, $F(1, 533) = 26.297$, $p < 0.001$, and to the degree of educational support in L1, $F(1, 533) = 60.978$, $p < 0.001$. The effects of the covariates were not statistically significant but there was a significant INLC by educational support interaction, $F(1, 533) = 6.724$, $p < 0.05$. Although a strong INLC in French was related to a lower degree of use of English, this effect was stronger when educational support in French was high than when it was low (see Table 13.2, H).

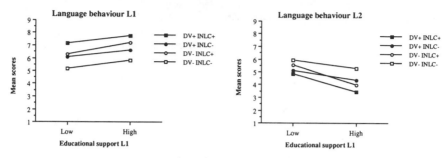

FIGURE 13.7 *Language behaviour in L1 and L2 for low and high levels of L1 demographic vitality (DV), INLC and educational support*

Discussion and Conclusion

Francophone minorities in Eastern Canada are among the most protected linguistic minorities in North America. Some gains in educational rights have been made by these minority groups (Foucher, 1985, 1988) and they seem to possess some of the 'empowering' factors (Cummins, 1986) that lead to ethnolinguistic vitality and additive bilingualism. Yet, the subtractive effects of the bilingual experience are still evident. These effects seem to be due to the factors identified by the macroscopic model of bilingual development presented in this chapter. Lack of vitality at the sociological level leads to a lower INLC (including educational support) and this lack of vitality in the different aspects of an individual's network of linguistic contacts is related to a lower level of competence and a weaker affective disposition towards the language. These effects at the psychological level are in turn related to less use of the language (Landry & Allard, 1987c).

In the present research, the intent was to look more closely at the relative impact of educational support as an agent of additive bilingualism. It was hypothesised that educational support in L1 would be more crucial for the promotion of additive bilingualism if the vitality of L1 was otherwise weak. It could be argued, however, that a linguistic minority (even a relatively strong one) will always be at risk if not educated in its own language (Landry & Allard, 1987a, 1987b; Cummins, 1986; Skutnabb-Kangas, 1983; Hamers & Blanc, 1983). But, as emphasised in the present model and as shown by other research (Mougeon & Canale, 1980; Mougeon & Heller, 1986), the school is not the only factor that favours language development. According to the 'counterbalance model' (Landry & Allard, 1987a, 1987b), the school is an essential contributor to additive bilingualism. Alone, however, it cannot fully compensate for the lack of linguistic vitality at the sociological level or for low levels of linguistic contacts in the family or the social milieu. The above hypotheses seem to be clearly supported by the present results.[3]

Communicative competence in L1 was positively related to demographic vitality and to INLC but not to educational support. This finding supports the model's hypothesis that L1 communicative competence is more strongly related to the network of interpersonal contacts than to educational support. The findings do indicate, however, that educational support is positively related to L1 communicative competence when L1 demographic vitality is low. In conditions of low ethnolinguistic vitality, therefore, schooling in L1 would be an important factor contributing to the promotion of communicative competence in L1.

Low L1 conditions in demographic vitality, INLC and educational support were related to stronger communicative competence scores in L2. In the theoretical model, it is hypothesised that when ethnolinguistic vitality and INLC favour L2 in a minority situation, schooling in the second language is not necessary for L2 communicative competence to develop. In that minority situation, communicative competence in L2 is favoured by the general social network. In the present study, this hypothesis was supported by a significant INLC by educational support interaction. Schooling in French was related to a lower level of communicative competence in English only when INLC in French was high.

The model also hypothesises that, in conditions of low ethnolinguistic vitality, schooling in L1 should contribute to a stronger cognitive-academic linguistic proficiency in L1. Furthermore, with regular second language courses, a relatively high level of L2 cognitive-academic linguistic proficiency is possible due to strong L1–L2 cognitive transfer (Cummins, 1984, 1981, 1979). This hypothesis was clearly supported. The three independent variables of demographic vitality, INLC and educational support were positively related to L1 cognitive-academic proficiency, but lower educational support in L1 was found to be less detrimental when L1 demographic vitality was high. Although the same three independent variables were negatively related to L2 cognitive-academic linguistic proficiency, when INLC in L1 was low, stronger educational support in L2 did not have a strong influence on cognitive-academic scores in L2. These results are similar to those of Hébert *et al.* (1976) who found that when minority francophones in Manitoba were schooled in French, their second language achievement scores were as good as those of French minority students schooled predominantly in English.

The role of the school was also found to be important in the promotion of strong personal beliefs in L1. Strong educational support in L1 tended to compensate for low L1 demographic vitality; in other words, the effect of schooling in the mother tongue tended to be stronger when French demographic vitality was lower. A strong INLC in L1 was also found to have an important influence on L1 personal beliefs. Inversely, low educational support in one's mother tongue paired with a weak INLC in L1 was significantly related to stronger L2 personal beliefs. Interestingly, personal beliefs did not seem to depend as much on demographic vitality as on the network of linguistic contacts experienced by the individual either through the educational system or through other social contacts.

Schooling had an interesting effect on the promotion of general beliefs. It is as if the experience of being educated in one's mother tongue led to a greater sensitivity to the vitality of the dominant group while at the same time contributing to a greater willingness to maintain the vitality of one's language (i.e. personal beliefs). This sensitivity to the dominant group's vitality favoured by educational support in L1 was more evident under conditions of low L1 demographic vitality. It is also interesting to note that, as should be expected, general beliefs were more dependent on demographic vitality than were personal beliefs.

Francophone and anglophone identity were also affected by the three independent variables. As was the case for personal beliefs, the effect was stronger for INLC and educational support, which reflect more directly on the personal linguistic experiences of the individual, than it was for demographic vitality whose influence is less direct. A very similar effect was found for the promotion of the standard variety of French; for the latter, educational support was found to be even more important if the INLC in L1 was low.

The contribution of L1 schooling was again evident when data on language behaviour was analysed. The importance of educational support in L1 was found to be greater when the INLC in L1 was low. Being schooled less in L1 was found to favour greater overall use of L2 even when INLC in L1 was high.

The results analysed in this chapter clearly show the importance of strong educational support in L1 for minority groups. Educational support in one's mother tongue seems to favour all aspects of additive bilingualism as defined in the present model. As already stated, additive bilingualism is more than linguistic competence: it encompasses the cognitive, affective and behavioural aspects of language experience. Restricting the definition of additive bilingualism could seriously hamper the full comprehension of linguistic assimilation in minority groups.

Notes

1. The present research was funded by the Secretary of State of the federal government of Canada and by the Department of Education, francophone division, of the Province of New Brunswick. We gratefully acknowledge their support. We also thank the grade 12 students and the school authorities who made the research possible by their active collaboration and participation.
2. A large-scale study has been undertaken to test the predictive validity of this model (Landry & Allard, 1987b). This study involved several groups of anglophone and francophone grade 12 students from the Maritime provinces and the province of Quebec in Canada. In the present chapter, we analyse the results for only the minority francophone groups involved in the study; other aspects of this study have been presented elsewhere (Allard & Landry, 1987b in press; Landry & Allard, 1987c in press). These analyses have provided empirical support to the predictive and construct validity of the model.
3. It could be argued that the results reported may have been influenced by uncontrolled variables or inter-provincial differences. The proposed model identifies several sources of ethnolinguistic vitality that were not controlled in the study (i.e. economic, political and cultural resources). Only demographic vitality was accounted for in the results reported. However, to be of relevance to bilingual development, uncontrolled variables would need to affect the network of linguistic contacts of the individuals. Since the latter was extensively measured and analysed in the present study, most ethnolinguistic vitality factors which could have affected bilingual development would have been indirectly controlled through INLC measures.

References

ALLARD, R. and LANDRY, R. 1986, Subjective ethnolinguistic vitality viewed as a belief system. *Journal of Multilingual and Multicultural Development* 7, 1–12.
— 1987a, Étude des relations entre les croyances envers la vitalité ethnolinguistique et comportement langagier en milieu minoritaire francophones. In R. THÉBERGE and J. LAFONTANT (eds) *Demain, la francophonie en milieu minoritaire*. Winnipeg: Centre de recherche du Collège de Saint-Boniface.
— 1987b, Contact des langues, vitalité ethnolinguistique subjective et comportement ethnolangagier. Paper presented at the Conference 'Contacts des langues: Quels modèles?', Nice, France.
— in press, Ethnolinguistic vitality beliefs and language maintenance and loss.

In W. FASE, K. JASPAERT and S. KROOM (eds) *Maintenance and Loss of Minority Languages*. Amsterdam: Benjamins.

ALLARDT, E. 1984, What constitutes a language minority? *Journal of Multilingual and Multicultural Development* 5, 193–205.

BENNETT, G.K., SEASHORE, H.G. and WESMAN, A.G. 1974, *Differential Aptitude Tests, Forms S and T* (5th edn). New York: Psychological Corporation.

BIBEAU, G. 1982, *L'éducation bilingue en Amérique du Nord*. Montréal: Guérin.

BLANC, M. 1987, Introduction. In M. BLANC and J. HAMERS (eds) *Theoretical and Methodological Issues on the Study of Languages/Dialects in Contact at Macro and Micro-logical Levels of Analysis*. Québec: International Center for Research on Bilingualism.

BLANC, M., CLÉMENT, R., DESHAIES, D. and HAMERS, J. 1984, Réseaux de communication. In A. PRUJINER *et al.*, *Variation du comportement langagier lorsque deux langues sont en contact*. Québec: Centre international de recherches sur le bilinguisme.

BLANC, M. and HAMERS J. 1987, *Problèmes théoriques et méthodologiques dans l'étude des langues/dialectes en contact aux niveaux macrologique et micrologique*. Québec: Centre international de recherches sur le bilinguisme.

BLISHEN, B.R. and MCROBERTS, H.A. 1976, A revised socioeconomic index for occupations in Canada. *Canadian Review of Sociology and Anthropology* 13, 71–9.

BOURDIEU, P. 1980, *La distinction*. Paris: Editions de Minuit.

BRETON, R. 1964, Institutional completeness of ethnic communities and the personal relations of immigrants. *American Journal of Sociology* 70, 193–205.

CARROLL, J.R. 1973, Implications of aptitude test research and psycholinguistic theory for foreign language teaching. *International Journal of Psycholinguistics* 2, 5–14.

CUMMINS, J. 1976, The influence of bilingualism on cognitive growth: A synthesis of research findings and explanatory hypotheses. *Working Papers on Bilingualism* 9, 1–43.

— 1978, Educational implications of mother tongue maintenance in minority-language groups. *Canadian Modern Language Review* 34, 395–416.

— 1979, Linguistic interdependence and the educational development of bilingual children. *Review of Educational Research* 49, 222–51.

— 1981, The role of primary language development in promoting educational success for language minority students. In CALIFORNIA STATE DEPARTMENT OF EDUCATION (ed.) *Schooling and Language Minority Students: A Theoretical Framework*. Los Angeles: Evaluation, Assessment and Dissemination Center.

— 1983, Language proficiency, bilateracy and French immersion. *Canadian Journal of Education* 8, 117–38.

— 1984, *Bilingualism and Special Education: Issues in Assessment and Pedagogy*. Clevedon, England: Multilingual Matters.

— 1986, Empowering minority students: A framework for intervention. *Harvard Educational Review* 56, 18–36.

CUMMINS, J. and MULCAHY, R. 1978, Orientation to language in Ukrainian–English bilingual children. *Child Development* 49, 1239–42.

CUMMINS, J. and SWAIN, M. 1986, *Bilingualism in Education*. London: Longman.

DEROSNAY, J. 1975, *Le macroscope: vers une vision globale*. Paris: Editions du Seuil.

DE VRIES, J. 1984, Factors affecting the survival of minorities: A preliminary comparative analysis of data for Western Europe. *Journal of Multilingual and Multicultural Development* 5, 207–16.

EDWARDS, J. 1985, *Language, Society and Identity*. Oxford: Basil Blackwell.

FOUCHER, P. 1985, *Les droits scolaires constitutionnels des minorités de langue officielle au Canada*. Ottawa: Conseil Canadien de documentation juridique.

— 1988, Six ans après: L'article 23 de la charte et les tribunaux. Presentation to the Bureau du Commissaire aux langues officielles et à l'Association Bugnet, Montréal, April.

GAUDET, A. 1986, *Colloque sur l'école acadienne*. Moncton: Association Acadienne pour l'administration de l'éducation.

GENESEE, F. 1976, The role of intelligence in second language learning. *Language Learning* 26, 267–80.

— 1978, Individual differences in second language learning. *Canadian Modern Language Review* 34, 490–504.

— 1983, Bilingual education of majority language children: The immersion experiments in review. *Applied Linguistics* 4, 1–46.

— 1987, *Learning Through Two Languages*. Rowley, MA: Newbury House.

GILES, H., BOURHIS, R.Y. and TAYLOR, D.M. 1977, Toward a theory of language in ethnic group relations. In H. GILES (ed.) *Language, Ethnicity and Intergroup Relations*. New York: Academic Press.

HAMERS, J. 1987, The relevance of social network analysis in the psycholinguistic investigation of multilingual behavior. In M. BLANC and J. HAMERS (eds) *Problèmes théoriques et méthodologiques dans l'étude des langues/dialectes en contact aux niveaux macrologique et micrologique*. Québec: Centre international de recherches sur le bilinguisme.

HAMERS, J. and BLANC, M. 1983, *Bilingualité et bilinguisme*. Brussels: Mardaga.

HARLEY, B. 1984, Mais apprennent-ils vraiment le français? *Langue et société* 12 (winter), 57–62.

HÉBERT, R. *et al.* 1976, *Rendement académique et langue d'enseignement chez les élèves franco-manitobains*. Saint-Boniface, Manitoba: Centre de recherches du Collège universitaire Saint-Boniface.

KRASHEN, S.D. 1981, Bilingual education and second language acquisition. In CALIFORNIA STATE DEPARTMENT OF EDUCATION (ed.) *Schooling and Language Minority Students: A Theoretical Framework*. Los Angeles: Evaluation, Assessment and Dissemination Center.

KREITLER, H. and KREITLER, S. 1972, The model of cognitive orientation: Towards a theory of human behavior. *British Journal of Psychology* 63(1), 9–30.

— 1976, *Cognitive Orientation and Behavior*. New York: Springer.

— 1982, The theory of cognitive orientation: Widening the scope of behavior prediction. In B. MAHER and W. MAHER (eds) *Progress in Experimental Personality Research, II*. New York: Academic Press.

LAMBERT, W.E. 1975, Culture and language as factors in learning and education. In A. WOLFGANG (ed.), *Education of Immigrant Students*. Toronto: Ontario Institute for Studies in Education.

LAMBERT, W.E. and TUCKER, G.R. 1972, *Bilingual Education of Children: The St Lambert Experiment*. Rowley, MA: Newbury House.

LANDRY, R. 1979, Caractéristiques des gradués d'une polyvalente francophone dans un milieu minoritaire. *Revue de l'Association canadienne d'éducation de langue française* 8(2), 8–21.

— 1981, Les Acadiens sont-ils des semilingues? *Revue de l'Université de Moncton* 14(1), 9–42.
— 1982, Le bilinguisme additif chez les francophones minoritaires du Canada. *Revue des sciences de l'éducation* 8, 223–44.
— 1984, Bilinguisme additif et bilinguisme soustractif. In A. PRUJINER *et al.*, *Variation du comportement langagier lorsque deux langues sont en contact*. Québec: Centre international de recherches sur le bilinguisme.
— 1985, Trois formes de réductionisme en éducation. *Revue de l'Université de Moncton* 18, 2–37.
— 1987, Additive bilingualism, schooling and special education: A minority group perspective. *Canadian Journal for Exceptional Children* 3(4), 109–14.
LANDRY, R. and ALLARD, R. 1984, Bilinguisme additif, bilinguisme soustractif et identité ethnolinguistique. *Recherches sociologiques* 15(2–3), 337–58.
— 1985, Choix de la langue d'enseignement: une analyse chez des parents francophones en milieu bilingue soustractif. *Revue canadienne des langues vivantes* 44, 480–500.
— 1987a, Développement bilingue en milieu minoritaire et en milieu majoritaire. In L. PÉRONNET (ed.) *L'école contribue-t-elle à maintenir la vitalité d'une langue minoritaire?* Moncton: Centre de recherche en linguistique appliquée.
— 1987b, Etude du développement bilingue chez les Acadiens des provinces Maritimes. In R. THÉBERGE and J. LAFONTANT (eds) *Demain, la francophonie en milieu minoritaire*. Winnipeg: Centre de recherche du Collège de Saint-Boniface.
— 1987c, Contact des langues et développement bilingue: Un modèle macroscopique. Paper presented at the Conference 'Contact des langues: Quels modèles?' Nice, France.
— in press, Ethnolinguistic vitality and the bilingual development of minority and majority students. In W. FASE, K. JASPAERT and S. KROON (eds) *Maintenance and Loss of Minority Languages*. Amsterdam: Benjamins.
McLAUGHLIN, B. 1984, Early bilingualism: Methodological and theoretical issues. In M. PARADIS and Y. LEBRUN (eds) *Early Bilingualism and Child Development*. Lisse: Swets & Zeitlinger.
MILROY, L. 1980, *Language and Social Networks*. Oxford: Blackwell.
MILROY, L. and MARGRAIN, S. 1980, Vernacular language loyalty and social network. *Language in Society* 3, 43–70.
MOUGEON, R. and CANALE, M. 1980, Maintenance of French in Ontario: Is education in French enough? *Interchange* 9, 30–9.
MOUGEON, R. and HELLER, M. 1986, The social and historical context of minority French language education in Ontario. *Journal of Multilingual and Multicultural Development* 7, 199–227.
PAULSTON, C.B. 1980, *Bilingual Education: Theories and Issues*. Rowley, MA: Newbury House.
PELLERIN, M. and HAMMERLY, H. 1986, L'expression orale après treize ans d'immersion française. *Revue canadienne des langues vivantes* 42, 592–606.
PRUJINER, A. 1987, Eléments de réflexion sur l'analyse des aspects sociétaux des contacts des langues. In H. BLANC and J. HAMERS (eds) *Problèmes théoriques et méthodologiques dans l'étude des langues/dialectes en contact aux niveaux macrologiques et micrologiques*. Québec: Centre international de recherches sur le bilinguisme.
PRUJINER, A., DESHAIES, D., HAMERS, J.F., BLANC, M., CLÉMENT, R. and LANDRY,

R. 1984, *Variation du comportement langagier lorsque deux langues sont en contact*. Québec: Centre international de recherches sur le bilinguisme.

RESNICK, L.B. 1987, Learning in school and out. *Educational Researcher* 16(9), 13–20.

ROGERS, E.M. and KINCAID, L.D. 1981, *Communication Networks: Toward a New Paradigm for Research*. New York: Free Press.

SKUTNABB-KANGAS, T. 1983, *Bilingualism or Not: The Education of Minorities*. Clevedon, England: Multilingual Matters.

— 1984, Why aren't all children in the Nordic countries bilingual? *Journal of Multilingual and Multicultural Development* 5, 301–15.

SKUTNABB-KANGAS, T. and TOUKOMAA, P. 1976, *Teaching Migrant Children's Mother Tongue and Learning the Language of the Host Country in the Context of the Socio-Cultural Situation of the Migrant Family*. Helsinki: The Finnish National Commission for UNESCO.

SPSS Inc. 1986, *SPSS^x User's Guide, Edition 2*. New York, McGraw-Hill.

SWAIN, M. 1985, Communicative competence: Some roles of comprehensible input and comprehensible output in its development. In S. GASS and C. MADDEN (eds) *Input in Second Language Acquisition*. Rowley, MA: Newbury House.

SWAIN, M. and LAPKIN, S. 1982, *Evaluating Bilingual Education: A Canadian Case Study*. Clevedon, England: Multilingual Matters.

TAJFEL, H. 1974, Social identity and intergroup behaviour. *Social Science Information* 13, 65–93.

TOUKOMAA, P. and SKUTNABB-KANGAS, T. 1977, *The Intensive Teaching of the Mother Tongue to Migrant Children of the Pre-School Age and Children in the Lower Level of Comprehensive School*. Helsinki: The Finnish National Commission for UNESCO.

WILLIG, A.C. 1985, A meta-analysis of selected studies on the effectiveness of bilingual education. *Review of Educational Research* 55, 269–317.

14 The Acquisition of Some Oral Second Language Skills in Early and Late Immersion

BIRGIT HARLEY

Introduction

The study examines students' use of verbs in an oral interview setting. The verb system was selected as a focus for the study because it is known to be a particularly problematic area of French for second language learners; indeed, linguists such as Palmer have suggested that 'for almost any language, the part that concerns the verb is the most difficult' (Palmer, 1974). Hence an important aim of this study is to provide teachers with diagnostic feedback that will be helpful in pinpointing specific problems that students are having in their communicative use of the French verb system. At the same time, the study is designed to examine in depth the relationship between age and aspects of the acquisition of a second language in an immersion setting, an issue of theoretical as well as practical interest. The investigation concentrates on three main questions in relation to the oral communicative use of the verb system: (1) the relative proficiency of young early and older late immersion students after a similar number of hours of in-school exposure to French; (2) the eventual in-school attainment of early and late immersion students who had started acquiring French at different ages; and (3) the process of acquisition by older and younger learners. The following brief review of the age literature provides the background to these questions.

Age and Second Language Acquisition

The relationship between age and second language (L2) acquisition is an issue of obvious practical concern to educators. In order to provide the best possible conditions for language learning in school, we need to understand how maturational and environmental factors interact to promote L2 acquisition. Some of the issues that have been debated are as follows: Are there advantages to beginning L2 acquisition in early childhood, and if so, to what extent can they be attributed to biological factors (Lenneberg, 1967), cognitive stage of development (e.g. Felix, 1985; Krashen, 1975), affective predisposition (e.g. Schumann, 1975), opportunities for authentic communication (Macnamara, 1973; Swain, 1981), or amount of time available for learning (Carroll, 1975)? Are there risks attached to the early introduction of a second language in school? What is the relationship between L1 and L2 acquisition, and are there circumstances where early L2 education may encourage academic failure and L1 loss (Cummins, 1981a; Skutnabb-Kangas & Toukomaa, 1976)? How best can one facilitate the process of L2 acquisition at different ages? Is this process essentially the same for older and younger L2 learners or it is more 'natural' (i.e. closer to L1 acquisition) in children than in those who are past puberty (e.g. Felix, 1985; Lenneberg, 1967; Rosansky, 1975)?

Most theorists have argued that there is at least some potential advantage to a childhood start to L2 acquisition, but there is little consensus on the precise nature of such an advantage, or its fundamental causes. As Snow (1979) has pointed out, the essential issue is to determine the relative contribution of maturational and environmental factors in language acquisition, not to assume that either can be eliminated from consideration. In order to sort out the contribution of 'Nature' and 'Nurture' in L2 acquisition we need to examine the findings of empirical studies of age-related differences in a wide variety of settings, and under different learning and testing conditions.

Most empirical studies of the relationship between age and second language acquisition have been concerned with the issue of success in mastering the L2. To make sense of the existing research findings and determine what further studies are needed, it is useful to view the research in the light of a number of distinctions that have been proposed: whether a study deals with initial rate of acquisition or eventual attainment (Krashen, Long & Scarcella, 1979); whether the assessment of success is based on academic (cognitively demanding and context-reduced) language tasks, or on conversational (cognitively undemanding and context-embedded) types of tasks (Cummins, 1983); whether what is at stake is absolute L2 proficiency or proficiency relative to native-speaker age norms (Cummins, 1981b); and whether the L2 is being acquired in a minority (usually immigrant) or majority L1 (usually classroom) setting.

When such distinctions are taken into account, patterns of findings emerge.

It appears, for example, that more mature, educated older learners in both minority and majority contexts tend to make more rapid initial progress on academic types of L2 tasks than do younger, less mature learners (e.g. Burstall *et al.*, 1974; Cummins, 1981b).[1] Typically, we may note, it is academic rather than communicative types of tasks that have been used in such age comparisons. In majority classroom contexts for L2 learning, it has been found, moreover, that an early start to an L2 programme does not necessarily produce any long-term advantage on academic types of tasks (e.g. Burstall *et al.*, 1974; Oller & Nagato, 1974). Taken together, these findings suggest that cognitive maturity, far from being a disadvantage, may be a positive advantage for certain aspects of L2 acquisition, and that time, *per se*, is no guarantee of greater success.

Does this mean that, contrary to the various theoretical arguments proposed in favour of an early start, there is no particular advantage to L2 acquisition in childhood? While some have arrived at this conclusion (e.g. Burstall *et al.*, 1974), there is evidence from minority settings to indicate that younger learners are more likely in the long run to be native-like on some listening and speaking skills assessed in more communicative contexts (e.g. Oyama, 1978; Patkowski, 1980; Seliger, Krashen & Ladefoged, 1975). It is not clear, however, how Nature and Nurture have interacted to produce these results. At least some advantage on such skills has also emerged in the eventual in-school attainment of classroom learners who started early (e.g. Burstall *et al.*, 1974; Swain & Lapkin, 1986) and it has been argued that changes to the environmental conditions provided might lead to more advantages for an early start (e.g. Genesee, 1987; Stern, 1976; Swain & Lapkin, 1986).

The findings with respect to communicatively oriented listening and speaking tasks have to be considered in relation to other findings on academic achievement and L1 maintenance. In some minority contexts, for example, early schooling in the L2 has been associated with low academic achievement and lack of L1 development, leading to the argument that, for such minority students who have little support for full L1 development in the environment, early schooling in the L1 may be beneficial (Cummins, 1983; Skutnabb-Kangas & Toukomaa, 1976). For majority students, on the other hand, there is no evidence that a long-term disadvantage in academic achievement or in L1 skills is associated with an early start to L2 acquisition (e.g. Burstall *et al.*, 1974), even when schooling takes place in the L2 under immersion conditions

(Genesee, 1987; Harley, Hart & Lapkin, 1986; Swain & Lapkin, 1982). The minority findings, however, point to the importance of not considering L2 acquisition in isolation from L1 acquisition.

While most empirical studies have been concerned with the relative L2 success of older and younger learners, a few have also investigated the issue of the acquisition process. Based on studies investigating the relative accuracy of grammatical morphemes produced by older and younger learners in the L2 and the kinds of errors made by children (in L1 or L2) and by older L2 learners (e.g. Bailey, Madden & Krashen, 1974; Cook, 1973; Fathman, 1975), there has been no evidence to show that the process of acquisition is actually different, or any less natural, among older learners than it is among younger learners. These findings have been interpreted as an indication that L2 learners of different ages have access to the same internal language acquisition capacities. However, such comparative studies of the acquisition process in different age groups have been restricted to learners in minority contexts rather than majority L1 classroom settings for L2 acquisition.

In the present study, the questions of relative success and process of acquisition in older and younger L2 learners are taken up afresh at a more detailed level of analysis. For the purposes of interpretation, it appears necessary to consider not only whether there are proficiency differences between age groups, but more precisely what the actual differences are. The study deals with students who are in an innovative type of L2 programme set in a majority L1 context for L2 acquisition, which is of considerable interest to educators because of the strong emphasis on communicative use of the second language within the classroom context. Of major concern in the investigation is the issue of whether older learners maintain the apparent advantage previously found on academic types of language tasks when the assessment focuses on morphology and syntax in a more communicative, context-embedded type of task (a face-to-face conversational interview). A further concern is the precise nature of any long-term advantages that emerge for those who have an early start. Given the previous findings that early immersion students suffer no long-term adverse effects on academic achievement and L1 skills, it may be assumed that, in this majority context, any eventual advantages in L2 skills for younger beginners can be considered additive in nature.

The Empirical Study

For the study, interviews with five groups of students were conducted, with 12 students in each of the groups. Three of the groups consisted of L2 learners in French immersion programmes: (1) a group of early immersion students in grade 1, (2) a group of late immersion students in grades 9 and 10, and (3) a second group of early immersion students in grades 9 and 10. Groups (1) and (2) were of different ages but had had the same number of in-class hours of exposure to French, while groups (2) and (3) were at the same age, but had had differing amounts of L2 exposure (greater for group (3)). In addition to the three immersion groups, two reference groups of native French speakers attending grades 1 and 10 in Quebec schools were included in the study. Further sample details are provided below in relation to the specific issues investigated.

The individual interviews were conducted by two native French-speaking Canadian young women, both of whom had had immersion teaching experience but were unfamiliar to the students in the study. The recorded interviews took place at school in a spare office or classroom and lasted approximately 30 minutes each. There were a series of questions that the interviewers were instructed to pose to students in the same way. These questions (see Appendix) provided contexts for the use of a variety of verbs and verb forms in the realisation of different semantic functions: for example, use of tenses to express time distinctions; the use of the *imparfait* to indicate incomplete or habitual past events; the expression of hypothetical events by means of the conditional; use of number agreement to distinguish singular and plural, and so on. The interview questions were, however, designed to focus students' attention on communicative content rather than the L2 code. Topics included favourite recipes, pastimes, personally experienced events, and the description of some humorous cartoons. Although there were set questions, the interviewers were encouraged to make the conversation as natural as possible by adding comments as appropriate. The interviews with native French speakers of comparable ages permitted verification of the validity of the questions in eliciting the anticipated verb forms. Scoring of the interviews was based on transcripts, with responses to different questions being scored for particular variables.

The findings of the study are summarised below in relation to each of the three main issues stated in the Introduction above. For a complete report of the study, the reader is referred to Harley (1986).

Proficiency after 1,000 hours of classroom exposure

The first question has to do with the amount of control of the target French verb system by the early and late immersion students after a similar number of hours of in-class exposure to French.

This question was investigated by comparing the interview performance of the group of 12 early immersion students near the end of their grade 1 year, with that of the matched group of 12 late immersion students in grades 9 and 10. At this stage, the students in both groups had had approximately 1,000 hours of classroom exposure to French. When interviewed, the early immersion students averaged 6;11 years of age; they had so far had a half-day kindergarten in French followed by full-day immersion in French in grade 1. The late immersion students were on average 15;4 years of age. They had started learning French in a 20-minute daily 'core' programme in grades 6 and 7, and had begun their immersion experience in grade 8 (i.e. about age 13) with 50 to 70% of the day in French. The early and late immersion groups each contained six boys and six girls and were selected from two programmes to be matched as closely as possible on additional variables such as socio-economic status (which was generally high), IQ, and exposure to French outside school.[2] Enrolment in both programmes was optional.

The findings indicated that after 1,000 hours of exposure to French in class, the older late immersion students were making significantly more use of some, though not all, features of the French verb system. Two of the three general areas where there were significant differences between the two age groups were primarily syntactic in nature: the older learners were more likely to mark number agreement in the verb, and they made greater use of a word order rule that involved placing pronoun complements in preverbal position — that is, in Subject-Object-Verb order. The third main area where the late immersion students scored higher than the early immersion students was in lexical variety: the older learners used a wider range of verb vocabulary in describing the cartoons than did the grade 1 students (see Table 14.1).

In the domains of time, aspect, and hypothetical modality, however, there were no significant differences found between the two age groups on the features that were studied; thus the early immersion students were just as likely as the late immersion students to use present, past or future forms in contexts where such forms were regularly used by native speakers to locate events in time. At the same time, the two immersion groups were alike in their non-use of the *imparfait* to mark past events in progress

TABLE 14.1 *Some significant differences between grade 1 early immersion (EI) and grade 9/10 late immersion (LI) groups*

Item	Context for scoring	Median scores		Signif.[a]
		EI %	LI %[b]	
2nd person plural	Q.40	0	61.1	0.01
2nd person polite	Q.11	7.1	70.0	0.05
3rd person plural	Qs.29,30,32,33	1.2	30.0	0.05
Pronominal verbs[c]	Qs. 9,10,12	3.3	65.3	0.01
SOV order (excl. pronom. verbs)	Qs. 5,9,10,12, 31,33	0.5	10.3	0.05
Lexical variety	Qs.9,10,29,30, 31,32,33	20.0[d]	27.5[d]	0.01

[a] Based on Mann-Whitney U Test, 2-tailed significance.
[b] Percentage scores are based on number of items produced in contexts for the relevant items.
[c] E.g. Il *se réveille*.
[d] Number of different lexical verbs used in describing cartoons.

or habitual past, and in their apparent inability to express the notion of the hypothetical via the conditional verb form.

As might be expected, after 1,000 hours of exposure to French, both the late and the early immersion students differed significantly, on almost all the features that were examined, from the native French-speaking age reference groups that were also included in the study. These groups were comparable in average age and socio-economic background to the immersion groups. They each included six boys and six girls, and the average IQ was 111.2 for the grade 1 native speakers and 110 for the grade 10 native speakers (Epreuve d'Habileté Mentale Otis-Lennon).

How do we account for the fact that the late immersion students were ahead of the early immersion students specifically in number agreement, preverbal placement of pronoun complements, and lexical variety? An interaction of maturational and environmental factors may be proposed. One important factor to consider is the kind of L2 experience that the older and younger learners have had. There are three things to note about the late immersion students: (1) they have been exposed to a considerable amount of written French; (2) they have been using audiolingual-style second language texts; and (3) they have been focusing on academic subject-matter such as geography and history that deals with non-immediate topics demanding a wide range of vocabulary. In contrast the early immersion students' L2 experience has been mainly oral since they are only beginning readers at the grade 1 level, and in keeping with their level of maturity the curriculum is firmly rooted in the immediate classroom context and experiences of the students. It makes sense to argue that their relative cognitive maturity — and familiarity with more concepts — interacts with the input that the late immersion students have received to promote acquisition of a larger vocabulary than that of the younger early immersion students. Indeed a significant difference ($p < 0.05$) was also found between the older (median $= 37.5$) and younger (median $= 33$) *native speakers* in lexical variety.

But what about number agreement and the placement of pronoun complements? With respect to number distinctions, one relevant factor may be that written French clearly indicates number agreement in the verb, even when singular and plural forms sound the same in spoken French (e.g. 'le(s) garçon(s) *joue(nt)* au football'). The regularity with which singular and plural verb forms are distinguished in written French would most likely help to draw attention to such distinctions in general. By means of their audiolingual second language texts, which focus heavily at first on the present tense, the late immersion students have also been provided with numerous opportunities to learn and practise such number distinctions. In other words, this may be a case where a rule that is relatively simple to 'learn' consciously in Krashen's (1981) sense may actually have helped subconscious 'acquisition'. The same kinds of observations can be made about preverbal pronoun complements. Such pronouns may sometimes be omitted in spoken French (e.g. 'Est-ce que tu aimes les fraises?' — 'oui, *j'aime bien*', instead of 'je *les* aime bien'), and in the third person may be virtually assimilated in oral discourse (e.g. the object pronoun in *il l'a vu* is scarcely discernible). In written French, however, they are always visibly 'there' to the eye. Such pronouns are also much featured in the second language texts which the late immersion students have been using.

Obviously the written input which the late immersion students have had is at least partly dependent on their relative cognitive maturity and experience in literacy. As noted earlier, the grade 1 early immersion students' L2 experience has naturally been mainly oral in nature. From an educational perspective, it is important to recognise that some grammatical distinctions may not occur with great frequency in natural oral communication, and indeed may often not be particularly important for getting one's message across. Thus when we say 'nos amis *viennent* chez nous ce soir' the information 'plural' is already available in the possessive *nos* and expressed only secondarily in the verb form *viennent*. It is interesting to note that the grade 1 native French speakers, who like the early immersion students had had little exposure to written French, also made occasional number agreement errors in the third person plural. This was, in fact, the only item on which there was a significant difference in percentage terms between the grade 1 (median = 98.8%) and grade 10 (median = 100%) native speakers.

These findings suggest that in French, number agreement in the verb is hard to acquire from natural oral input even for native speakers, and that in the context of an immersion programme, it may be that special opportunities need to be created for students to practise using such distinctions where they matter for conveying contrasts in meaning.

Eventual in-school attainment

We cannot assume that over time, early immersion students will automatically improve beyond the late immersion students (who were still a long way from native-like in the extent to which they were using number distinctions and clitic pronouns). The second question investigated in this study was how the eventual in-school attainment of early immersion students compared with that of late immersion students. This question was examined by comparing the interview performance of the same 12 late immersion students with that of another group of 12 early *partial* immersion students who had reached the grade 9/10 level. This group of students, also matched as closely as possible to the late immersion group, had had a 50% immersion programme from grade 1 on.[3] These early partial immersion students were significantly ahead of the late immersion students in range of vocabulary, and they tended to make greater use than the late immersion students of past time distinctions (Table 14.2). They also did significantly better than the late immersion students on a repétition task involving a range of verb forms. (See Harley, 1986, for details.) However, in the interview setting they were not significantly ahead of the late immersion students in the area of number distinctions, or in their use of preverbal pronoun complements, despite the considerably greater exposure to the second language that they had had. And like the late immersion students, they had also made minimal progress in expressing aspectual distinctions in the past via the *imparfait*, or in expressing hypothetical modality by means of the conditional.

Several complementary reasons could be put forward to explain why

TABLE 14.2 *Some interview scores of grade 9/10 early partial immersion (PI) and grade 9/10 late immersion (LI) groups*

Item	Context for scoring	Median scores		Signif.[a]
		PI	LI	
Past	Qs.14,22,23,34/35	41.9%[b]	21.3%	n.s.
Lexical variety[c]	Qs.9,10,29,30, 31,32,33	34.0	27.5	0.05

[a] Based on Mann-Whitney U Test, 2-tailed significance.
[b] Percentage scores are based on number of items produced in contexts for past time.
[c] Number of different lexical verbs used in describing cartoons.

the partial immersion students, despite their substantially greater exposure to French, had not made greater progress than the late immersion students in more areas of the verb system. One possible factor is that, given their social isolation from native speakers, they lacked motivation to make further progress in the second language once they had reached a level of communicative ability that was sufficient for their classroom needs. A second factor may once again be classroom experience. Over time the students, with input from each other, may develop a mutually intelligible and relatively stable classroom dialect, which differs in various respects from target language norms. It may be hypothesised that these students could have benefited from a greater focus on such apparent problem areas of French grammar as number, form and placement of pronoun complements, and the use of the *imparfait* and conditional.

However, one should not overemphasise the grammatical short-comings of the partial immersion students. Interestingly, the interviewer's impressions were that the early partial immersion students were in general more interesting to talk to, and seemed to be altogether more at ease in the interview situation than the late immersion students. This is an interesting area of research that could be followed up in further analysis of the interviews. The purpose of the present study, however, was to consider the acquisition of the target verb system from a diagnostic perspective, not to consider all aspects of the students' French proficiency.

Process of acquisition

The third question to be investigated in this study concerned the process of acquisition by the older late immersion and younger early immersion students. Did they appear to have the same relative difficulty with different features of the verb system? Were the errors they were making similar in nature, suggesting the same kind of approach to the acquisition of the system? These questions were investigated by a detailed analysis of the interviews with a subsample of six of the late immersion students and six of the grade 1 early total immersion students selected as representative of the range of proficiency in each group.

This analysis revealed some very similar patterns for each age group. One finding, for example, was that both early and late immersion students were invariably more accurate in their use of the present tense than in their use of the *passé composé* (conjugated with AVOIR) and almost invariably more accurate in their use of the *passé composé* than in their use of the future (ALLER + infinitive). This implicational pattern of present-past-future, which corresponds to a hypothesised universal hierarchy (Traugott, 1977), holds within the semantic domain of time distinctions for both groups. However, when another domain such as number distinctions is examined, one finds that it cannot be ordered in the same way for both groups relative to the time distinctions. Four of the late immersion students, for example, were more accurate on third person plural distinctions than they were in their use of the future, while none of the early immersion students was. However, within the semantic domain of number, as one would expect, there was an overwhelming trend towards more accurate use of unmarked singular forms relative to more marked plural forms in both age groups. Within semantic domains, then, these results suggest that both the older and younger students progress along similar paths, despite the input differences that have been noted in their programmes.

With respect to the kinds of errors that the students made, these tended also to be very similar across groups, although not every student made exactly the same error. At the same time, there was a trend in some instances for the early immersion students to make more of one kind of error and for the late immersion students to make more of another kind.

One example involves confusion in the present singular forms of the verbs ÊTRE and AVOIR. The form *est* was almost always used correctly in the third person singular of the verb ÊTRE, 'to be'. There are other uses of the same sound [e], however, which suggest that some students in both age groups are having a good deal of trouble sorting out the verbs ÊTRE and AVOIR ('to be' and 'to have' in English). There are two early immersion students, for example, who never produce forms such as *suis* (first person of ÊTRE) or *a* (third person of AVOIR) but use the same-sounding form [e] any time that either ÊTRE or AVOIR is required. One grade I student, explaining how she plays house with a friend, says, for example '[že] le bébé et mon amie *est* le maman' ([že] — *j'ai* (?) — instead of *je suis* meaning 'I *am* the baby'). The same child in another context says 'elle [e] juste un bras' (instead of 'elle n'a qu'un bras') meaning 'she *has* only one arm'. This sort of fusion of ÊTRE and AVOIR is a problem that is inherent in the French verb system, promoted by the homophony (or near-homophony depending on one's dialect of French) of the first person j'ai of AVOIR, and the second and third persons *tu es* and *il est* of ÊTRE. It is a problem that also arises to some extent for young children learning French as their mother tongue. For English speakers, the problem is compounded by the fact that there are circumstances where French requires AVOIR and English requires the verb TO BE (e.g. 'j'*ai* froid' is translatable by 'I *am* cold'). In other words, this is one of many cases where one can point to factors within the second language and to the students' mother tongue as combined sources of error.

At the risk of labouring the point, it may be suggested that differential L2 experience in the early and late immersion programmes can help to explain a lower incidence of errors in this area among the late immersion students. Written spelling distinctions between j'*ai* on the one hand, and tu *es* and il *est* on the other and an early emphasis in their second language texts on these two verbs have likely been helpful to the late immersion students. At the same time, it is possible that some kinds of routines that teachers are known to use in kindergarten and grade 1 may be contributing to the confusion of ÊTRE and AVOIR: for example, routines where the children are asked to recite their ages (j'ai cinq ans') where the student is probably, unbeknown to the teacher, identifying [že] with 'I am' as in English 'I am five years old'. (It might, in other words, be better to start with uses of AVOIR which correspond to HAVE in English.)

. The influence of written French and their L2 texts is not necessarily always positive for the late immersion students, however. One kind of error the late immersion students appeared to be making more often than the early immersion students was to use the present tense in obligatory contexts for past or future forms. While the early immersion students made as many errors, they tended to be more varied in nature — e.g. use of [prəne] (*prenez* or *prener*?) as a regularised first conjugation style of past participle for the verb PRENDRE, instead of *pris*. One reasonable explanation of this tendency on the part of the late immersion students is the long emphasis on present tense forms that characterises their second language texts. On other occasions the late immersion students appeared rather over-formal; they would use first person plural forms such as *nous allons* rather than conversational *on va*, or rather formal lexical items such as *placer* instead of the more usual *mettre*, 'to put'. In the same kinds of contexts we find native speakers and the early immersion students invariably using *on va* and *mettre*.

These examples do not suggest that the approach to second language acquisition is fundamentally different among the early or late immersion students, but rather that they have had somewhat different input on which to base their working hypotheses about how the verb system fits together. One finding, however, is more suggestive that the older students may have been taking a more analytic approach to the task of acquiring the French verb system. When their overall scores on the interview were rank ordered within each group, controlling for the effect of school class and outside exposure to French, it was found that there was a significant correlation of 0.62 between interview rank and verbal IQ scores among the 12 late immersion students, but no correlation (-0.02) was found in the grade 1 early immersion group. This suggests that for the older late immersion students, the kind of skills required for performance on an IQ test may have been more important for relative success in acquiring oral control of morphology and syntax in the second language than they have for the younger early immersion students.

Conclusion

In conclusion, it should be stressed that this study cannot be interpreted as a general assessment of the relative merits of early and late immersion. There are many considerations involved in this issue that have not been touched upon here (e.g. comprehension of academic content, willingness to participate in an immersion programme at different ages, etc.). Instead the purpose of this study was to compare the oral communicative control of a specific grammatical subsystem of the second language which is known to present continuing problems to second language learners. It is hoped that by comparing in detail the performance of groups with different programme backgrounds and starting points for L2 acquisition, it may be possible to establish more about the nature of the problems that students at different ages and stages encounter. It has been argued that, alongside their communicative experience in the L2, certain kinds of L2 input in the late immersion context (namely grammatically focused and written input), together with opportunities for practice, may have been conducive to the acquisition of particular features of the target verb system. This appears to be a profitable area for further research and experimentation among early classroom beginners as well (see e.g. Harley, 1989), in order to further clarify the weight that should be assigned to this kind of environmental factor *vis-à-vis* cognitive maturity and motivational considerations. The study has provided various indications that the English-speaking students of different ages pass through similar stages in their acquisition of different semantic domains in French. Thus, for educators, the important question that remains is how to promote this 'natural' course of development.

Notes

1. The finding that the academic L1 proficiency of older and younger school-aged learners is roughly equidistant from L2 native-speaker age norms (Cummins, 1981b; Walberg *et al.*, 1978) is not inconsistent with the results.
2. Eleven early immersion students and ten late immersion students had fathers who worked in professional or semi-professional occupations. IQ scores, based on grade-appropriate forms of the Canadian Cognitive Abilities Test were, on average, 114.1 for the early immersion students and 111.8 for the late immersion students. Home language use was in English for all the students but most of the late immersion students had made short tourist visits to French-speaking environments, while the grade 1 students in general had not. In addition, one late immersion student had spent two weeks with a French-speaking family.
3. This group's average age was 15;5 at the time of interview, and their mean IQ of 117 on the Canadian Cognitive Abilities Test was not significantly different from that of the late immersion group ($\bar{\chi}$ = 111.8). The small population of students enrolled in the partial immersion programme meant that matching was not quite as close as for the other groups, however. There was an unequal distribution of boys (N = 4) and girls (N = 8), for example, and the average socio-economic status was somewhat lower (five out of ten students reported fathers in professional or semi-professional occupations, while two could not be determined). Like the late immersion students, all the partial immersion students spoke English at home, but four of them had spent two or more weeks with a French-speaking family or in a French-speaking summer camp.

Appendix: The Interview

1. Tu as quel âge?
2. C'est quand, ta fête/ton anniversaire?
3. Quand c'est ta fête, qu'est-ce que tu aimes manger le plus?
4. Qu'est-ce que tu sais préparer toi-même (à la cuisine)?
4a. (Si rien) As-tu jamais aidé ta mère à faire un gâteau?

5. Est-ce que tu peux m'expliquer comment préparer . . . (ce que l'élève a répondu à 4)?
6. Où est-ce que tu habites? Quel est ton adresse?
7. Est-ce que c'est loin d'ici?
8. Si tu étais en retard pour l'école, qu'est-ce que le directeur/professeur ferait? Qu'est-ce qui'il ferait si tu arrivais souvent en retard?

A. 9. Je vais te montrer une petite histoire en images. Il y a une bonne idée pour aider les gens qui risquent d'être en retard le matin. Veux-tu me raconter l'histoire de ce pauvre monsieur? Ca commence ici et continue par ici, tu vois.
10. Oui, c'est ça. Et qu'est-ce qu'il va faire maintenant, tu penses?
11. Imagine maintenant que tu rencontres ce monsieur dans la rue et que tu veux savoir quelle heure il est. Alors, qu'est-ce que tu lui dis? Tu veux être très poli, n'est-ce pas, parce que tu ne le connais pas. Alors, moi, je fais le monsieur. Qu'est-ce que tu dis au monsieur?
12. D'habitude, qui est-ce qui te réveille le matin?
12a. (Si c'est pas la mère) C'est pas ta mère alors?
13. Qu'est-ce qu'elle faisait, ta mère, quand tu es parti pour l'école ce matin?
14. Est-ce que tu as un animal chez toi?
14a. (Si oui) Raconte-moi quelque chose que ton chien/chat/etc. a fait?
15. As-tu des frères ou des sœurs?
16. Est-ce qu'il(s)/elle(s) fait/font partie du programme d'immersion?
16a. (Si oui) En quelle année?
16b. (Si l'élève n'a pas de frères ou de sœurs) As-tu des amis qui habitent près de chez toi?
17. Qu'est-ce que vous aimez faire ensemble?
17a. (Si ce n'est pas dans la réponse à 17) A quels jeux jouez-vous?
18. Est-ce que tu peux m'expliquer comment jouer à . . . ? (ce que l'élève a mentionné en répondant à 17)
19. Qu'est-ce que tu feras ce soir après l'école?
19a. Et puis, qu'est-ce que tu feras? . . . Et puis? (jusqu'à ce que l'élève se mette au lit)
20. Pourquoi est-ce qu'on doit se coucher de bonne heure pendant la semaine?
21. Tu regardes la télévision quelquefois? Quel est ton programme favori?
22. Raconte-moi ce qui s'est passé la dernière fois que tu as vu . . .? (le programme mentionné)

23. Avez-vous déjà fait un voyage en famille, tous ensemble?
23a. (Si non) Avez-vous déjà fait une visite quelque part en classe?
24. Qu'est-ce que tu as aimé le mieux de ce que tu as vu?
25. Comment étai(en)t . . .? (quelque chose que l'élève a mentionné)
26. Et ta famille, avez-vous des projets pour les vacances de Noël/d'été/de Pâques qui viennent?
27. Qu'est-ce que tu aimes le mieux, l'été ou l'hiver? Pourquoi?
28. L'hiver/l'été passé, qu'est-ce que tu faisais d'habitude les fins de semaine (le weekend)?
B. 29. J'ai ici une petite scène d'été. Voici un homme avec un appareil photo. Qu'est-ce qui se passe?
29a. Qu'est-ce tu penses qu'il dit aux enfants?
29b. Pourquoi les enfants sont-ils contents à la fin?
C. 30. Voici une autre scène d'été. Qu'est-ce qui arrive ici?
30a. (Si *plonger* n'a pas été utilisé) Qu'est-ce qui'il fait ici (6e dessin)?
30b. Pourquoi est-ce qu'il y a tant de pieds dans le sable?
30c. Qu'est-ce que tous ces gens auraient dû faire avant de sauter?
D. 31. Bon, on va changer de saison, maintenant. On va regarder trois petites scènes d'hiver. Veux-tu me raconter l'histoire de cette image? (Montrez D)
31a. Pourquoi le Monsieur n'est pas content?
E. 32. Voici un accident de skidoo (moto-neige). Qu'est-ce qui se passe ici?
F. 33. Voici une autre sorte d'accident. Qu'est-ce qui est arrivé?
33a. Où est-ce qu'ils vont l'amener, tu penses?
34. As-tu déjà été à l'hôpital?
34a. (Si non) As-tu jamais eu une grande peur?
34b. (Si non) As-tu jamais fait un mauvais rêve?
35. Raconte-moi ce qui s'est passé.
36. Qu'est-ce que tu ferais, si tu avais beaucoup d'argent? Si tu gagnais la loterie, par exemple?
37. Et tes parents, qu'est-ce qu'ils feraient, eux?
38. Qu'est-ce que tu aimes le mieux faire à l'école?
39. Qu'est-ce que la classe faisait quand tu es sorti toute à l'heure?
40. Maintenant, imagine que tu es la maitresse/le professeur et que la classe fait des bêtises. Qu'est-ce que tu dis aux élèves? Voici la classe devant toi. Alors, qu'est-ce que tu nous dis?

References

BAILEY, N., MADDEN, C. and KRASHEN, S.D. 1974, Is there a 'natural sequence' in adult second language learning? *Modern Language Journal* 48, 420–4.

BURSTALL, C., JAMIESON, M., COHEN, S. and HARGREAVES, M. 1974, *Primary French in the Balance*. Slough: NFER.

CARROLL, J.B. 1975, *The Teaching of French as a Foreign Language in Eight Countries*. New York: John Wiley.

COOK, V.J. 1973, The comparison of language development in native children and foreign adults. *International Review of Applied Linguistics* 11, 13–28.

CUMMINS, J. 1981a, The role of primary language development in promoting educational success for language minority students. In CALIFORNIA STATE DEPARTMENT OF EDUCATION (ed.) *Schooling and Language Minority Students: A Theoretical Framework*. Los Angeles: National Assessment and Dissemination Center.

— 1981b, Age on arrival and immigrant second language learning in Canada: A reassessment. *Applied Linguistics* 2, 132–49.

— 1983, Language proficiency and academic achievement. In J.W. OLLER (ed.) *Current Issues in Language Testing Research*. Rowley, MA: Newbury House.

FATHMAN, A. 1975, The relationship between age and second language productive ability. *Language Learning* 25, 245–53.

FELIX, S. 1985, More evidence on competing cognitive systems. *Second Language Research* 1(1), 47–72.

GENESEE, F. 1987, *Learning Through Two Languages. Studies of Immersion and Bilingual Education*. Cambridge, MA: Newbury House.

HARLEY, B. 1986, *Age in Second Language Acquisition*. Clevedon, Avon: Multilingual Matters.

— 1989, Functional grammar in French immersion: A classroom experiment. *Applied Linguistics* 10, 331–59.

HARLEY, B., HART, D. and LAPKIN, S. 1986, The effects of early bilingual schooling on first-language skills. *Applied Psycholinguistics* 7, 295–322.

KRASHEN, S.D. 1975, The critical period for language acquisition and its possible bases. In D. AARONSON and R.W. RIEBER (eds) *Developmental Psycholinguistics and Communication Disorders*. New York: New York Academy of Sciences.

— 1981, *Second Language Acquisition and Second Language Learning*. London: Pergamon Press.

KRASHEN, S.D., LONG, M.H. and SCARCELLA, R.C. 1979, Age, rate and eventual attainment in second language acquisition. *TESOL Quarterly* 13, 573–82.

LENNEBERG, E.H. 1967, *Biological Foundations of Language*. New York: John Wiley.

MACNAMARA, J. 1973, Nurseries, streets and classrooms: Some comparisons and deductions. *Modern Language Journal* 57, 250–4.

OLLER, J.W. and NAGATO, N. 1974, The long-term effect of FLES: An experiment. *Modern Language Journal* 58, 15–19.

OYAMA, S. 1978, The sensitive period and comprehension of speech. *Working Papers on Bilingualism* 16, 1–17.

PALMER, F. 1974, *The English Verb*. London: Longman.

PATKOWSKI, M.S. 1980, The sensitive period for the acquisition of syntax in a second language. *Language Learning* 30, 449–72.

ROSANSKY, E.J. 1975, The critical period for the acquisition of language: Some cognitive development considerations. *Working Papers on Bilingualism* 6, 92–102.

SCHUMANN, J.H. 1975, Affective factors and the problem of age in second language acquisition. *Language Learning* 25, 209–35.

SELIGER, H.W., KRASHEN, S.D. and LADEFOGED, P. 1975, Maturational constraints in the acquisition of second language accent. *Language Sciences* 36, 20–2.

SKUTNABB-KANGAS, T. and TOUKOMAA, P. 1976, *Teaching Migrant Children's Mother Tongue and Learning the Language of the Host Country in the Context of the Socio-Cultural Situation of the Migrant Family*. Helsinki: The Finnish National Commission for UNESCO.

SNOW, C.E. 1979, Conversations with children. In P. FLETCHER and M. GARMAN (eds) *Language Acquisition: Studies in First Language Development*. Cambridge: Cambridge University Press.

STERN, H.H. 1976, Optimal age: Myth or reality? *Canadian Modern Language Review* 32, 283–94.

SWAIN, M. 1981, Time and timing in bilingual education. *Language Learning* 31, 1–15.

SWAIN, M. and LAPKIN, S. 1982, *Evaluating Bilingual Education: A Canadian Case Study*. Clevedon, Avon: Multilingual Matters.

— 1986, Immersion French in secondary schools: The 'goods' and the 'bads', *Contact* 5(3), 2–9.

TRAUGOTT, E.C. 1977, Natural semantax: Its role in the study of second language acquisition. In S.P. CORDER and E. ROULET (eds) *Theoretical Models in Applied Linguistics*. Paris and Brussels: Didier and AIMAV.

WALBERG, H.J., HASE, K. and PINZUR RASHER, S. 1978, English acquisition as a diminishing function of experience rather than age. *TESOL Quarterly* 12, 427–37.

15 Secondary Level Immersion French Skills: A Possible Plateau Effect

DOUG HART, SHARON LAPKIN and MERRILL SWAIN

Introduction

In retrospect, many French immersion graduates express a desire to have had more French in their programme (McGillivray, 1985). They appear to feel that their development of French language skills has not progressed as rapidly as they would have wished. In this chapter, we review the results of two evaluations conducted in several secondary schools of a large urban Ontario board. The findings are reviewed from two perspectives: (1) how the French language skills of senior secondary immersion students compare to those of francophone peers, and (2) evidence of progress in French proficiency from grade to grade within the secondary level immersion programme. The francophone comparison classes needed to address the first issue were drawn from a semi-rural board outside Quebec City. Grade 11 was used, as it is the final year of secondary school in the province of Quebec.

The comparison of senior secondary immersion students and francophones, not surprisingly, reveals that the immersion students have not achieved native-like proficiency. Their performance most strongly approaches that of native speakers in aspects of written production; it is more distant for oral production, and in particular, pronunciation. The comparison of junior and senior secondary level immersion students revealed few differences, providing evidence of a plateau in French achievement. The main exception is pronunciation, where senior immersion students appear weaker than students at the junior level.

Methodology

Samples

For ease of reference, the evaluation studies mentioned above are labelled the 1986 evaluation (four grade 12 immersion classes, four grade 11 francophone comparison classes) and the 1982–83 evaluation (four grade 9 and 10 classes, same students tested in 1982 at grade 9 and 1983 at grade 10). The 1982–83 study was thus longitudinal, while the 1986 study was cross-sectional. The secondary immersion programme taken by all students involved a variable number of courses offered through the medium of French, but in general, four such credits were taken at grade 9, four at grade 10, and two per year thereafter.

In selecting our sample for the 1986 evaluation, our intent was to bracket the normal range of abilities of both immersion and francophone students. Purposive rather than probability samples of classes were selected. In Ontario we obtained four classes, two early immersion, two late immersion, drawn from three schools representing all eligible classes in these schools.[1] Within each programme (early, late) one class was identified as academically strong, the other as academically weaker. This basis for selection reflected our expectation that programme alone would not provide substantial differences in levels of class performance.[2] In the Quebec board (semi-rural, and academically quite diverse), four classes were drawn from one school representing all eligible classes in that school.

Within classes, a simple random selection of eight students was made. In immersion classes, students with francophone home backgrounds or atypical programme backgrounds were excluded from the sampling list. For practical purposes, all students completed the written test; however, tests are scored only for the sample of eight students who completed the oral test items. In Quebec, two departures from this strategy occurred: first, the written test items were scored for all students to expand our pool of native-speaker data; second, practical difficulties prevented oral testing in two of the four classes.

Preliminary analysis of the Ontario immersion data revealed few significant differences (at the 0.05 level) among classes, contrary to expectations, given our sample design.[3] There are greater differences among francophone classes.[4] The differentiation occurs in areas where formal learning is important (e.g. there are no differences on measures such as pronunciation and use of communicative strategies, which are skill areas more dominated by informal learning outside the classroom). It likely represents an intended or *de facto* streaming process on academic ability. In what follows, immersion student performance is usually compared to the grade 11 francophone group as a whole; however, selective references are also made to the better grade 11 class for which we have complete data as approximating (from test scores) the standard of university-bound francophones.[5]

Some cautionary remarks are in order regarding interpretation of findings based on these data. First, no statistical claims can be made for the representativeness of selected classes regarding full board populations. In making comparisons between programmes we are thus, strictly speaking, making statements about the grade 12 French immersion students in three high schools and grade 11 students in one francophone school. Second, the statistical results of these comparisons use formulas, strictly speaking, applicable to simple random sampling. Our programme samples (excluding the francophone population data on written items) are stratified (by class) simple random samples with disproportional sampling fractions owing to differing class sizes. (The samples have not been weighted since sampling fractions differ appreciably only for immersion classes where, as noted above, there are few significant differences in class mean scores and standard deviations. Weighting would thus represent an exercise in false precision.)

The 1982–83 evaluation study had been conducted in the same Ontario board. It entailed administering À vous la parole to four grade 9 (two early immersion, two late immersion) classes in the winter term of 1982 (in two secondary schools made available to us by the board), and the same classes at grade 10, a year later. Students were excluded if they had not been enrolled in the relevant programme (early or late immersion) from its beginning to grade 9: thus any late immersion students who had some early immersion experience were excluded. Finally, any immersion students with French in their home background were excluded. Once the exclusions were made a sample of eight was selected from each class at grade 9, such that 25% had 'high' cloze test scores (administered prior to the main study), 50% had scored in the middle range on the cloze test, and 25% had 'low' cloze test scores. An attempt was made to include an equal number of boys and girls. These students were retested at grade 10. (The few that could not be retested were not replaced.)

The selection of classes for the 1982–83 evaluation study essentially relied on board officials' judgements of representativeness (within programmes). As is the case for our 1986 sample, few statistically significant differences were found among classes. Analysis of variance did not reveal significant differences among class performances on any measure. Pairwise comparisons using t-tests with Duncan's multiple range test isolated one statistically significant difference — on pronunciation — between the strongest and weakest of the four classes.

Once again, it is important to emphasise the limits of our data. Both the 1982–83 and the 1986 studies use purposive rather than random samples of classes. The grade 12 students in the 1986 study represent the cohort following, by one year, that sampled for the 1982–83 study.

Instruments

The French language test unit used in both evaluations is entitled À *vous la parole*, and is a unique attempt to create a series of theme-related tasks in a well developed communicative context (Swain, 1985). Thus students are given a colourful booklet which provides information on two fictional summer job opportunities. Based on the content of the booklet, they then write a composition on one of two topics (comparing the two job possibilities, or discussing their view of the ideal summer job), a task type which is quite familiar to them. Two further writing tasks introduce different target audiences: an informal note to pin up on a cafeteria bulletin board (at the job site), and a technical exercise in which point-form information provided in the student booklet is rewritten into continuous expository text. The oral tasks consist of a simulated job interview and a group discussion in which four students discuss the conditions of work and lodging at the chosen job site.

The unit was constructed as an operationalisation of a theoretical framework of communicative competence developed by Canale & Swain (1980; see also Canale, 1983). The framework distinguishes four components of communicative competence — grammatical, discourse, sociolinguistic and strategic — each of which is measured at least once in the tasks outlined above. The measures are briefly described in Table 15.1.

It should be noted that we changed the test tasks as we refined the À *vous la parole* test unit after 1983. As indicated in Table 15.1, the 1982–83 groups completed a letter task, while the 1986 groups wrote a composition. This means that the first two measures listed (number of different/sophisticated verbs) cannot be retained for the cross-sectional assessment of progress. We do retain the preposition errors in spite of the fact that the two tasks differed because the error count is conducted

TABLE 15.1 *French speaking and writing measures* (À vous la parole)

Area of competence	Task	Measure	Scoring method
Grammatical (written)	Letter (1982–83) Composition (1986)	No. of different verbs	Count of all verbs in the composition, excluding repetitions
		No. of sophisticated verbs	One point awarded for relatively infrequent verbs, i.e. those not appearing in *Le Français fondamental*
	Technical exercise	No. of preposition errors	Count of incorrect uses and omissions in a 50-word segment
		No. of grammatical spelling errors	Count of all non-homophonous morphological errors (in a 50-word segment), i.e. those errors which 'sound wrong' if the text is read aloud
		No. of incomplete sentences	Count of incomplete sentences (essential features omitted) in first three sentences. Possible ratings are 0–3
Grammatical (oral)	Interview	Pronunciation rating	Four-point rating (0–3) based on accurate pronunciation of the following phonemes: u, y, a, e, r, p, t, k

Discourse (written)	Note	Basic task fulfilment	One point awarded for each of five points of information required in the task instructions
	Composition	No. of tense errors	Count of tense errors in first 10 conjugated verbs. Possible ratings are 0 to 10
Discourse (oral)	Interview	Tense sequence	Percentage of tense errors in the response to the interview question: 'As-tu déjà visité une autre communauté francophone?' (number of erroneous verbs divided by total number of verbs used)
Sociolinguistic (written)	Note	Appropriate opening	One point for the use of an appropriate opening phrase
		Appropriate *tu/vous*	One point awarded for the appropriate use of *tu/vous* in the specific context established by the student
Strategic (oral)	Group discussion	Communicative strategies	Three-point rating (0–2) reflecting the degree to which coping strategies are used to avoid abandoning the message

on the first 50 words in each case, and the task demands can be considered similar in the two writing contexts.

Results

Comparing immersion and francophone performance at the senior secondary level

Table 15.2 provides a summary of immersion and francophone students' performance on *À vous la parole* at the senior secondary level. We will review these findings by dimension of communicative competence.

Grammatical competence

The pattern of results on measures of grammatical competence is particularly complex. On diversity of vocabulary and sophistication of vocabulary (as measured by verb counts) immersion students on average perform at the level of francophones. The slight edge held by immersion students regarding different verbs used is a fragile result dependent upon a few very exceptional scores. When immersion students are compared to the better grade 11 francophone class alone, there is no significant difference in variety of verbs used, and francophones produce on average significantly more sophisticated verbs. On measures of syntax (preposition, grammar and spelling errors) and on pronunciation immersion students on average do markedly worse than francophones. The incomplete sentences measure represents an exception with regard to syntax; here francophones on average somewhat more frequently fail to produce complete sentences than do immersion students. Again, this difference disappears if only the better francophone class is considered.

Figure 15.1 shows the distribution of immersion student and francophone scores for two grammatical measures. (Note: these distributions have been 'smoothed' without, however, altering lower end-points — see Tukey, 1977: Ch. 6.) In the case of use of sophisticated verbs, there is a close correspondence between immersion and francophone distributions. (However, if the comparison is restricted to the better francophone class, the correspondence is substantially reduced; no student in this class produced fewer than two sophisticated verbs and the median is six.) Regarding grammar/spelling errors, the two curves are very different. Although both are skewed to the left, the francophone distribution is much steeper and truncated. Not only do a much higher proportion of francophones make no errors (75.5 versus 37.5% of

TABLE 15.2 À vous la parole test results at the senior secondary level

	Immersion (Ontario)			Francophone (Quebec)			Significant Differences[a]	
	$\bar{x}$	SD	N	$\bar{x}$	SD	N	t-test (two-tailed)	Mann-Whitney
Grammatical: written								
No. of different verbs	19.34	6.34	32	16.56	6.85	100	I > F*	I > F*
No. of sophisticated verbs	3.69	2.89	32	3.81	2.68	100	I > F**	
No. of preposition errors	0.66	0.70	32	0.24	0.54	97	I > F***	I > F***
No. of grammar/spelling errors	1.13	1.26	32	0.28	0.51	102	I > F***	I > F***
No. of incomplete sentences	0.03	0.18	32	0.14	0.40	102	I < F*	
Grammatical: oral								
Pronunciation (max = 3)	0.70	0.56	23	3.00	0.00	15	I < F***	I < F***
Discourse: written								
No. of tasks fulfilled (max = 5)	4.31	1.06	32	4.62	0.81	101	I > F†	I > F*
No. of tense errors (in 10 verbs)	0.72	1.20	32	0.34	0.75	98		
Discourse: oral								
% of tense errors	11.97	21.20	26	1.69	3.08	15	I > F*	I > F*
Sociolinguistic: written								
Appropriate note opening (max = 1)	0.63	0.49	32	0.70	0.46	101		
Appropriate use of *tu/vous* (max = 1)	0.28	0.46	32	0.52	0.50	101	I < F*	I < F*
Strategic: oral								
Communicative strategies (max = 2)	1.18	0.39	28	2.00	0.00	14	I < F***	I < F***

* = < 0.1; ** = ≤ 0.05; *** = ≤ 0.01; **** = ≤ 0.001.
† = ≤ 0.10; * = ≤ 0.05; ** = ≤ 0.01; *** = ≤ 0.001.
[a] I = immersion, F = Francophone

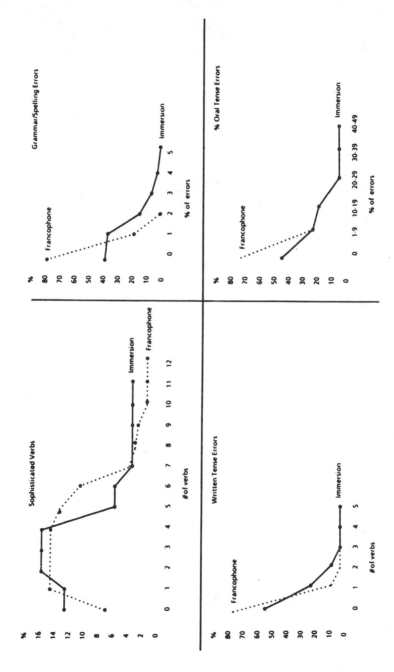

FIGURE 15.1 *Distributions on selected* À vous la parole *measures at the senior secondary level*

immersion students) but those making errors do so within a narrower range than immersion students. In the case of pronunciation (not shown), all francophones obtain the maximum score of '3', while no immersion students score above '2'; 61% obtain '1', and 35% a zero score. Finally, it should be noted that in the case of incomplete sentences, the marginally significant difference in mean score is the result of a somewhat larger proportion of francophones (11.2 versus 3.1%) making any errors. (Again, this difference disappears if comparison is restricted to the better francophone class.) For both groups, student performance levels have essentially reached the 'ceiling' of the measure.

Discourse competence

Francophones appear to do at least marginally better on all measures of discourse competence, but differences are significant only in the case of tense sequence measures. Majorities of immersion (62.5%) and francophone (73.3%) students include five pieces of relevant information in their notes (the 'task fulfilment' measure). However, 21.8% of immersion students include only three pieces of information or less, compared with 5% of francophone students. Differences on tense sequence error measures vary considerably between written and oral production (Figure 15.1). In the case of written production, a majority of both immersion (57.6%) and francophone (78.6%) students make no errors. As is the case for grammar/spelling errors, however, fewer francophones make any errors, and those who do, on average, make fewer errors than immersion students. The contrast between immersion and francophone student performance is sharper, however, with regard to oral tense errors. Almost three-quarters of francophones make no errors; the error rate for the rest is below 10%. Two-thirds of immersion students make at least one tense sequence error; over 30% have an error rate above 10%.

Sociolinguistic competence

Immersion students are equally able with francophone students to produce an appropriate note opening. They are, however, on average, significantly less able to use *tu* and *vous* appropriately in the contexts they have established in the note. It is worth noting, however, that almost half of our francophone sample (and 40% of the better class) also experienced difficulty in this area. (Over 80% of our grade 9 francophone sample received the maximum score on this measure. However, a grade 9 class of bilingual francophone students from the Ottawa-Carleton area, participating in our 1982–83 evaluation study, obtained a mean score similar to that of the grade 11 francophone sample.) This raises questions about either the reliability of the measure or the validity of the scoring procedures.

Strategic competence

Immersion students, on average, obtain lower scores on our measure of strategic competence than francophones. Most francophones do not, in the group discussion, encounter problems which threaten to disrupt communication and require repair (e.g. an inability to produce a particular vocabulary item). Most immersion students (82%) do encounter such difficulties but manage to cope with appropriate strategies (e.g. rephrasing in French rather than abandoning the attempt to communicate the message or lapsing into English).

Summary

Test results, not surprisingly, reveal that senior secondary level immersion students have not achieved native-like proficiency. Immersion students' performance most closely approaches that of native speakers in the production of diversified and sophisticated vocabulary (verbs), use of appropriate informal openings in written work, and to a lesser extent, production of relevant information content and coherent tense sequencing in written work. Weaknesses are evident in immersion students' ability to produce correct syntax, notably in their scores on measures of preposition errors and grammar/spelling errors. Immersion students' pronunciation and ability to maintain a coherent tense sequencing in oral discourse also do not approach native-speaker performance. Results for communicative strategies measures indicate that immersion students, unlike francophones, encounter difficulties in sustaining oral communication; they are, however, in most instances able to use repair strategies which allow communication to continue.

Areas of relative strength and weakness sometimes cross-cut competency dimensions. In part divisions appear to reflect sub-areas of dimensions: thus immersion students do comparatively well on vocabulary measures but relatively poorly on syntax measures. There is, however, another pattern: immersion students' areas of strength are concentrated in written production; their areas of weakness, in oral production.

Comparing immersion students' performance at the junior and senior secondary levels

Table 15.3 presents a summary of our comparative findings. Our data lend support to the hypothesis that immersion students reach a plateau in their French achievement at the secondary level, at some stage below the final year. Comparisons of grade 9 and 12 students show clear gains in the ability to incorporate relevant information in written work; comparisons of achievement at grades 10 and 12 show no gains.[6]

On two measures — pronunciation and appropriate use of *tu/vous* — there is evidence of a decline in proficiency over bilingual schooling. In the case of the sociolinguistic measure, the pattern by programme and grade level of comparison is irregular, which has heightened our concerns about the reliability and/or validity of the measure. In the case of pronunciation, results are wholly consistent by programme and grade level of comparison. Differences are, moreover, of sufficient magnitude that it is unlikely they can be explained by differences in sampling procedures in the two studies. The consistency of our scoring in 1982–83 and 1986 has been checked and verified. We are thus forced to conclude that students' pronunciation, in fact, worsens from junior to senior grades at the secondary level.[7]

It seems highly unlikely that this pattern reflects deterioration in the input received by students in the classroom. There is, in fact, a marked difference in the pattern of relationships between pronunciation and other measures of grammatical competence at the junior and senior secondary levels. At the junior level better pronunciation is associated with avoidance of both preposition, and grammar and spelling errors in written work. At the senior level, there is little relationship between pronunciation and other grammatical measures. From this we can infer that deterioration in pronunciation does not occur mainly among weaker students, but is a general phenomenon. This suggests that the academic environment is not the responsible agency, given that its effects would be expected to manifest themselves most strongly among weaker students. One possible explanation is that the deterioration in pronunciation occurs as students take fewer courses in French and have fewer opportunities to speak French. (It is also possible that subconsciously students are confirming their social identity as anglophones by marking their speech with a non-native-like accent.)

TABLE 15.3 *A comparison of junior and senior secondary immersion students' performance on À vous la parole*

Measures	Grade 9		Grade 10		Grade 12		Significant Differences t-test (two-tailed)	
	X̄	N	X̄	N	X̄	N	Grade 9/12	Grade 10/12
Grammatical: written								
No. of preposition errors	0.50	28	0.46	24	0.65	32		
No. of grammar/spelling errors	1.48	29	1.54	24	1.13	32		
Pronunciation	1.48	29	2.38	24	0.70	23	9 > 12***	10 > 12***
Discourse								
No. of tasks fulfilled	3.61	28	4.13	23	4.31	32	9 < 12**	
% of oral tense errors	14.24	27	6.13	24	11.97	26		
Sociolinguistic: written								
Appropriate note opening	0.75	28	0.67	24	0.63	32		
Appropriate use of *tu/vous*	0.61	28	0.67	24	0.28	32	9 > 12*	10 > 12**
Strategic								
Communicative strategies	0.96	28	1.13	24	1.18	28		

* = ⩽ 0.05; ** = ⩽ 0.01; *** = ⩽ 0.001.

Conclusion

The data presented above provide contradictory perspectives on the development of French language skills in secondary level immersion programmes. On the one hand, immersion performance approximates that of francophones in some respects by the end of secondary school. We also have information on areas of relative strength and weakness in their productive French language skills, which can be used in syllabus design. On the other hand, the apparent lack of progress from junior to senior secondary levels is discouraging.

In interpreting findings relating to both these issues (immersion and francophone outcomes compared, progress across secondary grades within the immersion programme), the nature of immersion programme design may constitute a key link. After grade 10, many immersion students take only two subjects in French — a level of exposure to the second language which, in light of our results, appears inadequate to foster continuing development of French language skills. Elsewhere (Swain & Lapkin, 1986) we have argued that such development will occur in classrooms where students are given ample opportunity for extended and varied writing and speaking in French.

It is our belief that not only the *amount* of instruction through the medium of French, but the *quality* of classroom interaction will play an important role in continuing progress in students' second language skills towards a native-speaker norm. Further experimentation is needed to examine the effects of varying 'doses' of French, and more innovative classroom activities promoting sustained student use of French so that a possible plateau effect can be avoided in the future.

Notes

1. In 1970–71 the Carleton and Ottawa Boards of Education established ten experimental kindergarten 'early immersion' classes in their schools. These early immersion pupils had all of the regular curriculum taught to them in French for their kindergarten and grade 1 years. In grade 2, one period (60 minutes) of English language arts was introduced, and by grade 7 or 8, approximately one-half of their school subjects were taught in French and one-half in English. In 1973–74, 'late immersion' programmes were also initiated in the two boards. These involved a grade 6 or 7 start, with the intensive exposure to French varying from between 50 to 100% of the school day.
2. Some background information is needed here on our decision to combine early and late immersion students for the purpose of the analyses needed to address the two issues identified in the opening paragraph of this chapter. Previous

work with the *À vous la parole* test unit, specifically the development of norms based on province-wide testing at grade 9 in New Brunswick (Lapkin & Swain, 1984), had revealed only one significant between-programme difference – on the pronunciation measure. The decision to combine programme groups for norms development was based on a desire to mirror as broad a range as possible of proficiency in French. The 1986 and 1982–83 data utilised here similarly revealed little difference in the achievement of early and late immersion students. Our analyses comparing the test scores of the early and late immersion students once again showed differences only on the pronunciation measure.

Past research (e.g. Lapkin & Swain, 1984; Morrison *et al.*, 1986; Pawley, 1986) has suggested that many differences in the measured French proficiency of early and late immersion students disappear during secondary level bilingual schooling. Generally speaking, some differences persist in listening and speaking, while performance is similar in reading and writing.

The ratio of late to early immersion accumulated hours of class time in French is, of course, falling substantially over the secondary grades. However, another factor may be at work, one which may also account for the limited differences among early immersion classes. This is the appearance of a 'plateau' in immersion student achievement at the secondary level, identified by some educators (and as will be seen later, suggested by our own data). The reasons suggested for both the appearance of a plateau and for a certain 'fossilisation' of immersion students' French proficiency relate to the limited native-speaker input students receive and lack of opportunities to use French, where learning occurs mainly in the classroom. Beyond its immediate consequences for learning, lack of native-speaker input is a likely source of students' frequent over-confidence in their own proficiency.

In summary, there are reasons to think that the relative absence of differentiation among early and late immersion classes in our sample does not mean these are unrepresentative of the actual range of abilities in the student population.

3. Analysis of variance revealed significant differences among classes on preposition errors and communicative strategies measures. In both instances, these differences reflected multiple significant contrasts among pairs of classes. In addition, pairwise comparisons using t-tests (with Duncan's multiple range test) revealed localised differences between particular classes on two measures (pronunciation and appropriate use of *tu/vous*). Significant t values are also obtained for the note opening measure, but are not confirmed by the Duncan test.

4. On five of 12 measures, analysis of variance revealed significant differences among francophone classes. These include four of six grammatical measures (number of different verbs, number of sophisticated verbs, number of preposition errors, and number of incomplete sentences) and one discourse measure (number of tasks fulfilled). In addition, t-tests revealed localised significant differences on number of grammar/spelling errors. On these five measures, there were significant differences between the two classes for which we have both written and oral data.

5. The proper francophone reference group for immersion students will likely become a subject of increasing debate as the student populations in immersion programmes, and their educational and occupational destinations, become

more heterogeneous. For the moment, however, the implicit reference group is the university-bound francophone student. By this standard (and only by this standard) a grade 9 francophone group to which we were given access prior to the 1982–83 evaluation is more appropriate than our grade 11 sample. In fact, t-tests reveal that our grade 11 sample performs significantly below the grade 9 sample on five measures (different verbs, sophisticated verbs, preposition errors, grammar/spelling errors and appropriate use of *tu/vous* in the note). The better of the two grade 11 classes for which we have complete data is broadly similar to our grade 9 sample in terms of test results. There are significant differences on two measures: the grade 11 class does better than our grade 9 class on task fulfilment, worse on written tense errors. However, on both measures of sociolinguistic competence, grade 11 students obtained lower scores than those at grade 9, with near significant differences ($p \leqslant 0.10$).

6. It is interesting to note that gains in all cases primarily reflect results for early immersion students.
7. The longitudinal 1982–83 study had shown striking *gains* in pronunciation from grade 9 to grade 10 (e.g. the early immersion mean was 1.77 at grade 9 and 2.77 out of a possible 3 at grade 10). It is thus all the more surprising that the drop between grade 10 and 12 should be so dramatic (even though it is based on cross-sectional results).

References

CANALE, M. 1983, From communicative competence to communicative language pedagogy. In J. RICHARDS and L. SCHMIDT (eds) *Language and Communication*. London: Longman.

CANALE, M. and SWAIN, M. 1980, Theoretical bases of communicative approaches to second language teaching and testing. *Applied Linguistics* I(1) 1–47.

LAPKIN, S. and SWAIN, M. 1984, Final report on the evaluation of French immersion programs at grades 3, 6 and 9 in New Brunswick. Toronto: The Ontario Institute for Studies in Education (mimeo).

McGILLIVRAY, R.W. (ed.) 1985, *More French, s'il vous plaît!* Ottawa: Canadian Parents for French.

MORRISON, F., PAWLEY, C., BONYUN, R. and UNITT, J. 1986, *Aspects of French Immersion at the Primary and Secondary Levels*. Toronto: Ontario Ministry of Education.

PAWLEY, C. 1986, French immersion — where do we need to know more? Paper presented at the Tenth Annual Conference of Canadian Parents for French, Ottawa (mimeo).

SWAIN, M. 1985, Large-scale communicative language testing: A case study. In Y.P. LEE, A.C.Y.Y. FOK, R. LORD and G. LOW (eds) *New Directions in Language Testing*. Toronto: Pergamon Press.

SWAIN, M. and LAPKIN, S. 1986, Immersion French in secondary schools: 'The goods' and 'the bads'. *Contact* 5(3), 2–9.

TUKEY, J.W. 1977, *Exploratory Data Analysis*. Reading, MA: Addison-Wesley.

16 The Role of Language Factors in Second Language Writing

MARGARET S.S. YAU

Introduction

The current study is an attempt to explore the interplay of linguistic ability and cognitive ability on students' writing performance. Writing research suggests that there is a strong relationship between cognitive ability and linguistic ability, a relationship reflected especially in the speaker or writer's ability to employ increasingly complex syntactic structures. Evidence for this suggestion comes from two sources: firstly, developmental research shows that linguistic development is closely related to cognitive development. Studies investigating syntactic development across grade levels showed that in writing, the ability to employ complex syntactic structures increases with age. (This ability is henceforth termed 'syntactic complexity'.[1] Syntactic complexity is in turn commonly measured by the length of clauses and T-units[2] achieved by the individual in speaking or writing.) Hunt (1970) showed that syntactic complexity is related not only to chronological age, but to mental age as well; he observed that even within the same grade levels, students with higher IQs wrote significantly longer T-units and clauses than students with lower IQs. A more recent study (Prato & Mayo, 1984) showed that cognitive developmental level exerted a significant main effect on syntactic complexity; grade 10 students who are operating at a transitional stage wrote more clauses per T-unit than students operating at the concrete operational stage (the stages being defined in a Piagetian sense and measured by the Renner scale (Renner, 1977)).

Two views have been proposed to explain the relation between the development of syntactic complexity and the development of conceptual capacity. Kerek (1981) sees the growth in syntactic complexity as a result of the growth in working memory capacity so that with such growth, children are able to retain a larger chunk of language. This ability in turn

266

enables them to produce more complete syntax. Mellon (1979) sees the growth in syntactic complexity as a result of the development of conceptual knowledge. He argues,

> . . . as young persons' conceptual knowledge grows broader in scope and richer in structure, this growth causes them to see *more* things interrelated in *more complex* detail. . . . As a result, the names persons make, first to represent and then to say what they see, necessarily grow more complex in content and therefore also in form, with the passing of time. (p. 18)

Secondly, syntactic complexity is a reflection of the cognitive demand made by different kinds of writing on the writer. Writing that is conceptually more complex induces more complete syntax. This is evident from the fact that the argumentative or the informative modes of writing tend to elicit a higher level of syntactic complexity than the descriptive or narrative mode (Rosen, 1969; San Jose, 1972; Perron, 1976; Crowhurst & Piche, 1979; Crowhurst, 1980). The higher level of conceptual complexity in the argumentative or the informative mode is in turn established by the pausal analysis studies (e.g. Matsuhashi, 1981, 1982) which show that writers writing in the argumentative mode make more and longer pauses (an indication of more elaborate planning activities) than when writing in the narrative or descriptive mode. On the other hand, Maimon & Nodine (1978) showed that students' inability to grapple with complex subject matter leads to a deterioration in syntactic performance. Similarly, Ney (1976) showed that unless students have acquired the necessary level of conceptual capacity, they will not be able to produce syntactically complex sentences no matter how intensively they are drilled. This also seems to explain why, at the high school level, sentence combining practice, the aim of which is to induce students to produce more complex syntax, is more effective with high-ability students who presumably are more developed cognitively than the low-ability students (Mellon, 1969; O'Hare, 1973).

The data reviewed above suggest that increases in syntactic complexity in writing is a certain manifestation of the level of conceptual complexity inherent in the writing that comes as a result of mental growth, or as a result of the demand made by a particular mode of writing. The question of interest is whether the converse is also true, that is, will the level of linguistic ability achieved by the writers affect their ability to write conceptually complex content? The answer to this question has important pedagogical implications in teaching English as a Second Language (ESL). While it is clear from the studies above that with native speakers, growth in conceptual and linguistic complexity is commensurate with age, with ESL learners, the situation is quite different. Depending on the stage of ESL learning, the learner's linguistic ability in the second language may lag far behind his or her conceptual capacity. If the relation between linguistic ability and conceptual capacity is unidirectional, that is, if conceptual complexity induces linguistic complexity and not vice versa, language ability should not affect writing ability because, depending on their language ability, writers apparently can make use of either simple or complex syntax, or sophisticated or unsophisticated vocabulary, to convey their ideas or to fulfil their intention (Scardamalia, 1981). Therefore, to help improve the writing performance of ESL students, using a process approach to writing (an approach aiming at improving the execution of various aspects of writing) may be as useful as, or more useful than, a product-oriented approach (an approach aiming at improving the language aspect of writing), a conclusion reached by some ESL writing researchers (e.g. Zamel, 1976, 1982, 1983; Liebman-Kleine, 1986). However, if writers' linguistic ability sets certain limits to what they can do conceptually or affects the writing process itself, then something more should be done than just developing the writing processes of ESL writers. Although we should not cripple our students' interest in writing through an undue stress on grammatical correctness, the influence of second language factors on writing performance is something we have to reckon with and not pretend that concentrating on the process would automatically resolve the difficulty caused by these factors. Therefore, clarifying the nature of the relationship between cognitive ability and linguistic ability has significant implications for classroom writing practice.

The Study

The current study, then, is an attempt to explore the relation between linguistic ability and cognitive ability. Its goal is to find out how the two interact to affect the writing task. This study singles out the effect of language ability by comparing students' writing performance in L1 and L2 on two dimensions: syntactic complexity and conceptual complexity. The question this study attempts to answer is whether ESL writers' limited proficiency in the second language will have a direct effect on the content of the writing. Two kinds of L1 and L2 writing are compared in two separate investigations, which are detailed below.

Investigation 1

Investigation 1 is a comparison of the English writing performance of two groups (20 subjects in each) of Chinese students learning English as a second language (ESL) at two grade levels (grades 9 and 13) who were randomly chosen from a secondary school in Hong Kong. Students at the grade 9 level were just beginning to produce free writing in English, and so the group is considered to be beginning ESL writers. The grade 13 students, on the other hand, had about five years of experience writing free English compositions as well as writing English essays in the content area, and so the group is considered to be advanced ESL writers. The purpose of the comparison was to find out how the two groups, at two distinct stages of second language learning, differ in their writing performance. The English writing performance of the grade 9 ESL students was also compared with the writing performance of a comparable group (in terms of general academic achievement and socio-economic status) of Canadian grade 9 students who are native speakers of English (L1) chosen from a school in Toronto. The purpose of this comparison was, controlling for age and maturation factors, to see how the difference in language proficiency affects writing.

The three groups of students were asked to produce an expository essay of about 200 words in a 40-minute session. The topic was to write about their ideas of an ideal person. Prior to the writing session, a series of pre-writing procedures (see Appendix) was administered uniformly to the three groups to ensure that idea generation or topic familiarity would not be a confounding factor. These procedures were similar to those used by Anderson, Bereiter & Smart (1980) which have been found useful to elicit better writing performance from students.

Analysis

Two kinds of analyses were performed on the student compositions. The first analysis is a measure of the level of complexity achieved by the students in elaborating a line of argument, an ability related to the level of cognitive development attained by the students (Scardamalia, 1981); the second is a measure of their linguistic abilities as reflected in the employment of certain syntactic structures. The methods for the two analyses are detailed below.

Complexity analysis: The unit of analysis is a 'logic' or 'idea' unit. Such a unit is defined as a proposition that is independent of its immediate surrounding propositions. Complexity of elaboration is defined as level 1, 2, 3 and 4 according to the number of logic units the student has to co-ordinate to develop a line of argument. A paragraph from an ESL grade 13 student will make this clear:

> To be an ideal father, one must be kind. This means that between his children and him, there must be love because it is an essential component which links them together. However, he has to be strict too, for instance, in case the children have done wrong he should not be too lenient to them; otherwise this will spoil the children.

The above paragraph can be represented schematically as in Figure 16.1.

The listing of an attribute (be kind) is defined as level 1 because the student merely needs to co-ordinate the attribute with the central thesis (i.e. important qualities for an ideal father). The second sentence, which tells what it means to be kind and why it is important, develops the line of argument further: they are respectively a level 2 and level 3 elaboration. In the third sentence, the student listed another attribute (i.e. to be strict); this attribute, however, is subsumed under the first attribute as a qualifying statement. Therefore it is put at level 2 because the student has to co-ordinate three logic units: the central thesis, the first attribute and the second attribute. The next two logic units further

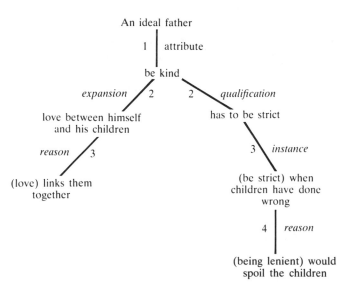

FIGURE 16.1 *A schematic representation of the complexity of elaboration in a written paragraph*

elaborating the second attribute are then put at level 3 and level 4.

After the idea units were graded at their respective level of complexity, they were scored. The lowest score was 0 and was given to logic units not coherent to a line of argument. While the students might stray from the given topic, as long as the line of argument was clear, the idea units were scored. A level one co-ordination was given a basic score of 2, level two was 4 (2^2); level three was 8 (2^3) and level 4 or above was 16 (2^4). As higher level of co-ordinations had to be built on lower level ones, such a scoring scheme differentiates more clearly students who showed higher levels of idea co-ordinations (i.e. level 3 or 4) from students who merely had a lot of level 2 co-ordinations. Then the mean score per logic unit achieved by the students in the three groups was calculated. Another measure, mean complexity level, looks into what the students could do at the top level of their performance. Three logic units which were graded at the highest level of complexity were taken out and the mean level for the three was calculated. An analogy to this procedure is averaging the three fastest times clocked by a sprinter, which should reflect more accurately how fast he can run than averaging the times in all the races he has run.

Syntactic analysis: The syntactic analysis includes calculating the mean T-unit length and mean clause length, two measures most commonly used in recent studies investigating language development (Larsen-Freeman & Strom, 1977; Stewart, 1978; Sharma, 1979; Yau, 1983). Two other measures, mean length of complex nominals per T-unit and mean length of complex nominals per clause, were also used. The reason for introducing these two measures is that T-unit length and clause length analyses 'do not discriminate the various ways length can be achieved' (O'Donnell, 1976: 33). But as Mellon (1979) argued, growth in clause and T-unit length caused by non-restrictive modifiers is not the same as growth produced by restrictive modifiers such as prepositional phrases and relative clauses with dominant noun phrase. The former kind of lengthening merely reflects the students' skill as writers because non-restrictive modifiers represent little more than surface structure ellipsis, a skill that can be taught and learnt quickly. In developmental terms, Mellon suggests, a true reflection of growth is the slow rise in restrictive modification which comes as a 'direct and unavoidable consequence of the development of conceptual knowledge' (p. 18). Complex nominals, as defined in the current study, are headed nominals expanded by adjectives, nouns, relative clauses or relative clause reductions, prepositional or infinitive phrases, participles or participial phrases, and non-headed nominals such as infinitive phrases and noun clauses (excluding noun clauses serving as direct objects of verbs, to avoid inclusion of instances like 'I think . . .'), all used in a restrictive sense.

Statistical procedure

The six dependent variables (mean complexity score, mean complexity level, mean words per T-unit, mean words per clause, mean words in complex nominals per T-unit and mean words in complex nominals per clause) were tested at 0.05 level of significance by a one-way analysis of variance (Glass & Stanley, 1970). A Pearson-Product Moment Correlation Coefficient (Glass & Stanley, 1970) between the six variables was also calculated with the three groups pooled together and within individual groups.

Results

The average number of words written by the ESL grade 9 students, the L1 grade 9 students and the ESL grade 13 students in the compositions are respectively 186.8 (SD 38.34), 363.2 (SD 56.82) and 229.3 (SD 40.97). The average number of logic units per composition written by the three groups are 18.8 (SD 4.37), 20.6 (SD 4.67) and 17.3 (SD 3.60) respectively. The mean scores and standard deviations on the six dependent variables achieved by the three groups are presented in Table 16.1.

As can be seen from the table, on both complexity measures the ESL grade 13 students scored the highest while the ESL grade 9 students scored the lowest; scores on these two measures for the L1 students thus fell between these two groups. Analysis of variance indicates that the differences among the three groups on both measures were statistically significant. The F-values and the corresponding probability level for the two measures are: complexity score: $F(2,57) = 23.97$, $p < 0.0001$; complexity level: $F(2,57) = 14.57$, $p < 0.0001$. Newman Keuls tests (Glass & Stanley, 1970) further indicate that there was a significant difference between any combination of the three groups on these two measures.

The picture is somewhat different on the syntactic analysis. As can be seen from Table 16.1, on all four syntactic scores, while the ESL grade 9 students scored substantially lower than the other two groups, the differences between the L1 grade 9 students and the ESL grade 13 students were not very great. Analysis of variance further indicates that there was a significant difference on all four measures among the three groups. The F-ratio and corresponding probability levels are: words per

TABLE 16.1 *Mean scores and standard deviations on six dependent variables achieved by three groups*

Group	Complexity score		Complexity level		T-unit length		Clause length		Nominals per T-unit		Nominals per clause	
	Mean	SD	Mean	SD	Mean	SD	Mean	SD	Mean	SD	Mean	SD
ESL G9	2.69	0.65	2.17	0.68	10.82	2.09	7.62	1.14	2.37	0.82	1.72	0.65
L1 G9	3.52	0.66	2.68	0.45	17.00	2.93	9.63	1.14	6.71	1.93	3.80	1.09
ESL G13	4.71	1.31	3.12	0.60	15.54	3.62	10.48	1.77	6.00	2.31	4.09	1.45

T-unit: $F(2,57) = 24.00$, $p < 0.0001$; words per clause: $F(2,57) = 22.67$, $p < 0.0001$; nominals per T-unit: $F(2,57) = 33.49$, $p < 0.0001$; nominals per clause: $F(2,57) = 26.84$, $p < 0.0001$. Newman Keuls tests indicate, however, that the significant difference was caused by the markedly low scores achieved by the ESL grade 9 students on all four measures; there was no significant difference between the ESL grade 13 and L1 grade 9 students on these measures.

Table 16.2 shows the pooled correlation coefficient between individual variables with the three groups pooled together and within

TABLE 16.2 *Correlation matrix of six dependent variables with three groups pooled together and within individual groups*

	Complexity score	Complexity level	T-unit length	Clause length	Nominals per T-unit	Nominals per clause
Three groups pooled						
Com Sc	1.00					
Com Le	0.89	1.00				
T-unit	0.24	0.23	1.00			
Clause	0.33	0.29	0.68	1.00		
Nom/T	0.30	0.27	0.82	0.67	1.00	
Nom/C1	0.34	0.30	0.62	0.77	0.91	1.00
ESL grade 9						
Com Sc	1.00					
Com Le	0.91	1.00				
T-unit	0.21	0.18	1.00			
Clause	0.18	0.16	0.80	1.00		
Nom/T	0.29	0.29	0.48	0.35	1.00	
Nom/C1	0.21	0.21	0.18	0.19	0.91	1.00
L1 grade 9						
Com Sc	1.00					
Com Le	0.91	1.00				
T-unit	0.12	0.08	1.00			
Clause	−0.21	−0.16	0.35	1.00		
Nom/T	−0.02	−0.24	0.56	0.28	1.00	
Nom/C1	−0.26	−0.42	0.11	0.50	0.81	1.00
ESL grade 13						
Com Sc	1.00					
Com Le	0.87	1.00				
T-unit	−0.31	−0.41	1.00			
Clause	−0.27	−0.37	0.54	1.00		
Nom/T	−0.24	−0.24	0.77	0.60	1.00	
Nom/C1	−0.15	−0.14	0.49	0.76	0.89	1.00

individual groups. As Table 16.2 indicates, measures belonging to the same category show a medium to high degree of correlation, which is to be expected, because they measure the students' skill or knowledge in the same cognitive domain. There is a positive, though moderate, correlation between the complexity and syntactic measures when the three groups are pooled together. However, when the coefficients are calculated for the individual groups, only the ESL grade 9 students retained this positive correlation between the two types of scores, while the L1 grade 9 students and the ESL grade 13 students showed a near zero, or negative, correlation. While the lack of a strong positive relationship between the two kinds of measures may indicate that there is not a direct causal relationship between them, it is still possible that the complexity and syntactic measures are linked by some underlying factors. Hunt (1983) compared the relation between development in writing abilities and development in syntactic complexity to the relation between the increase in height and the gain in weight as children grow. He suggested that while there may not be a correlation between height and weight among children of the same age group, when children of different age groups are compared, the relation between age, height and weight would be much more apparent. The present results could be interpreted in a similar way.

Investigation 2

The second investigation was conducted as a follow-up study of the first. The first investigation shows that the ESL grade 9 students wrote English compositions that were scored significantly lower than the compositions written by their Canadian counterparts on both the conceptual and syntactic aspects, while the more advanced ESL grade 13 students scored higher than the Canadian students on the conceptual measures, though not on the syntactic measures. There may be a number of reasons, other than those attributed to the ESL students' ability with the English language, that account for the significantly lower scores achieved by the ESL grade 9 students. One possible reason is the difference in the two schooling systems (it is reasonable to assume that the schooling system in Hong Kong is not the same as the schooling system in Canada). Another possible reason is that the ESL grade 9 students' English writing performance was affected by negative transfer of rhetorical features from their first language, Chinese. (Negative transfer, which results in interference errors, is found to affect beginning second language learners more than advanced second language learners, (cf. Taylor, 1975), and therefore the English writing performance of the grade 13 students should be less prone to such kind of interference.) The notion of rhetorical conventions acquired in L1 writing being negatively transferred to L2 writing was popularised by Kaplan (1972), who analysed ESL writings produced by students of different ethnic groups and found striking differences in the way that these different groups developed and organised English expository essays. Such a notion, though, has been refuted by Mohen & Lo (1985) who pointed out that, at least for English and Chinese expository essays, many rhetorical conventions that underlie these essays are similar, rather than different, as exemplified by literary texts or instructions given in writing textbooks on how to write such kind of essays. Therefore the rhetorical aberrations found in Chinese students' English writing cannot be wholly attributed to the notion of negative transfer. But still, in the current study, it is possible that both sources may be in operation to affect the English writing performance of these students. As a result, the second investigation was conducted that compared the writing performance of these students when they were writing in L1 (Chinese) and when they were writing in L2 (English). Such a comparison would help to clarify two issues. Firstly, since the students being compared had identical schooling experience, if their writing performance in the two languages still showed a difference, the difference should be attributed to factors other than schooling experience. Secondly, if it could be shown that the students wrote conceptually complex essays in Chinese, the fact that they were not able to do so in English should less likely be a matter of negative transfer of rhetorical features from the first language and was more likely to be the result of the linguistic constraint imposed by the second language.

Methodology

Two groups (30 subjects in each) of Chinese ESL subjects at the grade 9 level were randomly chosen from the same school as in Investigation 1. One group wrote in English on either of the following two opinion essays:

(1) Should students be allowed to choose the subjects they study in school?
(2) Should parents decide for their children the kind of friends they should have?

The other group wrote on the same two opinion essays in Chinese under the same test condition. No pre-writing procedures were administered to either group.

Since Chinese and English belong to two distinct language families, and the validity of comparing the essays on language-related aspects (such as length of sentences, etc.) has not been established, no syntactic analysis was performed on the essays. However, the conceptual complexity analysis was not affected by which language was used since it measured the level of idea elaboration within an argument, a measurement that is related to the content, rather than the language, of the writing. Accordingly, the essays written by the two groups were compared using the mean complexity score. The results are as follows.

Results

No word count was performed on the essays for reasons explained above. But a comparison of the average number of idea units written by the students in the two languages indicated that the students were including more ideas into their Chinese essays. The mean and standard deviation on the number of idea units for essays written in English and for essays written in Chinese are respectively 12.3 (SD 3.43) and 22.6 (SD 3.88). When the mean complexity score for the two types of essays was computed, the Chinese essays were found to display a higher level of conceptual complexity: the mean complexity score in the Chinese essays was 4.50 (SD 0.96) while the mean for the English essays was 3.04 (SD 0.62). One-way analysis of variance indicated that the difference in the complexity score between the two types of essays was highly significant. The F-value obtained from the analysis was 48.56, $p < 0.0001$.

Discussion

The two investigations indicated that language ability does affect cognitive processing. Both Investigations 1 and 2 indicated that the ESL grade 9 students' conceptual performance was seriously impeded because they had not achieved a certain level of linguistic ability in the target language they were writing. Controlling for native language background (comparison 1) and maturation factors (comparison 2), Investigation 1 shows that the grade 9 students' ability to manipulate conceptually complex content was significantly inferior to that of a more advanced group of ESL learners (the grade 13 students) and to that of a comparable group (in terms of age and years of schooling) of native English speakers. Investigation 2 further indicated that the deterioration in conceptual performance was more likely to be a result of limited linguistic ability in the target language than a result of differences in schooling experience or negative transfer of rhetorical features from the first language.

While evidence reviewed before suggests that conceptual complexity induces syntactic complexity, results from the two investigations suggest that the converse may also be true. The implication is that thinking and language processing are interrelated cognitive processes rather than completely independent of one another. A strong claim supporting a dependency of thinking on language is the Whorfian hypothesis (Whorf, 1956) which suggests that language both embodies and imposes upon the culture a particular world view. Such a view has since been refuted (see, for example, Rosch, 1977). However, interpreted in the context of writing using an information processing perspective, language (specifically, language ability) can exert considerable influence on the thinking process.

Since human beings are limited-capacity information processors, to account for their ability to process large amounts of information and develop complex social, linguistic and cognitive skills, one has to turn to the concept of 'chunking' (Miller, 1956). By integrating input into existing cognitive structures, individuals can become more efficient processors; this is done by creating a more inclusive cognitive structure that subsumes the new input and existing cognitive structures (cf. Schank, 1980). Or individuals can 'procedurise' (Anderson, 1982; Lesgold, 1984) certain sub-components of a cognitive task so that execution of these sub-components can become an automatic process, thereby sparing mental energy for other controlled processes.

Viewed in this context, language ability can be seen as an indication of how much the use of syntactic structures and lexicons has been procedurised so that these structures and lexicons are readily available to the writer. We may call this aspect 'proficiency'. It can also be seen as how rich the individual's linguistic repertoire is: semantically, this means establishing a repertoire of lexicons with their associative conceptual network and subsuming individual lexicons into more inclusive terms; syntactically, this means establishing a repertoire of syntactic structures and subsuming discrete structures into larger structures which makes the relation between propositions more explicit. We may refer to this aspect as 'development'. Second language learning, of course, involves both acquiring proficiency in the use of the language and developing the linguistic repertoire. As the learners become more advanced in their stage of language learning, they should also become more efficient users of the second language because of increased proficiency and having a more developed network of linguistic resources. One indication of this efficiency is their ability to produce more complex syntax, as suggested by developmental research in syntactic processing.

Extending the above discussions to the present study, the ESL grade 9 students' limited ability in English affected their writing performance by imposing an extra burden on the writing task. Limited by their linguistic resources and not having these resources readily available, these students would have great difficulty with the written language production process. Their difficulty in retrieving the necessary lexicons to realise their intention would cause additional difficulty in syntactic processing (Bock, 1982), which in turn would induce them to opt for syntax that would be least straining to their memory, typically syntactic structures that show a clear relation between the agent and the action (Kerek, 1981). This explains the very low scores achieved by these students on all the syntactic measures. On the other hand, the strain exerted on their working memory capacity in processing language also leaves them little room for more global concerns such as idea development, leading to a kind of 'associative writing' (Bereiter, 1980), which consists of putting down whatever that comes into the mind in whatever order it comes.

Conclusion and Implications

The two investigations reported in this study indicate that in writing, there is a close relation between the students' syntactic performance and their conceptual performance. This suggests that writing performance is as much a result of the students' use of strategies in various sub-processes of writing as it is of their handling of language (i.e. whether they can raise their syntactic resources to a conscious level to serve the purpose of the writing). One implication that can be drawn from this suggestion is that composition instructional techniques should take account of both strategy development and language skill development to derive the maximum benefits for students, especially in a second language writing classroom.

Notes

1. Different researchers have coined different names to refer to this ability to produce increasingly complex syntax: syntactic maturity (Hunt, 1965), syntactic fluency (Mellon, 1969) and syntactic complexity (Crowhurst, 1980). For a discussion on the appropriateness of the three terms, see Faigley (1980). For this chapter, 'syntactic complexity' is used as it is the most neutral of the three terms.

2. The term 'T-unit' was first coined by Hunt (1965). A T-unit is one main clause plus any subordinate clauses or non-clausal elements attached to, or embedded in, it.

Appendix

Prewriting activities:
* (H) indicates that the students are to prepare the work at home.

Session 1 (suggested duration: 2 min.)

(a) Distribute the writing instructions to students.
(b) (H) Ask students to read over the instructions and be prepared to discuss it for next day.

Session 2 (suggested duration: 7–10 min.)

(a) Clarify with students the concept of 'ideal'.
(b) Ask students to suggest more qualities that an ideal student should possess.
(c) (H) Ask students to think about which ideal person they are going to write. Ask them to think about all words that would describe the·ideal person.
Ask them to bring the list of words to class the next day.

Session 3 (suggested duration: 10–15 min.)

(a) Divide the students into groups of 4.
(b) Ask students to share their lists with other group members who should contribute more words and expressions to the list.
(c) (H) Ask students to think about 5 details that will bring out or explain the qualities that the ideal person should possess.

Session 4 (suggested duration: 10–15 min.)

(a) Divide students into the same grouping as Session 3.
(b) Ask students to share their best three ideas with other group members.
(c) Ask each group to share the best detail with the class.
(d) (H) Ask students to think over how they would use the words and details in their compositions.

Session 5 (suggested duration: 15 min.)

(a) Ask students to write a rough draft. The draft may be an outline, the first paragraph, or just rough notes on how they will write.
(b) Collect the drafts from students. Tell them that they will' be given back the drafts the next day.

Actual writing session (40 min.)

(a) Give back the drafts to students.

(b) Ask them to write the composition working from their drafts.

References

ANDERSON, J.R. 1982, Acquisition of cognitive skill. *Psychological Review* 89, 369–406.

ANDERSON, V., BEREITER, C. and SMART, D. 1980, Activation of semantic networks in writing: Teaching students how to do it themselves. Paper presented at the annual meeting of the American Educational Research Association, Boston.

BEREITER, C. 1980, Development in writing. In L.W. GREGG and E.R. STEINBERG (eds) *Cognitive Processes in Writing*. Hillsdale, NJ: Lawrence Erlbaum.

BOCK, J.K. 1982, Toward a cognitive psychology of syntax: Information processing contributions to sentence formulation. *Psychological Review* 89, 1–47.

CROWHURST, M. 1980, Syntactic complexity in narration and arguments at three grade levels. *Canadian Journal of Education* 5, 6–12.

CROWHURST, M. and PICHE, G.L. 1979, Audience and mode of discourse effects on syntactic complexity in writing at two grade levels. *Research in the Teaching of English* 13, 101–9.

FAIGLEY, L. 1980, Names in search of a concept: Maturity, fluency, complexity, and growth in written syntax. *College Composition and Communication* 31, 291–6.

GLASS, G.V. and STANLEY, J.C. 1970, *Statistical Methods in Education and Psychology*. Englewood Cliffs, NJ: Prentice-Hall.

HUNT, K.W. 1965, *Grammatical Structures Written at Three Grade Levels*. Urbana, IL: NCTE.

— 1970, Syntactic maturity in school-children and adults. *Monograph of the Society for Research in Child Development* 35.

— 1983, Sentence combining and the teaching of writing. In M. MARTLEW (ed.) *The Psychology of Written Language: A Developmental Approach*. London: Wiley.

KAPLAN, R.B. 1972, *The Anatomy of Rhetoric: Prolegomena to a Functional Theory of Rhetoric*. Philadelphia: Center for Curriculum Development; Concord, MA: Heinle and Heinle.

KEREK, A. 1981, The combining process. In M.C. HAIRSTON and C.L. SELFE (eds) *Selected Papers from the 1981 Texas Writing Research Conference* (Austin, Texas, Aug. 1981). (ERIC Document Reproduction Service ED 208 417.)

LARSEN-FREEMAN, D. and STROM, V. 1977, The construction of a second language acquisition index of development. *Language Learning* 27, 123–34.

LESGOLD, A.M. 1984, Acquiring expertise. In J.R. ANDERSON and S.M. KOSSLYN (eds) *Tutorials in Learning and Memory*. New York: W.H. Freeman.

LIEBMAN-KLEINE, J. 1986, In defence of teaching process in ESL composition. *TESOL Quarterly* 20, 783–8.

MAIMON, E.P. and NODINE, B.F. 1978, Measuring syntactic growth: Errors and expectations in sentence combining practice with college freshmen. *Research in the Teaching of English* 12, 233–44.

MATSUHASHI, A. 1981, Pausing and planning: The tempo of written discourse. *Research in the Teaching of English* 15, 113–34.

— 1982, Exploration in the real time production of written discourse. In M. NYSTRAND (ed.) *What Writers Know: The Language, Process, and Structure of Written Discourse*. New York: Academic Press.

MELLON, J.C. 1969, *Transformational Sentence-Combining: A Method for Enhancing the Development of Syntactic Fluency in English Compositions*. Urbana, IL: NCTE.

— 1979, Issues in the theory and practice of sentence combining: A twenty-year perspective. In D.A. DAIKER, A. KEREK and M. MORENBERG (eds) *Sentence Combining and the Teaching of Writing*. Akron, Ohio: University of Akron.

MILLER, G.A. 1956, The magic number seven, plus or minus two: Some limits on our capacity for processing information. *Psychological Review* 63, 81–97.

MOHEN, B.A. and LO, W.A. 1985, Academic writing and Chinese students: Transfer and developmental factors. *TESOL Quarterly* 19, 515–34.

NEY, J.W. 1976, Notes towards a psycholinguistic model of the writing process. *Research in the Teaching of English* 10, 157–69.

O'DONNELL, R.C. 1976, A critique of some indices of syntactic maturity. *Research in the Teaching of English* 10, 33–8.

O'HARE, F. 1973, *Sentence Combining: Improving Student Writing Without Formal Grammar Instruction*. Urbana, IL: NCTE.

PERRON, J.D. 1976, The impact of mode on written syntactic complexity. Part III: Fifth grade. *Studies in Language Education*, Report No. 27. Department of Language Education, The University of Georgia. (ERIC Document Reproduction Service No. ED 128 827.)

PRATO, D.L. and MAYO, N.B. 1984, Cognitive developmental level and syntactic maturity. *Journal of Research and Development in Education* 17, 1–7.

RENNER, J.W. 1977, *Evaluating Intellectual Development Using Written Responses to Selected Science Problems*. Normans: University of Oklahoma. A report to the National Science Foundation.

ROSCH, E. 1977, Linguistic relativity. In P.N. JOHNSON-LAIRD and P.C. WATSON (eds) *Thinking: Readings in Cognitive Science*. Cambridge: Cambridge University Press.

ROSEN, H. 1969, An investigation of the effects of differentiated writing assignments on the performance in English composition of a selected group of 15/16-year-old pupils. Unpublished Ph.D. thesis, University of London.

SAN JOSE, C.P.M. 1972, Grammatical structures in four modes of writing at fourth grade level. Unpublished Doctoral Dissertation, Syracuse University.

SCARDAMALIA, M. 1981, How children cope with the cognitive demands of writing. In C.H. FREDERIKSEN, M.F. WHITEMAN and J.F. DOMINIC (eds) *Writing: The Nature, Development and Teaching of Written Communication*. Hillsdale, NJ: Lawrence Erlbaum.

SCHANK, R.C. 1980, Language and memory. *Cognitive Science* 4, 243–85.

SHARMA, A. 1979, Syntactic maturity: Assessing writing proficiency in a second language. Paper presented at the International Conference on Frontiers in Language Proficiency and Dominance Testing (Carbondale, IL, 26–28 Sept. 1979). (ERIC Document Reproduction Service No. ED 185 105.)

STEWART, M.F. 1978, Syntactic maturity from high school to university: A first look. *Research in the Teaching of English* 12, 37–46.

TAYLOR, B.P. 1975, The use of overgeneralization and transfer learning strategies by elementary and intermediate students in ESL. *Language Learning* 25, 73–108.

WHORF, B.L. 1956, *Language, Thought and Reality*. New York: Wiley.

YAU, M. 1983, Syntactic development in the writing of ESL students. Unpublished MA thesis, University of British Columbia.

ZAMEL, V. 1976, Teaching composition in the ESL classroom: What we can learn from research in the teaching of English. *TESOL Quarterly* 10, 67–76.

— 1982, Writing: The process of discovery meaning. *TESOL Quarterly* 16, 195–209.

— 1983, The composing processes of advanced ESL students: Six case studies. *TESOL Quarterly* 17, 165–87.

17 Towards a More Language Oriented Second Language Classroom

JOAN E. NETTEN

Introduction

The purpose of this chapter is to reappraise some currently held views on second language instructional techniques in the light of data obtained observing French immersion classrooms. Three classrooms are described here, and differences in these classrooms with respect to three areas of instruction are discussed. Questions are raised with respect to the effectiveness of current practices, in enhancing second language learning. The three questions investigated in this chapter are:

(1) Should the use of more cognitively, or language, oriented aids to comprehension be encouraged?
(2) Should teachers make more use of negative as well as positive affect in interacting with pupils?
(3) Should techniques other than 'echoing' be developed for correcting pupils' responses?

Suggestions are made as to ways in which present views may need to be revised or re-examined. It is hoped that this information will be useful in developing more effective teaching strategies for immersion classrooms, and thus for bilingual education programs in general.

Larger Classroom Processes Study

The data on which this chapter is based come from a study of classroom processes undertaken in the provinces of Newfoundland and

Labrador. The study was undertaken in 23 grade 1, 2 and 3 classrooms during the 1985–86 school year. Virtually all the French immersion classrooms in the province participated in the study. Consequently, both rural and urban classrooms, as well as a variety of class sizes, were represented. In all, 524 children and 23 teachers were included in the study. A preliminary analysis of three of the 23 classrooms in the larger study has yielded some interesting information about the differences between classrooms with respect to the instructional strategies used. It is data from the preliminary study which will be discussed here.

The study focused on communication patterns in the French immersion classrooms by recording the number and certain characteristics of messages between pupils and the teacher. Data were gathered by trained observers who recorded their observations on a form developed by researchers for the project. Six target pupils were observed in each of the classrooms, three of whom were identified as high achieving pupils, and three as low achieving pupils. High and low achieving pupils were selected on the basis of teacher observations and achievement data. Differences in the communication patterns of the high and low achievers were compared. It was felt that contrasting the communication patterns of high and low achievers in each classroom would be a simple and effective method of discovering those classroom processes which appeared to enhance learning.

Tables 17.1, 17.2 and 17.3 have been included here in order to give background information for the discussion which follows.

Table 17.1 gives an indication of the number of messages coded in

TABLE 17.1 *Communication patterns within three classrooms*

Message initiator	% Messages in classroom		
	A	B	C
Teacher	44.2	58.7	62.1
Pupils	54.7	35.7	29.8
Target pupils	28.9	22.0	13.7
From teacher to targets	17.1 (336)*	9.4 (244)*	6.6 (134)*
From targets to teacher	13.2 (260)*	3.2 (83)*	2.1 (43)*
Total number of messages	1967	2594	2032

* Approximate number of messages given in brackets.

TABLE 17.2 *Percentage of class time spent on selected activities*

Process activity	Classroom		
	A	B	C
Lecture	1.3	8.9	20.2
Questions	12.6	11.0	9.8
Drill	2.9	10.9	15.1
Discussion	5.0	1.9	0.9
Group work (piloting)	10.1	6.2	3.7
Seatwork (piloting)	26.8	34.8	17.6

each of the classrooms described. It is to be noted that there were many more messages between teacher and target pupils in Classroom A than in either Classrooms B or C. Table 17.2 gives a brief picture of the process structure of the three classrooms. In Classroom A there was less formal teaching, and more opportunities for interaction between teacher and pupils. Classroom C tended to be a class where more emphasis was placed on formal learning situations and attending to the teacher, even though a number of game type activities were used. Table 17.3 gives some indication of the degree to which messages in each classroom related to the purposes set by the teacher. Classroom B tended to be the class in which most off-task behaviour was tolerated. There was a considerable amount of off-task behaviour in Classroom A, but a much larger proportion of these behaviours were not disruptive than was the case for Classroom B. It is interesting to realise that Classroom A had the most pupils, while Classroom C had the least.

In the larger study, classroom processes were compared with

TABLE 17.3 *Task orientation of messages given as percentage of total messages per classroom*

Messages	Classrooms		
	A	B	C
Organisation	13.9	12.3	15.5
Control	0.8	0.2	0.7
On-task	82.9	79.9	92.1
Off-task	15.9	19.4	7.9

achievement outcomes. Achievement was measured by the use of two tests. The Canadian Cognitive Abilities Test (CCAT) was used as a measure of scholastic ability in English. The Tourond *Test diagnostique de lecture* was used as an indicator of French language achievement. The assumption was made that the results of the CCAT testing would give an expected level for achievement in the classroom. The Tourond test was considered as a measure of French language competence. The assumption was also made that reading ability depends on communicative competence to a considerable degree. In this way the Tourond test could be considered as an indirect measure of achievement in oral French. For the purposes of this discussion, it is worthy of note that achievement in Classroom A was considerably higher than anticipated, while that in Classroom C was lower than might have been expected. Achievement outcomes for Classroom B were at expected levels. Variance in the classrooms was also observed. Year-end results for Classroom A were more homogeneous than expected, while those for Classroom C were more heterogeneous than might have been anticipated. These results suggest that the learning environment created in Classroom A tended to enhance language acquisition for all pupils, but particularly low achievers, while the environment in Classroom C tended to have less positive results, particularly for low achieving pupils.

In addition to the classroom observation data, individual interviews were conducted with the 23 teachers involved in the study. Data gathered from these interviews gave information on teacher priorities, practices, perceptions and concerns with respect to French immersion programmes. Reference is made to this data in explaining or interpreting the classroom observation data discussed in this chapter.

Instructional Strategies in the Three Classrooms

In this section each classroom will be described with respect to the practices followed for the use of instructional strategies in the following areas:

(1) aids to language comprehension;
(2) use of affect in motivation and responding to pupils;
(3) correction of oral expression.

Differences between the classrooms will be discussed, and reference made to the relative levels of achievement attained by each class. Some suggestions will be made as to the possible connection between the instructional strategies used and their effectiveness in enhancing the learning environment for the immersion pupils. No direct cause–effect relationships may be established by the analysis. However, some questions are raised and indications given which might well be investigated with respect to current practices in second language methodology.

Aids to language comprehension

One of the most important aspects in the teaching of a second language by a direct method is the question of establishing meaning. In recent years in the second language classroom it has been accepted that pupils should be encouraged to use whatever clues, linguistic, paralinguistic, or other, which they can detect in order to extract meaning from the sounds which they hear. Much attention has been paid to situational context and to the concept of 'general' comprehension. Learners have been encouraged to guess intelligently in order to understand the gist of what is being said. Teachers have been encouraged to use visual, aural, paralinguistic and linguistic aids to assist in this process. In the immersion classroom, where subject matter is learned through the second language, the question of establishing meaning for the pupils would appear to be of considerable import. It would also seem reasonable to anticipate that some pupils would be able to derive much more precise meaning from the language flow presented to them than· others. The two questions which were of particular interest in the study were the following: To what extent do immersion teachers focus on assisting the pupils to comprehend the target language? What means do immersion teachers use to help pupils comprehend the language being learned?

Teacher perceptions

The question of the amount of attention given to the actual teaching of comprehension of the target language in the immersion classroom is very difficult to determine. The interview data gathered suggested that concern about the pupils' level of comprehension in the second language was generally expressed most by teachers at the kindergarten level. Teachers in grades 1 to 3 did not appear to be consciously influenced in their teaching, for the majority of the time, by the need to teach the second language. Teachers expected that the pupils would learn the target language as they were learning the content of the prescribed curriculum. In most cases, it appeared to be very difficult for teachers to separate linguistic from semantic instructional goals in the immersion classroom situation in grades 1 to 3.

Teachers reported that pupils beyond the kindergarten year generally appeared to comprehend what was said to them. If they did not, most pupils would indicate that they were experiencing difficulty, either overtly or covertly. It was suggested that some pupils did present a problem in this regard, particularly the timid child. Teachers did have to check on an individual basis with such pupils to make certain that comprehension had been achieved, but this verification often took place after the presentation part of the lesson was over.

Most teachers admitted to assisting with comprehension on occasion, though views with regard to the amount of such assistance needed in the immersion classroom were varied. Two of the teachers described here indicated that they simplified the language used in the classroom from that which they would use normally with native francophones, but one teacher claimed that she did not use language that was in any way different from that which she would use in teaching young francophones of the same age. One teacher indicated that she generally introduced new vocabulary to the pupils at the beginning of instruction, while one teacher felt that she gave clarification of items only when it became apparent that assistance was needed.

Clarification, according to the teachers, was usually sought from other members of the class, and was often obtained. Clarification given by pupils was sometimes given in the mother tongue. Intervention on the part of the teacher was given when there was no appropriate response from the pupils. Clarification supplied by the teachers more often took the form of identifying a morphological form or explaining a syntactical construction. On some occasions, identification of a vocabulary item was required. In general, the impression given by the teachers was that their primary goal was to assist pupils to learn the material prescribed in the curriculum, not to comprehend the second language.

Observational data,

In attempting to observe the way in which the second language was treated in the immersion classroom, attention was given to the number and type of messages about second language comprehension which were used in each classroom. As shown in Table 17.4 some interesting patterns did emerge. The total percentage of messages with respect to language comprehension was about the same in the three classrooms, and, as anticipated, was not particularly high. However, given the absolute number of messages coded for each classroom, the total number of messages with respect to language comprehension was highest in Classroom A.

TABLE 17.4 *Percentage of messages about language comprehension*

	A	B	C
High achievers	1.7	4.8	3.5
Low achievers	5.0	0.7	2.6
Total %	6.7	5.5	6.1

Note: Percentages are given on a per classroom basis.

The three classrooms showed marked differences with respect to the target pupils. Messages about language comprehension tended to be directed primarily to the high achievers in Classrooms B and C. When this information is combined with the number of messages between target pupils and teachers in these classrooms, it may be seen that low achieving . pupils received very few messages about language comprehension. On the other hand, in Classroom A approximately five out of every seven messages about language comprehension were directed to low achievers. In Classroom A there was much more emphasis on the comprehension of the second language for low achieving pupils.

A further interesting development emerged when the types of comprehension aids used were observed. As indicated in Table 17.5, the traditionally accepted comprehension aids for second language classrooms were used quite extensively in Classrooms B and C.

TABLE 17.5 *Percentage of non-verbal messages to assist with comprehension of the target language*

		A	B	C
Aural aids	H*	0	15.4	3.5
	L**	1.4	6.5	2.6
Paralinguistic aids	H	0	13.5	24.6
(body language)	L	0.9	14.4	22.1
Visual graphic aids	H	0	24.0	19.3
(pictures/drawings)	L	0	34.5	22.0

H* = High achievers
L** = Low achievers
Note: Percentages are given on a per classroom basis.

Almost 90% of the comprehension aids used in Classroom C were either visual (pictures, drawings) or paralinguistic (i.e. gestures, body language) aids. About equal use of both types of aids was recorded for both high and low achieving pupils, though there was tendency to use visual aids more with low achievers. In Classroom B visual aids were used more often than body language, and more often with low achievers. Aural aids (such as phonemic contrast) were sometimes used with high achieving pupils. Classroom A depicted a very different learning environment. Virtually none of the traditionally accepted types of comprehension aids for second language classrooms were used. When used, they were employed only for low achieving pupils. This difference is further reinforced by the information given in Table 17.6.

When observing the types of comprehension aids used in the classrooms, the use of verbal aids, as contrasted with non-verbal aids, was recorded. It is to be noted that no verbal aids to comprehension · were used in Classroom C. Some use of such aids was observed in both Classrooms A and B. Given the difference in the absolute number of messages between target pupils and the teacher in the classroom, these data suggest an interesting difference between Classroom A and

TABLE 17.6 *Percentage of verbal messages to assist with comprehension of the target language*

Type of aid		A	B	C
Simplification	H*	0.8	0.9	0
	L**	3.6	0	0
Definition/association	H	0	0	0
	L	0	1.4	0
Syntactic/morphological	H	0	0	0
	L	0	0	0
Memory jogging	H	0.8	0	0
	L	2.7	2.9	0
Phonetic contrast	H	0	0	0
	L	0	1.4	0

H* = High achievers
L** = Low achievers
Note: Percentages are given on a per classroom basis.

Classrooms B and C. There were more verbal messages relative to language comprehension in Classroom A. These messages were most often directed to low achievers. Very little use was made of non-verbal comprehension aids. As there was a limited amount of teacher talk in this classroom in general, it may be hypothesised that the messages about language comprehension became a much more predominant part of the learning environment, particularly for the low achiever.

This difference would appear to be supported by self-report in the interview data. The teacher in Classroom A placed a high priority on the cognitive goals of instruction. The concern that pupils should understand what they were hearing/learning, it may be hypothesised, resulted in more emphasis being placed on accurate comprehension of the language being used, particularly for low achieving pupils. The teacher in Classroom A was also more reserved than the teacher in the other two classrooms. It was not her nature to use body language or visual and kinesic depictions · of meaning. Consequently, comprehension was established through the use of language. This procedure, it may be suggested, created for pupils a more language oriented learning environment. It is also of some interest that this teacher is one of those who admitted that she was aware of simplifying the language which she used in the classroom. On the other hand, the teacher in Classroom C was vivacious, and very much oriented to the use of body language. She used many examples of visual aids, sketches, drawing and gesture in her teaching style. It is also of interest that this teacher is the one who claimed that she did not simplify the language that she used in the classroom from that which she would normally use with young francophones.

Some questions

This data would appear to raise some questions about the types of comprehension aids which may be most effective for second language learners, particularly in immersion classrooms. The teacher in Classroom A appears to have created a learning environment in which considerable attention is directed to the accurate comprehension of the second language. In addition, comprehension is most often developed by the use of verbal strategies. It is interesting to note that this emphasis on language and cognition appears to be an enhancement of the learning environment, particularly for the low achieving pupil. It is to be remembered that this is the classroom in which actual levels of achievement were well above those anticipated for the group. In addition achievement levels were considerably more homogeneous than expected.

Several questions may need examination with respect to the use of comprehension aids in the immersion or second language classroom. If more verbal aids to comprehension were used, would this help to create for the pupil more connections amongst the various aspects of the target language which would ultimately assist in learning the language? Would the development of such connections be particularly helpful for the low achieving pupils? Would the use of more verbal comprehension strategies by the teacher give models for the use of more effective communication strategies on the part of the learners, particularly low achievers?

Use of affect to motivate and respond to pupils

In the field of second language education the need for motivating the student and developing positive attitudes towards learning the second language has been emphasised. The importance of acknowledging positively pupils' attempts at oral expression and encouraging them to make further attempts are well known to the practitioner. These types of behaviours have been recommended to second language teachers as a means of assisting the learner to talk, and thus practise the second language. In addition to the immediate goal of encouraging the pupil to talk, there has been the implication that the appropriate use of praise will assist in developing in the pupils the desire to learn the second language and give them feelings of success as they participate. In the primary classroom as well, there is a concern for the overall social and emotional development, of the child, and the need to incorporate the learning of the second language into the school life of the pupil in such a manner as not to interfere with normal affective development.

These considerations become even more important when one examines the immersion classroom. The child in the immersion classroom is communicating in a language which is not used at home, and is therefore apt to feel some degree of insecurity. In addition, pupils must be encouraged to talk, as it is only through the production of oral language that teachers can make judgements as to the degree of competence in the second language which is being attained by the pupils. Consequently, the use of affect made by the teachers in attempting to motivate and encourage pupils in the immersion classroom was of considerable interest in this study. Three questions were of particular interest:

(1) To what extent do immersion teachers make use of affect in motivating pupils to participate in the lesson?

(2) To what extent do teachers make use of affect in responding to the
    questions or answers of pupils?
(3) Are the expressions of affect by the teachers verbal or non verbal?

Teacher perceptions

The interview data appeared to support currently held views on
motivation and second language learning. Teachers indicated that they
felt children in the immersion programmes needed to receive regular
positive feedback. The teachers appeared to be very conscious of
establishing a friendly and supportive atmosphere in the classroom for
the immersion pupil. They suggested that they tried to minimise the use
of negative feedback as much as possible, in order not to undermine the
child's confidence. All three teachers described here indicated that they
were concerned about the emotional development of the children in their .
classrooms. One teacher, however, expressed the feeling that this aspect
was generally subordinate to that of the cognitive goals of instruction.

Observation data

To investigate the use of affect in the immersion classroom, messages
in the classroom were observed with respect to their affective content.
Each communication act was divided into three parts: the initial message,
the response to the initial message, and the reaction to this response.
This third aspect of the total communication act was termed the 'redirect'.
It was felt that the redirect was of particular significance in the context
of second language learning. An indication of the degree of affect
expressed with both the initial message and the redirect was recorded by
using a scale of one to five, grading from positive through neutral to
negative expressions of affect.

In addition, since the immersion classroom is one in which the
learning of language is a major goal, it was thought that the extent to
which verbal, rather than non-verbal, expressions of affect were used
might be worthy of note. Therefore an attempt was made to record
whether the affective content of the message was expressed verbally or
non-verbally.

The findings with respect to the use of affect are reported in Tables
17.7 and 17.8. It is perhaps interesting to note that considerably less
affect was used overall than one might expect, particularly given the
expressed concern of the teachers with encouraging the immersion pupil.
In the three classrooms under study, the use of affect was not as great

TABLE 17.7 *Percentage of teacher use of affect accompanying verbal messages to students*

		A	B	C
Initial Message				
Positive	H*	0	5.1	10.5
	L**	0.4	9.5	7.8
Neutral	H	100	89.8	80.7
	L	91.9	79.5	83.1
Negative	H	0	5.1	8.8
	L	7.7	11.0	9.1
Redirect				
Positive	H	6.9	23.1	17.5
	L	5.0	15.8	11.7
Neutral	H	90.5	75.8	82.5
	L	91.8	77.7	87
Negative	H	2.6	1.4	0
	L	3.2	6.5	1.3

H* = High achievers
L** = Low achievers
Note: Percentages are given on a per classroom basis.

as anticipated, and very different patterns emerged with respect to its use.

As indicated in Table 17.7, much more encouragement was expressed in the initial message in Classrooms B and C. In Classroom A the initial message was virtually devoid of any affective content. In Classrooms B and C affect was used to motivate the pupils to answer the question or participate in the learning experience, while in Classroom A this technique was not used. There was a further interesting difference between Classrooms B and C. More encouragement to answer or participate was expressed to high achievers in Classroom C, while more was expressed to low achievers in Classroom B. These data would suggest that different teachers respond differently to high and low achievers. Low achievers in some classrooms may not receive as much encouragement to participate in the learning process as is the case in other classrooms.

When the third part of the communication, the redirect, is examined,

TABLE 17.8 *Percentages of messages expressing verbal and non-verbal affective content*

		A	B	C
Initial teacher message				
Verbal	H*	0	8.6	8.8
	L**	5	10.1	5.2
Non verbal	H	8.8	4.3	10.5
	L	5.2	11.5	22.1
Redirect teacher message				
Verbal	H	11.1	18.3	10.5
	L	10.9	15.8	6.5
Non verbal	H	2.6	13.5	7.0
	L	3.2	10.1	9.1

H*   = High achievers
L** = Low achievers
Note: Percentages are given on a per classroom basis.

several interesting differences between classrooms were noted. In Classroom C, there were more neutral messages at this point in the interchange, particularly for low achievers. While this strategy may be the teacher's way of refraining from expressing disapproval so as not to discourage the pupils, it may have the effect of leaving pupils, particularly low achievers, unable to determine whether or not their response is acceptable. Because of the number of neutral messages, nearly 90% of the messages in this classroom may be termed ambiguous. The percentage of messages receiving positive feedback in this classroom is somewhat higher for high achievers, and about the same for low achievers as for the initial message, again suggesting that the high achiever in this classroom receives more praise.

In Classroom B considerably more positive affect was expressed on the redirect than the initial message for both high and low achievers. Low achievers receive about the same number of neutral messages for both the initial message and the redirect, while high achievers receive somewhat more positive reinforcement of their answers. Pupils in this classroom appeared to be encouraged to respond, and shown approbation when their responses were suitable. Some use is made of contrast between negative and positive affect, particularly for low achieving pupils. Approximately one out of every three expressions of affect to low achieving pupils had some negative connotation. However, approximately 75% of the redirect messages in this classroom were ambiguous, and there was a somewhat greater degree of ambiguity for the low achiever than for high achieving pupils.

Classroom A presented a rather different learning environment. In this classroom, though 90% of the initial messages were neutral, the data suggested considerably less ambiguous feedback for the pupils. There was much more use of positive feedback for both low and high achieving pupils in the redirect than for the initial message, and some use of negative feedback for both groups. Therefore, it would seem that pupils in this classroom were much more aware of the suitability of their response. Since the teacher uses almost no affective overtones in her initial message, the use of even limited positive affect in the redirect, it can be hypothesised, was more noticeable to the pupils. Also, the use of negative feedback almost half as often as positive feedback suggests that pupils were alerted to signs of both approval and disapproval with respect to their responses. These data would suggest that high and low achieving pupils in this classroom received similar amounts of positive and negative feedback. This feedback was probably of considerable import as it did not form part of a more generalised use of motivation to encourage the pupil to attend to the lesson.

Verbal expression of affect

A second aspect of the question of the use of motivation in the immersion classroom was examined by observing whether the source of teacher reinforcement, or the affective content of messages, was expressed verbally or non-verbally. Different patterns in the use of language to express affect were noted in the three classrooms. These data are summarised in Table 17.8.

With respect to the initial message, more non-verbal than verbal expressions of affect were used in Classrooms A and C. In Classroom C, more non-verbal expressions of affect were used for all pupils, but particularly for low achievers. In Classroom A, more non-verbal expressions of affect were used with high achieving pupils, and about equal amounts of verbal and non-verbal expressions of affect with low achievers. In Classroom B more verbal expressions of affect were used, particularly with high achievers.

With respect to the redirect, there was more use of verbal than non-verbal affect in all three classrooms. In Classrooms B and C, however, more positive reinforcement was offered to high achievers than to low achieving pupils. In Classroom A the amount of verbal affect expressed was more nearly similar for both groups of pupils.

Overall, for the initial message and the redirect combined, low achievers in Classrooms A and B received a considerable percentage of verbal messages of affect, though the absolute number of such messages would be much greater in Classroom A. Low achievers in Classroom C regularly received more non-verbal expressions of affect.

These data would seem to indicate that there was much more use of verbal expressions of affect in Classroom A. They would also suggest that verbal expressions of positive affect were used with both high and low achieving pupils, but, overall perhaps more often with low achievers. In Classroom B, affective content of messages was expressed somewhat more often verbally, but more positive encouragement appeared to be directed to high achievers. In Classroom C affective content of messages was expressed non-verbally about 50% of the time. More positive affect was expressed to high achievers, and little use was made of expressions of negative affect. In Classroom A both positive and negative feedback was expressed to all pupils, and the affective content of messages increased considerably as the interchange between teacher and target progressed. In Classroom C, by contrast, the exchange became more neutral, particularly for low achievers. It may be hypothesised that the appropriate use of both positive and negative feedback is essential to the learning process to avoid ambiguous feedback, particularly for low achieving pupils. It is interesting to speculate on whether the use of verbal expressions of affect may have some importance in a language oriented classroom. In interpreting these findings it is important to remember that the levels of achievement were higher than anticipated and more homogeneous in Classroom A. This use may have some importance in a language oriented classroom.

Some questions

These findings raise several questions with regard to the use of expressions of affect in the immersion or second language classroom. Is affect used for motivational purpose as important as affect used in accepting or rejecting pupil responses? Does the expression of negative affect when accepting/rejecting a pupil's response really cause discouragement? Does the low achieving pupil, particularly, require more direct expressions of positive and negative feedback in order to interpret whether or not the response made is acceptable? Does the use of verbal, rather than non-verbal, expressions of affect enrich significantly the language learning environment to which the immersion pupil is exposed? Do verbal expressions of affect have more significance for the pupil than non-verbal expressions of affect?

Correctness of oral expression

Concern with correctness of oral expression was investigated since it was felt that attention to this aspect of second language learning would affect the degree to which immersion pupils used appropriate language forms. Much concern has been expressed about the extent to which errors appear to become 'fossilised' in the speech of immersion pupils. On the other hand, because of the need to be attentive to the social and emotional development of second language learners, particularly in the primary grade levels, there is a hesitancy to be too stringent in the correction of error. There is also much discussion from the point of view of language acquisition/learning as to what type of, and how much, error correction is productive in the early stages of developing competence in a language.

Questions examined in this part of the study focused on the amount of correction which actually took place in the classroom and the methods which were used for correcting pupils' language. The language studied was only that produced by the pupils.

Teacher perceptions

From the interview data it appeared that there were a wide variety of practices followed by teachers, although there seemed to be considerable agreement on generally accepted principles. Oral errors are corrected as unobtrusively as possible, usually by echoing the pupil's response. Encouragement for communicating was given rather than focusing attention on errors. The priority which was placed on error correction, however, varied considerably. One teacher claimed that she corrected all errors, while the others indicated that they corrected only selected ones. In general, the points of view expressed were not markedly different from those expressed by teachers of the first language where there is, at the present time, also a tendency to de-emphasise the correction of grammatical errors in order to encourage expression and other communicative goals.

Observational data

Several interesting differences occurred amongst the classrooms with respect to the treatment of oral errors. There were wide differences relating both to the number of correct messages which were heard in the classrooms and the pattern developed for correction. Table 17.9 indicates that there were considerably more correct messages in Classroom C.

Nearly two-thirds of the messages from both high and low achievers were correct. In Classroom B about two-thirds of the messages from high achieving pupils and one-half from low achieving pupils were correct. In Classroom A, however, only about one-third of the messages from both high and low achieving pupils were correct. These percentages must be interpreted in the light of the actual number of messages in the classrooms. In Classroom A the number of messages was approximately double the number in Classroom B, and four times the number in Classroom C. With respect to the number of messages from low achievers the difference was considerably more extreme. Therefore, in absolute terms, there was much more language being used by the pupils in Classroom A, particularly the low achievers.

Further differences are evident when one examines the correction patterns for low and high achieving pupils. In Classroom C, both high and low achieving pupils were corrected, but the low achieving pupils received more messages about the errors in their utterances. In Classroom B it was again the low achievers who received a considerably higher percentage of messages correcting their oral expression. In Classroom A, while both groups received messages about the correctness of their responses, it was the high achievers who received the greater proportion

TABLE 17.9 *Percentage of messages respecting correctness of oral expression*

		A	B	C
Form correct	H*	35.2	62.7	63.0
	L**	33.1	50.0	62.5
Teacher corrects form	H	5.7	1.7	3.7
	L	3.2	7.1	6.2
Number of messages coded target teacher	H	105	59	27
	L	159	28	16
Number of messages coded in classroom		1967	2594	2032

H* = High achievers
L** = Low achievers
Note: Percentages are given on a per classroom basis.

of such messages. Thus, though the total percentage of messages about correction in all three classrooms was about the same, the group receiving particular attention was not. In addition, though the total percentage of messages corrected was similar in each classroom, the absolute number of messages corrected was considerably higher in Classroom A. As a result, there was considerably more correction of the utterances of pupils in Classroom A than in either of the other two classrooms.

By referring to Table 17.2, which gives a summary of the type of activity taking place in the classrooms, it may be seen that the structure of the learning activities gave much more opportunity to the teacher in Classroom A to interact with the pupils, often on a one-to-one basis. Pupils also had the opportunity to receive correction in an informal, and perhaps less threatening situation than those in Classrooms B and C. It is also interesting to note from Table 17.3 the types of messages coded in the three classrooms. In Classroom A the orientation was towards a high number of on-task messages at all times. Given again the difference in absolute number of messages, it may be seen that there are considerably more on-task messages from low achieving pupils. Communication in this classroom appears to be 'purposeful' for all pupils most of the time, and correction may therefore be more significant.

It may also be worthy to note that, in Classroom A, the high achievers receive a considerable amount of correction, being corrected almost twice as often as the low achieving pupils. This pattern was different from that in Classrooms B and C. The question of why the high achieving pupils in Classroom A required so much correction is probably related to two factors:

(1) the average initial scholastic ability in this classroom was lower than that in the other two classrooms, and
(2) much more language was being produced by all pupils.

There is a further interesting difference which appeared in the interview data which may be of some importance. The teachers in both Classrooms B and C indicated that they used 'echo techniques' for correction, with very little use of affect or of explanation. The incorrect response of a pupil was quietly restated in its correct form. Concern was expressed by both teachers about the necessity not to discourage, or embarrass, the young learner. In Classroom A, however, while attention was still paid to the feelings of the children, much more direct correction practices were employed. Pupils were sometimes asked to repeat the correct form, and on occasion, brief explanations were required or given. However, there was very little use of affect, so that even when an answer was not accepted, the communication that ensued did not have overtones of disapproval or rejection. There was created, nonetheless, a definite feeling that correct language expression was of some importance in communicating in the second language.

This information raises some questions about the effectiveness of 'echoing' techniques as devices for correction in the second language classroom. Is it possible that the absence of affective reinforcement tends to lessen the importance which the pupil places on the correction offered? Does the technique suit the higher achieving student better than the low achiever? Do low achievers even realise that something significant in what they have said has been altered in the repetition by the teacher? Do teachers tend to repeat pupils' answers in other contexts, so that the learners are not aware that this particular type of repetition is a different kind which contains a message of significance about the language being learned?

Summary and Conclusions

There appears to be considerable indication from the data that some of the perceptions which are generally held about appropriate instructional strategies to be used in second language or immersion teaching may need modification, and that several widely used practices might fruitfully be re-examined. Teacher behaviours appear to have a significant effect in determining the amount of real communication which can be achieved by each pupil in a classroom. Therefore, it would seem that the findings of this study have significant implications for the education and supervision of immersion teachers.

Several perceptions currently held with respect to teachers may need modification. These include:

(1) The role of the fluency of the teacher. Beyond a certain level of fluency, use of appropriate instructional strategies may be of much more significance in creating an effective learning environment than native-like ability in the target language.
(2) The role of the personality of the teacher. An environment in the classroom which is comfortable and not stressful may be more important than a highly enthusiastic one.
(3) The role of the teacher as 'encourager'. The appropriate reinforcement of particular language behaviours may be more effective in helping pupils to acquire the second language than the creation of general motivation to participate in the learning experience.

(4) The role of the teachers as 'model'. Interaction between teacher and pupils, and amongst the pupils themselves, may permit more experimentation with the language, leading to higher levels of competence in the second language. The need for the teacher-talk as a model may have been somewhat overemphasised in second language classrooms.

(5) The role of physical arrangements in the classrooms. The actual instructional strategies used by the teacher appear to have more impact in enhancing language learning than factors such as classroom organisation or size.

These considerations suggest some cautions which may need to be exercised by those involved in supervising immersion programmes. These areas would include:

(1) Emphasis placed on native, or native-like, fluency in the second language rather than teacher effectiveness.

(2) Dependence on classroom organisation as a stimulation of communication rather than process structure in the classroom.

(3) Concern with the ability of the teacher to create enthusiasm in the classroom rather than an effective learning climate.

With respect to teacher education for the immersion classroom, there would appear to be a need to sensitise teachers to two important considerations:

(1) What constitutes real and active communication in the classroom. Pupil participation in games, or activity, does not necessarily ensure active language use on the part of the child.

(2) Which teacher behaviours enhance second language learning. An enthusiastic teacher, or one who 'echoes' pupil responses, does not necessarily enhance the second language learning environment for all pupils.

In addition, it would seem that teachers should be encouraged to consider the following practices:

(1) The use of more verbal aids to the comprehension of the second language. It would appear that teachers should be made aware of the tendency to assume comprehension of the target language, perhaps more than may be warranted for some pupils, particularly the lower achievers in the classroom. Teachers should be encouraged not to rely on non-verbal depictions of meaning for the second language, but should develop as many verbal connections as possible for the pupils. They should also be alerted to the tendency to use fewer

verbal messages with low achievers, and be aware of the probable need for the low achievers to receive more rather than less verbal stimulation. Teachers should also be alerted to the potential of encouraging pupils, particularly low achievers, to use more 'achievement' rather than 'reduction' communication strategies by employing more verbal aids to comprehension with these pupils.

(2) A more sophisticated use of affect in the classroom. The use of affect as a motivational device appears to have less effect on learning than the use of affect in reaction to the pupil's response. In addition, the use of both positive and negative affect appears to be essential if reinforcement is to be effective for the pupil. Less ambiguous feedback appears to be important, particularly for the low achieving pupil.

(3) The exploration of different techniques for the correction of errors in oral expression. It may be that simply 'echoing' a response is not a sufficient way of indicating to pupils, particularly low achievers, that modification of their utterance is of some significance in order to communicate clearly in the target language.

It has been the purpose of this chapter to reappraise some current practices and perceptions with respect to immersion teaching. This task has been undertaken to understand more fully the process of teaching a second language and to assist in making this process more effective for a larger group of learners. It is hoped that the avenues explored here will contribute to the discovery of those instructional strategies which will enhance learning in the immersion classroom and benefit all those involved in bilingual education programmes.

Acknowledgements

The data on which this chapter is based was collected in connection with a larger study being undertaken with Dr William H. Spain of the Institute for Educational Research and Development. The project was funded by the Social Sciences and Humanity Research Council of Canada and the Office of the Secretary of State through the Department of Education of the Province of Newfoundland and Labrador.

Contributors

Réal Allard obtained a master's degree in psychology from the University of Ottawa and pursued doctoral studies at the University of California (Santa Barbara) and at the Université de Montréal. He is presently Professor of Education at the Faculté des sciences de l'éducation of the Université de Moncton. His present research interests revolve primarily around the use of attitudes and beliefs in the prediction of language behaviour in inter-ethnic contexts.

Louise Burton is presently a professor of Special Education at California State University, San Bernardino, School of Education. She teaches special education courses, has presented scholarly papers and has published major articles in the areas of bilingual special education, parental involvement, career education, and special education curriculum. Dr Burton has written and directed grants in transition programmes for severe and learning handicapped individuals.

Janice Chavez is currently a professor of Special Education and Programme Administrator of the Bilingual Special Education Teacher Training (BSETT) grant at California State University, Fresno, School of Education and Human Development. To meet an urgent need in California, the BSETT programme had trained Spanish-speaking graduate students to assess and instruct bilingual learning handicapped children and to work effectively with their parents. She has numerous conference presentation and scholarly publications in the areas of bilingual special education, parental involvement, nondiscriminatory assessment, learning disabilities and microcomputer technology. Dr Chavez serves as the National Council for Exceptional Children (CEC) co-Chair for the Hispanic Caucus.

Jim Cummins received his Ph.D. from the University of Alberta in 1974. He subsequently worked in the Educational Research Centre in Dublin where he conducted several studies related to the consequences of

Irish–English bilingualism and bilingual education. He has also carried out research on cognitive processing and reading difficulties at the Centre for the Study of Mental Retardation at the University of Alberta. He is at present a professor in the Modern Language Centre of the Ontario Institute for Studies in Education in Toronto.

Georges Duquette received French language elementary and secondary education in north-eastern and eastern Ontario. He pursued university studies in both English and French in Toronto, Sudbury and Ottawa. He obtained his Ph.D. from the State University of New York at Buffalo. Before completing graduate studies, he taught English for 11 years in French language secondary schools. He also taught French as a second language in English elementary and secondary schools, English as a second and foreign language at the undergraduate level, and education courses at graduate and undergraduate levels. He has published in the *Canadian Modern Language Review, The New York State Association of Foreign Language Teachers, Education Canada, Language and Society*, and the National Association for Bilingual Education's *Theory, Research, and Application: Selected Papers*. His research interests include studies and applications in bilingual (first and second language) education, the role of the home culture in language development, and bilingualism and special education. He taught at the Faculty of Education of Saint Mary's University in Halifax and is now Professor at the School of Education at Laurentian University in Sudbury.

William T. Fagan, Professor at the University of Alberta, Edmonton, Alberta, has a Ph.D. from the University of Alberta and also studied at the University of Toronto and the University of Michigan. He has been a teacher of all grade levels. He has been the recipient of the International Reading Association Outstanding Dissertation of the Year, the National Council of Teachers of English Promising Research Award, and the Alberta McCalla Research Professorship. His present research interests include literacy development, adult literacy, and second language learning.

Alvino E. Fantini, Director of Bilingual–Multicultural Education, Master of Arts in Teaching Programme, School for International Training, Brattleboro, Vermont, USA, holds a Ph.D. from the University of Texas. He has worked for more than 25 years in both language and intercultural education, in the USA and abroad. Internationally recognised in the field of applied linguistics, he was distinguished with an International Award for sociolinguistic research from the Academia de la Lengua in Mexico, and received a post-doctoral research grant on bilingualism from the

National Endowment for the Humanities. He has authored numerous books and articles, and is currently President of the prestigious international Society for Intercultural Education, Training and Research (SIETAR).

Joan E. Friedenberg is currently a research specialist in Bilingual Vocational Education at the Ohio State University. She received her Ph.D. in Bilingual Multicultural Education from the University of Illinois as a Title VII fellow. She is the coauthor of thirteen books and over 50 articles and chapters related to the employment issues and dropout prevention for Limited English Proficient (LEP) persons.

Birgit Harley (Ph.D. University of Toronto) is an associate professor in the Department of Curriculum of the Ontario Institute for Studies in Education, where she teaches courses in second language teaching and learning. Author of *Age in Second Language Acquisition*, she has conducted a number of studies of second language development in French immersion. She recently participated in the National Core French Study, a curriculum renewal project of the Canadian Association of Second Language Teachers, as convener of the task force on research and evaluation.

Doug Hart was born and educated in Canada, and obtained his Ph.D. in sociology from York University. He is currently a research associate at the Ontario Institute for Studies in Education, having spent the past decade as a research officer first in the Department of Sociology and subsequently in that department and the Modern Language Centre. Over this period he has mainly been involved in survey research in education and research concerning the relationship of schooling to work. Over recent years, however, he has been engaged in evaluation studies of French bilingual education programmes looking at linguistic outcomes, social characteristics of students, and student attitudes.

Rodrigue Landry obtained an MA (Ed.) in educational psychology from the Université de Moncton and a Ph.D. in the same field from the University of Wisconsin. He is presently Full Professor at the Université de Moncton in the Faculty of Education. His research has focused on the social, cognitive, affective and behavioural dimensions of bilingualism.

Sharon Lapkin was born and educated in Canada, and obtained her Ph.D. from the University of Toronto. Her doctoral research involved a linguistic comparison of continental and Canadian French. After three years of language teaching at the university level, she joined the staff of the Modern Language Centre, Ontario Institute for Studies in Education where she is now an associate professor and Centre Head. Most of her research has been in the area of the evaluation of bilingual education programmes, including the development of language tests and of scoring procedures designed to reflect current theories of communicative language proficiency. She has worked as a consultant to several provincial Departments of Education in Canada and to the California State Department of Education.

David Lopez is a professor of Education at California State University, Fresno, School of Education and Human Development. He presently teaches courses in curriculum and instruction, social studies, parental involvement, and the Bilingual Special Education Teacher Training Programme (BSETT); he has been involved in developing specific expertise and conducting research in the area of Hispanic parental involvement and communication. He is in the process of formulating faculty/student exchange programmes in Spain and Germany.

Lilliam Malavé, Ph.D., is Assistant Professor Director of the Graduate Bilingual Education programme at the State University of New York at Buffalo. She was the 1985/86 Vice-President and was the 1986/87 Co-Chairperson of Publications of the National Association for Bilingual Education (NABE). In addition, she is the editor of the NABE Conference annual publication. She was a member of the Bilingual Advisory Council of the New York State Commissioner of Education and the National Clearinghouse for Bilingual Education Advisory Council. Dr Malavé has been an education consultant to the US Department of Education and to the US Office of Bilingual Education and Minority Languages Affairs. Among her many activities in the area of research and bilingual education we find a publication entitled *Bilingual Education: Research, Theory and Application* and another, co-authored with A. Papalia, *Developing Bilingualism and Multiculturalism*.

Joan Netten is Professor in the Faculty of Education at Memorial University of Newfoundland, where she holds a joint appointment in the Department of Curriculum and Instruction and the Institute for Educational Research and Development. For the past several years she has been Co-ordinator of the French Teacher Education programme at Memorial. She has studied at the universities of Saskatchewan, Toronto, McGill and Laval, and has degrees in both French and Education. She has had experience teaching French at all grade levels from primary to university, as well as with adult learners, and has taught French methodology for over fifteen years. In recent years she has been a member of the Editorial Board of the *Canadian Modern Language Review* and of *Contact*. She has contributed reviews to many journals, as well as reviewing various curriculum materials for several publishers. Most recently she was appointed a member of the Policy Advisory Committee on French Programmes established by the Minister of Education in the Province of Newfoundland and Labrador. She is currently on leave from the University in order to assist the Newfoundland Department of Education in its evaluation and re-organisation of French programmes in the province.

John Oller, Jr is the author of eight books and over 130 articles in linguistics and closely allied areas. In 1984, he won the Mildenberger Medal, an international prize offered annually by the Modern Language Association. Invited lecture tours have taken him to Europe, the Middle East, Japan, Taiwan, Mexico, Canada, and throughout the United States. He is best known for his studies on the relation between language and intelligence. His latest book, *Language and Experience: Classic Pragmatism*, appeared in 1989 under the University Press of America Imprint. Formerly an associate professor at UCLA, he is now Professor of Linguistics at the University of New Mexico.

Erlinda B. Reyes, Assistant Professor, the University of Wisconsin, Stevens Point, received her Ph.D. from Texas Women's University. She holds an MA in Education from the Philippines Normal College, Manila, and has studied in the graduate programme (reading) at the University of Alberta. She has taught elementary grades in the Philippines and was an instructor at the Philippine Normal College. She is a member of the Wisconsin State Reading Association.

Herbert Seliger is Professor in the Department of Linguistics at Queens College in Flushing, New York. He obtained his Ph.D. from Columbia's Teachers College, and has published extensively in such journals as *Language Learning, The Modern Language Journal, TESOL Quarterly, The Indian Journal of Education, The International Journal of Applied Linguistics*, and *Interlanguage Studies Bulletin*.

Larry Selinker (Ph.D., Georgetown) is Professor of Linguistics and former Director of the English Language Institute at the University of Michigan. His most recent research efforts include exploring the inter-actions and interrelations between Language for Specific Purposes and

Interlanguage. With Dan Douglas he has recently co-edited a special issue of the *English for Special Purposes Journal* (6(2), 1987) on this topic.

Merrill Swain was born in Canada and educated in Canada and the United States. She received her Ph.D. from the University of California at Irvine. Her doctoral research was undertaken in Quebec city where she studied the acquisition of French and English by pre-school children being raised in bilingual homes. She was formerly Head of the Modern Language Centre at the Ontario Institute for Studies in Education and Professor in the Department of Curriculum of that Institute. She is also cross-appointed to the Department of Linguistics at the University of Toronto. Her research has been concerned with many facets of bilingualism and second language learning and teaching. Her current research interests include bilingual education for majority and minority language children, the development of bilingual proficiency, and the effectiveness of communicative language teaching. She has worked as a consultant to the Secretary of State of the Canadian Government, the Singapore Ministry of Education, and the California State Department of Education, and has lectured in Singapore, Belgium, Holland, Sweden and Denmark as well as in many cities across Canada and the United States. She has also served as Chair of the Academic Advisory Panel of the Social Sciences and Humanities Research Council of Canada.

Claudette Tardif (Ph.D. University of Alberta) is Associate Professor at Faculté Saint-Jean of the University of Alberta where, for many years, she directed the Education Programme. Currently, she teaches courses related to second language acquisition and on the curriculum and methodology of language teaching in immersion and in minority language settings. Her research interests include the curriculum of teacher education, language acquisition and teaching, and education in a minority milieu.

Henry T. Trueba is Professor of Educational Psychology and Cross Cultural Studies at the University of California, Santa Barbara. He has a Ph.D. from the University of Pittsburgh and was recently awarded the Outstanding Hispanic Education Award by the American Educational Research Association. Professor Trueba has written extensively on bilingualism and multiculturalism. His works have been published in *The National Association for Bilingual Education Journal, Learning and Disability Quarterly*, the *Journal of Multilingual and Multicultural Development* and in various books and research documents. He is the author of the book *Bilingual Bicultural Education for the Spanish-Speaking*.

Sandra Weber is Associate Professor of Child Studies in the Department of Education at Concordia University in Montreal. Her publications include articles on second language sense-making strategies, teacher education, and qualitative research methodology. She is currently investigating second language classrooms for immigrant children.

Margaret Yau obtained her Ph.D. from the Ontario Institute for Studies in Education in 1987. She is now teaching writing at the University of Western Ontario. Before, she taught ESL teacher training courses at the University of Manitoba. Her articles on ESL writing have appeared in the *TESL Canada Journal* and the *English Quarterly*.

Index